THE PATHS TO PRIVITY

A HISTORY OF THIRD PARTY BENEFICIARY CONTRACTS AT
ENGLISH LAW

To Brian Simpson —
In gratitude, best wishes,
and deepest esteem,
Vernon

Vernon Valentine Palmer

Thomas Pickles Professor of Law
Tulane University

Library of Congress Cataloging-in-Publication Data

Palmer, Vernon V.
  The paths to privity of contract: the history of the third party beneficiary contract at English law/ Vernon Valentine Palmer.
  250p.   cm.
  Includes bibliographical references.
  ISBN 1-880921-15-4 (pbk.): $39.95. -- ISBN 1-880921-16-2 (cloth): $64.95
  1. Contracts--Great Britain--History. 2. Third parties (Law)--Great Britain--History.   I. Title.
  KD 1573.P35   1992
  346.41'02--dc20
  [344.1062]   92-29490
                                                                      CIP

Editorial Inquiries:

Austin & Winfield, Publishers
534 Pacific Avenue
San Francisco, CA 94133
Fax: (415) 434-3441

Order Fulfillment:

Austin & Winfield, Publishers
P.O. Box 2529
San Francisco, CA 94126
Fax: (415) 434-3441

To the memory of my father who died while I was in Oxford, and in remembrance of a conversation in which he expressed the dream that all his children -- all seven -- would pursue doctoral degrees. Without his personal inspiration I would not have begun or finished this work.

CONTENTS

I.   Introduction 1

II.   The Nature of Privity 6

III. The Formative Period 26

IV.   The Chancery Phase 84

V.   The Rise of the Parties-Only
      Principle 158

VI.   Reflections and Conclusions 237

PREFACE

Time is the theme of all history, but history itself, or the writing of it, is a great consumer of time. This book has been my travelling companion for many years. It was begun in Oxford, revised in New Orleans, rewritten in Strasbourg, submitted for the D.Phil. degree in Oxford, and readied for final publication here in Paris. It covers, from the perspective of beneficiary contracts, a period of four hundred years of cloudy history which had not been systematically examined by prior authors. This work, however, also accounts for a good part of my own personal history, and I have accumulated many obligations along the way.

To Barry Nicholas, formerly Principal of Brasenose College, who remained an invaluable adviser and friend through the long process of completing my studies at Oxford, I owe an unrepayable debt. He once described the ideal D. Phil. candidate as possessing the qualities of a marathon runner, not those of a sprinter. The remark seems equally true of the ideal supervisor who encourages and perseveres with the runner all the way to the finish line. I was doubly blessed to have two supervisors of this type in Brian Simpson and Barry Nicholas.

To Brian Simpson, an eminent legal historian and presently professor at the Michigan Law School, I owe a debt of gratitude that is difficult to express. He read and reread the manuscript many times, and he freely shared with me his enormous historical expertise, pointing out new paths to explore and pitfalls to avoid. Where merit can be found in this study, it is often the byproduct of Brian Simpson's keen intellectual insights.

I should also like to express my profound gratitude and thanks to my thesis examiners, Professor Patrick Atiyah and Professor John Baker, for their careful and thoughtful review of the work. Their vast erudition and meticulous observations led me to revise my initial draft and improve many portions of the thesis.

Finally, I would like to give special thanks to Mary Ricart, my secretary at the Tulane Law School, who over many years has done everything possible to assist me in this and other domains. My special thanks are also due to Stephanie Mitchell in Tulane's Word Processing Center for her outstanding skill in preparing this book for camera-ready publication.

Paris, The Sorbonne
December 1992

INTRODUCTION

"The controversy over the right of a stranger to the consideration to sue upon a promise made for his benefit involves the most momentous issue raised in the law of contract since the decision of *Slade's Case*."

- Thomas Street

The principle of privity of contract is deeply embedded in the history of every European system.[1] Continental systems of law have had neither the doctrine of consideration nor the writ of assumpsit, and European jurists do not easily recognize the term "privity of contract." Yet an equivalent principle obtained in European law long before its discovery in English law. This is a principle of universal law, embodying policies and socio-economic factors more general and ancient than the uniquely-expressed English doctrine may suggest.[2]

The principle attains its maximum force in the sphere of "personal" contracts,[3] where it takes the form of two prohibitions: the parties to a contract cannot impose the contract obligation upon a third person, nor can

---

[1] The civilians refer to the principle of relativity of contracts, as to which see the following authorities. Roman Law: REINHARD ZIMMERMANN, THE LAW OF OBLIGATIONS, 34 ff. (Juta 1990); BARRY NICHOLAS, AN INTRODUCTION TO ROMAN LAW (Oxford University Press, 1962), p. 199; Scots Law: T.B. Smith, "Pollicitatio—Promise and Offer; Stair v. Grotius," [1958] Acta Juridica 141; French Law: FCC Art. 1121; HENRI ET LEON MAZEAUD ET JEAN MAZEAUD, LECONS DE DROIT CIVIL, 6th ed. (Montchrestien 1969), vol. II, sec. 774; Italian Law: Civil Code Art. 1141; German Law: due to its late codification in 1900, the German Code generally permits contracts in favor of a third person BGB sec. 328; E.J. COHN, MANUAL OF GERMAN LAW (Stationery Office, 1950), p. 73; ZWEIGERT AND KöTZ, AN INTRODUCTION TO COMPARATIVE LAW, vol. II, p. 124 & ff.; M.A. Millner, "Ius Quaesitum Tertio: Comparison and Synthesis" [1967] 16 I.C.L.Q. 446.

[2] Discussed below, p. 2.

[3] This study will not deal with contracts translative of title (*i.e.* so-called "real" contracts), for in every legal system contracts of this nature, such as sales and mortgages, produce rights that can be asserted against the world. Andrew Tettenborn, "Covenants, Privity of Contract and the Purchaser of Personal Property" 41 Camb. L. J. 58 (1982). Josserand has written: "La grande régle de la relativité des conventions cesse d'être exacte dans la mesure ou les contrats sont par eux-meme productifs ou translatifs de droits réels opposables aux tiers." WEILL, LA RELATIVITÉ DES CONVENTIONS, 308 (Paris 1939). Likewise this study will not deal with the doctrine of *Tulk v. Moxhay* (1848) 2 Ph. 774 (restrictive covenants on freehold land) nor with the doctrine of the *Strathcona* case [1926] A.C. 108 (notice of prior ship charter).

a third person sue upon a stipulation in his favor. Whereas the first prohibition remains unquestionably in force in all systems, the second has been fully overcome on the Continent,[4] and in nearly all jurisdictions in the United States.[5] The law of England stands alone among modern systems in its rigid adherence to the view that only the parties to a contract can sue upon it.[6] The modern controversy over the beneficiary action perhaps no longer holds the intense interest it once held for the learned Thomas Street.[7] Yet if there is diminished importance, there still remains ample mystery as to the historical basis of this principle and why it is steadfastly retained. Originally, whether in early Rome or early England, this principle received reinforcement from a combination of legal and natural factors that have largely disappeared in modern times:

> (1). An extreme personal conception of the contractual tie made it appear impossible to transfer rights to a stranger.[8]
> (2). A harsh system of physical execution, whereby the debtor engaged his person and the creditor held enormous powers of self-redress, caused the creditor's personal qualities (leniency, fairness etc.) to become an important part of any bargain.[9]

---

[4] See the authorities *supra* note 1 and the discussion below at pp. 180-185.

[5] *See,* Restatement (2nd) of Contracts, § 302 (1981); HAMILTON, RAU, & WEINTRAUB, CONTRACTS, 748-767 (West 1984).

[6] Sixth Interim Report of the Law Revision Committee 1937 (Cmd. 5449).

[7] THOMAS A. STREET, FOUNDATIONS OF LEGAL LIABILITY (Thompson 1906), vol. II, p. 160.

[8] NICHOLAS, *supra* note 1, at 199. "It is safe to assume," writes Reinhard Zimmermann, "that in early Roman law 'privity of contract', in this sense, was so much a matter of course that it hardly needed to be emphasized: legal acts and their effects were seen as a unity." *Supra* note 1. For an analysis linking the personal factor to Roman law's hostility to the beneficiary action, see SIR FREDERICK POLLOCK, A FIRST BOOK OF JURISPRUDENCE pp. 195-197 (Franklin reprint 1970).

[9] Every system where execution against the person was originally imposed has shown a resistance to the transfer of personal rights. At Rome, for example, in the case of the nexi, who were plebians forced to borrow from patricians, the creditor's right was close to that of a slave owner. The obligor engaged his person, and upon default could be chained in the creditor's house, put to death, or sold as a slave. The logic of the Roman prohibition against assignments and stipulations for third persons is understandable in light of the gruesome consequences of default. If the creditor could freely transfer his rights of enforcement to anyone else, then a new and harsher creditor choosing to execute to the letter of the law could severely prejudice the debtor. The very notion of a personal obligation, as opposed to a real right, did not appear at Roman law until the means of constraint became more humane. Zimmermann notes that "the very word 'obligatio' always reminded the Roman lawyer of the fact that, in former times, the

(3). Relatively less trade and fewer institutions for the exchange of credits and debts existed in an agrarian economy.[10]

(4). Fear of the danger of litigational maintenance was widespread.

(5). The simple parole promise was not yet enforceable.[11]

Instead, the contractual system was based upon formulas, actions, or

---

person who was to be liable, that is, over whose body the creditor acquired the pledge-like power of seizure, was physically laid out in bonds; ...." *Supra* note 1, at p. 5.

The personal hazards to which defaulting debtors were subject continued to be a concern in the modern era. However, when debtor's prison was finally abolished in France in 1867, the overthrow of the relativity principle found in Art. 1165 of the Code Napoleon soon followed. In effect when the debtor's patrimony rather than his person became the security for his debts, the transfer of enforcement rights into third party hands was considered less hazardous. (MAZEAUD & MAZEAUD, *supra* note 1, vol. II, sec. 33.) (On the overthrow of Art. 1165, see MAZEAUD & MAZEAUD, *supra* note 1, vol. II, sec. 774. For the history of execution against the person in France ("de la contrainte par corps"), see JEAN B. BRISSAUD, A HISTORY OF FRENCH PRIVATE LAW, trans. from 2nd French ed. by Howell, (Rothman Reprints, 1968), secs. 408-412; ROBERT J. POTHIER, OEUVRES (PICHON-BECHET, 1827), vol. IX , p. 284.

In England a similar pattern emerged. Debtor imprisonment was largely abolished in 1869 and within four years the courts, overturning centuries of resistance, recognized that assignments of choses in action were permissible in principle. This correlation is pointed out in Bailey's historical study of assignment. Stanley J. Bailey, "Assignments of Debts in England from the Twelfth to the Twentieth Century," [1931] 47 L.Q.R. 516; [1932] 48 L.Q.R. 547. On the English background to execution against the person, see A.W.B. SIMPSON, A HISTORY OF THE COMMON LAW OF CONTRACT (Oxford University Press, 19?5), p. 587 & ff.

[10] After France's agricultural economy had given way to greater trade and urbanization, expanding capitalism, banking institutions, and finally, the industrial revolution, the courts were impressed by the social utility of many beneficiary contracts, such as life insurance, accident insurance and the carriage of goods. Though required to circumvent code articles that faithfully reflected the old Roman prohibition, the French courts transformed that prohibition into an enabling text and held all *stipulations pour autrui* to be valid. Meanwhile, English courts steadfastly clung to the rule against assignment of choses in action, but trade necessities in the 19th century prompted Parliament to pass no less than 12 statutes in derogation thereof. By these statutes Parliament exempted all sorts of bonds, bills of lading, debentures and insurance policies from the common-law rule. In 17th century Holland as well, the needs and usages of the rapidly expanding Dutch economy explained why the "elegant" jurisprudence of the Netherlands turned away from the Roman principle of *alteri stipulari nemo potest.* ZIMMERMANN, *supra* note 1, at 42.

[11] *See* SOHM, INSTITUTES OF ROMAN LAW §§ 78-82 (3rd ed. 1907).

writs,[12] and the beneficiary might be accommodated under one action or writ (*e g. account*) but not under another (*e.g. stipulatio, covenant*).

The advance of the beneficiary action in modern European systems was in a sense founded upon the progressive breakdown of these conditions, yet strangely enough in England the old prohibition survived despite their disappearance. The tenacity of this prohibition in England is not easy to explain as a matter of logic or justice. The refusal to admit the beneficiary action often frustrates the expectations of the parties, penalizes reasonable reliance, and rewards the bad faith of the promisor.[13] Lord Dunedin once observed[14] that the English rule "make(s) it possible for a person to snap his fingers at a bargain deliberately made, a bargain not in itself unfair, and which the person seeking to enforce it has a legitimate interest to enforce." Nor does the rule apparently produce a consistent policy. English law is already riddled with statutory exceptions,[15] and an equivalent result can be routinely achieved by an assignment of a contract to a third person, by establishing a trust in his favor, or by treating him as an agent.[16]

In light of the common law's supposed immunity to rigidity and dogma, foreign observers find it puzzling how stubbornly English law clings to the view that a *jus quaesitum tertio* is inadmissible.[17] In 1925, a writer prophesied that it was only a question of time before English judges surrendered to the inexorable and placed their law in accord with Continental

---

[12] Formalism demands the presence of the parties and inevitably requires the strictest notions of privity. Where an obligation can only arise after the parties pronounce a certain oath or the exact words of the *stipulatio* as at Rome, then it is clear that the formality itself precludes the possibility that a third person, who has not pronounced these words, can be liable or benefitted. HENRI LEVY-ULLMANN, COURS DE DOCTORAT, p. 448 (Paris 1927-28); WEILL, *supra* note 3 at 42 (Paris 1939). The *stipulatio alteri* at Roman law did not comply with the set form of question and answer of the *stipulatio* procedure. One difficulty is that "a stipulation had to contain the word 'mihi', and it thus had to secure performance to the stipulator, not to [a third person] Titius." ZIMMERMANN, *supra* note 1, at 35.

[13] Some English judges have noted that the rule is repugnant to justice: *e.g.* Ld. Pearce in *Beswick v. Beswick*, [1968] A.C. 58, and Ld. Denning in *Jackson v. Horizon Holidays Ltd.*, [1975] 1 W.L.R. 1468.

[14] *See Dunlop v. Selfridge* [1915] A.C. 847, 855 (dissenting opinion).

[15] *See e.g.*, The Law of Property Act, 1925, §§ 56(1) and the list of statutes *infra* p. 245.

[16] *See* Note, "Third Party Beneficiary Contracts in England," 35 U.Chi.L. Rev. 544 (1968); ATIYAH, AN INTRODUCTION TO THE LAW OF CONTRACT, 227-241 (2nd ed. 1971).

[17] ZWEIGERT AND KöTZ, *supra* note 1, Vol. II, at 134.

systems.[18] Nearly seventy years have passed without significant change, and perhaps now one is not only more skeptical about the future, but increasingly amazed by the peculiar hold of the past upon the present and future. The subject has a particularly opaque history, from which all sides in the contemporary controversy have drawn support, comfort, and corroboration. Thus, there is a need to study this history more carefully -- to follow the paths of privity conceptually and consecutively -- and this is the task undertaken in the present work.

---

[18] Haitami, "La Stipulation Pour Autrui en Droit Anglais et en Droit Anglo-Américain," (Thèse 1925).

CHAPTER I

THE NATURE OF PRIVITY -- ORIGINS, MEANINGS AND HISTORICAL QUESTIONS

I. ORIGINS

The challenge of tracing the history of privity of contract begins with "the mysterious and undefined term, 'privity'."[19] It is surely a generic term that has acquired diverse meanings and functions in different periods and contexts, thus greatly complicating our understanding. This word conceals a lengthy evolution and a vast inventory of ideas, rules and principles.

We must begin with the fact that early law was virtually silent as to the definition of privity and that the etymology of the term is very distant from our present usage. In some legal texts, such as Rastell's *Termes de La Ley* (1624) and Edmund Wingate's *Maximes of Reason* (1658), privity was given much attention and several kinds of privity were listed, together with numerous examples, but the authors ventured no definitions and conveyed little hint of its function in the law.[20] These writers had to proceed cautiously because privity connoted a series of ideas: privacy, secrecy, knowledge, interest, and relationship.[21]

---

[19] ARTHUR L. CORBIN, CORBIN ON CONTRACTS (West Publishing, 1951), vol. IV, § 778.

[20] Rastell's entry on p. 321 reads " "Privy or privities: Privy or privities is, where a lease is made to hold at will for years, for life, or a feoffment in fee, and in divers other cases; now because of this that hath passed between these parties, they are called privies, in respect of strangers, between whom no such conveyances have been." Edmund Wingate entitles his entry "The Law Favoureth Privity," but in more than ten pages of examples and citations, he neglects to explain why the law favors privity. WINGATE, MAXIMES OF REASON (reprint ed. Garland Publishing, 1980).

[21] For entries dealing with each of these meanings, see OXFORD ENGLISH DICTIONARY, Vol. VIII, p. 1393 (1933) and MIDDLE ENGLISH DICTIONARY, Part P. 7, p. 1339 (Mich. Press 1983).

Dr. Johnson's first dictionary (1755)[22] stated that the word originally came from the old French term *privauté* meaning privacy, but this dictionary also noted that the contemporary 18th century meaning was "joint knowledge" and "great familiarity." In Kelham's *Dictionary of the Norman or Old French Language* (1779), the French term "privities" is rendered in English as "secrets",[23] and the notion of secrecy lingers in another definition current in the 18th century: "Private knowledge, as a woman is said to do a thing without her husband's privity."[24] The noun privy derived from the French *privé* and originally signified a friend or acquaintance (as opposed to a stranger). When used as an adjective or an adverb, privy came to be identified with intimate knowledge and familiarity, as in the expression "he is privy to the affair."[25] The transition from the concept of privacy *(privauté)* to that of knowledge and familiarity is perhaps understandable. In the privacy of the family, for example, persons were permitted to know one another's affairs, and in the privacy of correspondence[26] and meetings, personal knowledge was shared, though not with the world at large. But privity acquired more abstract legal connotations such as "interest" and "relationship," an evolution which seems more difficult to explain. The transition is shown in John Cowell's statement in 1607: "Privie commeth of the French (privie i. familiaris) and signifieth in our common lawe, him that is partaker, or hath an interest in any action, or thing."[27] A modern legal dictionary similarly indicates that while privity originally meant "knowledge," it now denotes in a secondary sense "a peculiar relation in which a person stands either to a transaction or to some other

[22] SAMUEL JOHNSON, A DICTIONARY OF THE ENGLISH LANGUAGE (1755) (reprint ed. AMS Press, 1967 ("Privity")). *See also,* ERNEST KLEIN, COMPREHENSIVE ETYMOLOGICAL DICTIONARY OF THE ENGLISH LANGUAGE (Elsevier Publishing, 1971).

[23] Divine secrets were described in medieval English as heavenly privities, and thus the "Book of Privities" had reference to the Apocalypse. See, MIDDLE ENGLISH DICTIONARY, at p. 1341.

[24] JAMES BUCHANAN, LINGUAE BRITANNICAE VERA PRONUNCIATIO (1757) ("Privity").

[25] *See* JOWETT, DICTIONARY OF ENGLISH LAW ("Privity").

[26] Thus Chief Justice Holt: "though these are worthy persons, yet bad may succeed them, who may search and open men's letters, and none be the wiser, or able to fix it upon them; being transacted in their own office, and lying only in the offender's privity, who thus may with impunity abuse the trust reposed in him." *Lane v. Cotton* (1702) 12 Mod. 472, 482.

[27] THE INTERPRETER (Cambridge, 1607); A LAW-FRENCH DICTIONARY (1701) by an anonymous author similarly states: *"Person privie,* is who has an interest in the thing demanded."

person."[28]

This transition suggests that privity *the fact* became a source of obligations when legal meaning was attached to the personal bond or "inward relation" resulting from knowledge and familiarity.[29] Contracts, for example, have a recurrent factual basis in the privacy of meetings, discussions, and personal dealings.[30] The word covenant still indicates this original basis. Well before it came to signify a promise or an action at common law, covenant meant a convening, an assembly, or a "coming together," and those who were not there could not know nor perhaps accurately relate what had transpired.[31] From the fact of close relationship would follow the concept of the closed circle. Outside the circle are strangers who can be neither benefitted nor burdened by the rights or duties concerned. The number of these circles is almost infinite, but duties and relationships are kept quite distinct. A's debt to his friend B places them together in the duty circle, but B would be a stranger toward A with respect to A's dealings with someone else. The size of the circle and the number of privies within it would vary, depending upon the scope of the duty and its real or personal nature.[32] Furthermore, those originally outside the circle may be drawn into it when they acquire rights or assets with knowledge or notice of the existing state of affairs between parties.[33]

Privity, then, has possessed a broad inventory of meanings, a reason why contemporary usage seems confused, almost intuitional. In large measure, the modern controversy between the monist and dualist schools of thought (discussed below) would not exist but for the indiscriminate blending of various meanings of the term. The present day gulf between American and

---

[28] JOWETT, DICTIONARY OF ENGLISH LAW. ("Privity").

[29] JOHN KERSEY, DICTIONARIUM ANGLO-BRITANNICUM (1708 reprint ed., Scholar Press, 1969) ("Privity").

[30] This connection still survives in Fifoot's happy phrase "the dogma of contractual privacy." He seems to be the sole modern writer to link the doctrine back to this source. C.H.S. FIFOOT, HISTORY AND SOURCES OF THE COMMON LAW, 337 (London, 1949).

[31] KLEIN, *supra* note 22, ("Covenant").

[32] See *supra* note 3.

[33] For example, if a trustee defrauded A by transferring trust property to B (who had knowledge of the trustee's fraud), then B became "privy to the wrong" and was seised to the first use. See SIMPSON *supra* note 9, at 361; see also Y.B. (1406) 7 Hen. IV 14, pl. 8. On assignments and suretyship, see generally, I Eq. Ca. Abr. 44, "Assignment and Privity, Cap. VIII. Tothill, pp. 161-162, and 180, ("Surities").

English usage is also a striking illustration of the broad spectrum of meaning carried by the word "privity."

To American jurists in this century, privity is but a legal conclusion rather than a factual precondition of duty. It has been called an "effect rather than a cause," and "a relationship not what creates it."[34] According to this view, privity necessarily follows once a court has determined what rights a party or beneficiary should have. "Therefore, to say that there is no right because there is no privity, rather than that there is no privity because there is no right is a plain case of transposing cart and horse."[35] Reflecting this same thinking, Black and Gilmore contend that privity is in reality an "empty container" into which the courts are free to pour meaning.[36] Corbin stated with admirable plainness that privity means "nothing more than one person is under an obligation to the other."[37]

Perhaps a system that generally accepts the third party beneficiary contract (as the American states do) finds it easier to equate privity with obligation than does a system that rejects the action in principle. Equating privity with "right" or "duty" follows in the tradition of Holmes who once proposed a scientific classification of law expressly based upon privity.[38] Holmes made the term synonymous with any legal duty and classified all duties of individuals by their privity to the sovereign, to all the world, or to persons in particular situations or relationships.[39] At this level, privity approached the abstractness of a semantic blank deriving its content from subsidiary concepts like furnishing consideration, receiving notice, forming a trust, or any other ground offered by a court. In English legal literature, however, privity has never been accepted as a synonym for duty. The privity demanded in assumpsit was viewed as a component of a duty relationship, but not the duty itself. Formulated narrowly in terms of the consideration doctrine, it was neither the only measure of duty nor a precondition to every

---

[34] Per Stone J., *Peterson v. Parviainen* (1928) 219 N.W. 180, 183. (concurring opinion).

[35] *Ibid.*

[36] GRANT GILMORE AND CHARLES F. BLACK, THE LAW OF ADMIRALTY, 877 (2nd ed. Foundation Press, 1975).

[37] CORBIN, *supra* n. 19 vol. IV, at 28.

[38] Oliver W. Holmes, "The Arrangement of the Law -- Privity," [1872] 7 Amer. L. Rev. 46. In this article Holmes offered a systematic chart of the common law in which all legal duties were classified in terms of privity to the sovereign, to all the world, or to persons in particular situations or relationships.

[39] In the last category, he placed privity of contract.

contract duty. The American position stands at one extreme from the English position, but it demonstrates that the scope and purpose of the term has changed in the course of history and in the geographical dispersal of the common law. To postulate a fixed constant definition, even within one tradition, can only lead to false conclusions.[40] Indeed the contrary is the case: we can only understand its meaning in relation to period, context and function.

II. FUNCTION AND MEANING

The functions of the doctrine of privity of contract are an essential tool in analyzing its evolution and in clarifying its meaning. Historically there have been at least four functions of the doctrine in the law of contract:

a.   to classify contractual duties (schematic);
b.   to regulate evidence and proof of obligations (evidentiary);
c.   to denote particular relationships necessary to satisfy the contract writs (interior);
d.   to mark off the boundaries between contract and other fields of law (exterior).

Certain functions exploit particular meanings more than others and are not always directly related to the subject of third party beneficiary contracts. The schematic function employs privity in the abstract, relational sense of the term. The evidentiary function emphasizes privity in the sense of a party's interest in a cause and the jury's knowledge of the facts. Both of these functions include, but largely exceed, the dimensions of the beneficiary problem. The interior function descends to the level of specific beneficiary doctrines. For example, in assumpsit privity may be conceived as a consideration-based relationship; in debt the reference may be to a *quid pro quo*-based relationship. The exterior function occurs outside of the contract actions and invariably uses privity in its parties-only sense for instrumental purposes.

a.   The schematic function.

Interestingly, when the phrase "privity of contract" first appeared in the common law it was used in a schematic sense remote from the subject of third party beneficiary contracts. Writing in the early 17th century, Lord Coke listed four kinds of privity recognized by the common law: privies in estate (*e.g.* lessor and lessee), privies in blood (*e.g.* ancestor and heir), privies in

---

[40] For an example of this assumption, see Note, "Privity of Contract" [1954] 70 L.Q.R. 467.

representation (*e.g.* testator and executor) and privies in tenure (*e.g.* lord and tenant).[41] Coke's "quadruplex," as it was then called[42] was not an attempt to list all of the various privity expressions flourishing in his day, such as "privity by judgment,"[43] "privity of condition,"[44] "privies in the trespass,"[45] "privity of estoppel,"[46] "privity of bailment,"[47] "privity of right"[48] and many others. Coke was using the privity concept as a classification tool, and he confined himself to the main sources of legal duties, thus providing the early model for the systematic pursuits of Holmes.[49] Nevertheless, Coke's failure to include privity of contract into his scheme seems remarkable since the case of *Walker v. Harris* (1587) (see below) had already been decided and reported by him.[50] Even when Coke's scheme was later enlarged by his annotators, privity of contract was only mentioned in a footnote as a subcategory of privity of estate. This property classification presented no anomaly in early ways of thinking since contract and the "real" action of debt were considered substantially the same. More than a century later both Viner and Lilly still adhered to this classification scheme.[51]

The question of the proper classification of real and personal rights

---

[41] SIR EDWARD COKE, A COMMENTARY UPON LITTLETON, 15th ed. by Hargrave & Butler, (Brooks, 1794), vol. II, Lib. 3, Cap. 8, sec. 461, 271a.

[42] *See* SIR HUMPHREY DAVENPORT, AN ABRIDGEMENT OF THE LORD COKE'S COMMENTARY ON LITTLETON (1651) (reprint ed. Garland Publishing 1979) in the index under "Privity".

[43] Y.B. (1471) 10 Edw. IV, 11.

[44] JOHN PERKINS, A PROFITABLE BOOK, (15th ed. 1827; reprint ed., Garland Publishing, 1978), secs. 830-835. DAVENPORT, *supra* n. 42 sec. 336, pl. 5; WINGATE, *supra* note 20, No. 55, pl. 23.

[45] WINGATE, *supra* note 20, No. 55, pl. 29.

[46] *Id.*, pl. 74.

[47] SIR WILLIAM STAUNFORD, LES PLEES DEL CORON (1557, reprint ed., Garland Publishing, 1979), Bk. I, Cap. 15, p. 25.

[48] *Lampet's Case* (1613) 10 Co. Rep. 46b, 48b.

[49] Holmes, *supra* note 38.

[50] 3 Co. Rep. 22a.

[51] CHARLES VINER, A GENERAL ABRIDGEMENT OF LAW AND EQUITY (1743), vol. 16, pp. 534, 535, "Privity" (Hereinafter cited as VINER AB.). JOHN LILLY, THE PRACTICAL REGISTER (Nutt & Gosling, 1719), p. 366.

had been previously raised in 1565 by a lessor's action in debt to recover rent.[52] The lessee's defense was that he had already assigned the lease to another, and the lessor should be forced to proceed against the assignee. It was urged there was no privity of estate to ground an action in debt against a lessee who had assigned over. Several judges were inclined to hold for the defendant because "the privity between lessor and lessee is gone," and "a new Privity is created which goes with the land between the lessor and the assignee."[53] The reporter of the case then posed the other position left open by the case -- "Yet quaere whether the privity of contract does not remain between the parties to the first contract because it is personal." This question was later answered in the case of *Walker v. Harris* (1587),[54] which held that the original lessee to a lease remained liable, despite an assignment to a third person, because there was still "privity of contract" between him and the lessor.[55] The court used the privity concept to describe the type of obligation created by a lease. It reasoned that there were three types of privity involved in a lease following an assignment: estate only, contract only, and estate and contract together. Thus, privity of contract was legal shorthand for the distinction between real and personal duties.[56] The action of debt was no longer purely real.[57] A new variety of privity had entered the schematic ranks via a lessor-lessee dispute that had virtually nothing to do with third party beneficiaries.

b.   The evidentiary function.

In medieval law certain rules of evidence were based on privity, and these gave rise to a distinctive set of privity objections. One such rule was that the parties litigant and "interested" persons generally were barred from

---

[52] *Anonymous* (1566) 2 Dyer 247b.

[53] *Id.* at 247b, 248b.

[54] 3 Co. Rep. 22a.

[55] *Walker's Case* supports Fifoot's thesis that debt had completed the transition from being a purely "real" action to one also connoting a personal form of liability. FIFOOT, *supra* note 30, p. 227 *et seq.*

[56] "Privity of contract only is personal privity and extends only to the person of the lessor and to the person of the lessee as in the case at bar...." *Walker's Case, supra,* at p. 23a. The common law derived the distinction "real and personal" from the civilian commentators. *See* POLLOCK, A FIRST BOOK OF JURISPRUDENCE, p. 81; SIR JOHN SALMOND, JURISPRUDENCE pp. 206-207 (2nd ed. 1907).

[57] FIFOOT, *supra* note 30, p. 227 *et seq.*

testifying in a cause on the assumption that their testimony would be biased.[58] Consequently a promisee of a promise for the benefit of a third person was normally disqualified as a witness if he himself brought the action.[59] Being plaintiff and in privity, the promisee was not a trustworthy witness. The promisee's testimony would be admitted, however, in cases where the third party beneficiary asserted the action, for then the promisee's own action was barred and "[he] is become a mere stranger and might be a witness in this action."[60]

Privity was also pivotal to the mode of process available in the medieval court. Trial by jury presupposed that facts were notorious enough that the country (not simply the litigants) could know of them. Wager of law, on the other hand, was an appeal to the supernatural under the pain of eternal punishment,[61] and it demanded highly certain knowledge of the facts--swearable knowledge--obtained through first-hand dealings with the plaintiff or the transaction.[62] Thus, it was generally believed that wager should not be allowed in circumstances where *a priori* the defendant might be mistaken and might imperil his soul by a false oath. For similar reasons, courts did not permit the defendant to wager contrary to a certainty, and thus the basis of the maxim that no man shall wage his law against a specialty.[63]

The danger of false proof was increasingly felt when third parties became involved in a past transaction. One class of cases posing the danger were those of executors and administrators sued in a representative capacity on the contracts of a deceased person, or an abbot sued upon a contract made

[58] See *Anonymous*, (1670) 1 Mod. 107; J. H. BAKER, AN INTRODUCTION TO ENGLISH LEGAL HISTORY P. 289 (2nd ed. 1979), p. 289.

[59] The problem was acute if he was the sole witness to the promise, as in *Dutton v. Poole* 1 Freem. 471 (1680). See below at p. 76.

[60] *Sprat v. Agar* (1658) Cremer Ms., pp. 380-381 (Gray's Inn Library Ms. H-1792, Eng. Leg. Ms. Project, Ed. J.H. Baker.)

[61] SIR FREDERICK POLLOCK AND FREDERICK MAITLAND, THE HISTORY OF ENGLISH LAW, 2nd ed. (Cambridge University Press, 1968), vol. II, p. 598.

[62] This ancient basis for the privity rule was noted in Comyns' Digest: "The rule itself depends, first, upon the maxim (now nearly obsolete) that no stranger to a contract real or personal, shall by his own pleading derive directly or indirectly any advantage from it . . .; he is regarded as having no *legal* knowledge, the only knowledge that can be useful to him of its existence." SIR JOHN COMYNS, A DIGEST OF THE LAWS OF ENGLAND, 5th ed. by Hammond, (Strahan, 1822), p. 304, n. (p), "Assumpsit."

[63] *Core's Case* (1537) 1 Dyer 20a; *Hooper's Case* (1587) 2 Leon. 110.

in the time of his predecessor. These defendants were third persons who could not be absolutely sure whether their deceased principal may have contracted the debt, received *quid pro quo*, or had paid the plaintiff. The situation was too unsafe to allow the use of wager. It was explained in 1594,

> The reason why debt lies not against an executor upon the contract of the testator is, because the law does not intend that he is privy thereto, or can have notice thereof; and he cannot gage his law for such a debt as the testator might....[64]

Since the "country" might have no knowledge of such a contract either, there was no process to try the matter and consequently no liability. The result produced a direct correlation between the absence of privity, the failure of proof and the inability to impose liability. It was but a short step from the evidentiary objection to the substantive position that the plaintiff had no right of action, and this would explain what medieval judges intended by the statement, "the action of debt cannot be maintained without privitie."[65] An immunity originally deduced from the defendant's inability to wage law[66] was transformed into the lack of a right to sue.

The same problem did not arise in account. A third party plaintiff under the action of account was permitted to have an action despite his lack of personal nexus to the defendant. The "third hand" situation in account was considered an instance in which proof by wager was ousted. If the defendant was sued upon a receipt from the hand of someone other than the plaintiff, he could not wage his law because of the inherent uncertainty. Yet the action in account was not necessarily stymied, because if a third person was involved, the country could know of it.[67] As trial by jury increasingly ousted wager of law and became the standard process of courts in the 15th and 16th century, the importance of privity declined as an evidentiary factor.[68]

---

[64] *Stubbins v. Rotherham* (1595) Cro. Eliz. 454.

[65] Y.B. (1490) 5 Hen. VII, 12, pl. 18.

[66] S. F. C. Milsom, "Sale of Goods in the Fifteenth Century," [1961] 77 L.Q.R. 257, 264-265.

[67] *Id.* at 261.

[68] Milsom's research on the action of debt for the sale of goods shows that the choice exercised by defendants steadily swung over to jury trial in the fifteenth century (*Id.*, p. 266). In assumpsit, however, trial was always by jury after 1375 (SIMPSON, *supra* note 9, at pp. 219-220), and consequently, the privity factor was never an evidentiary barrier during the development of the doctrine of consideration. The exclusive use of trial by jury partly explains

c.   The relationships demanded by the writs

The diversity of the forms of action called forth individual "interior" privities adapted to the scope and aim of the particular writs. In this sense our law of contract did not begin with one invariable notion of privity, but with separate strains found in covenant, account, debt and, later on, assumpsit. The history of assumpsit shows that this "interior" privity would change over time, and these changes have left us with a number of terminological problems. Since assumpsit was not wholly divorced from the influence of the older actions, it will be useful to review these, both to illustrate the privity function inside the writs and to lay the proper groundwork for the detailed study of assumpsit in Chapter II.

Covenant

After covenant lost its informality in the reign of Edward I, the rule became established that covenant would only lie on a deed under seal.[69] However, an important effect flowed from the distinction between deeds *inter partes* and unilateral declarations under seal, such as a deed poll. Covenants *inter partes* were highly-formal bilateral contracts containing a "parties clause" in which all parties were named. A person who was not named as a party was a "stranger" who could not sue.[70] The use of plaintiff's seal was not the key to his right to sue. A plaintiff named in the parties clause, though he did not seal the agreement, could maintain an action.[71] Generally, this privity meant a promisee suing a promisor. Consideration passing between them was

---

the initial deemphasis of privity during the Formative Period, 1550-1680. Much of the period was prior to the time when a substantive privity rule based upon consideration was finally established. See the discussion of *Bourne v. Mason* 1 Vent. 6 (1669) below at pp. 68-75.

[69] THEODORE F.T. PLUCKNETT, A CONCISE HISTORY OF THE COMMON LAW. (5th ed. Little, Brown, 1956), p. 366.

[70] *Gilby v. Copley* (1684) 3 Lev. 138; *Foame v. Vandeteram* (1587) Cro. Eliz. 56; *Salter v. Kidgly* (1690) Carth. 76; *Quick & Harris v. Ludborrow* (1616) 3 Bulst. 29; *Lowther v. Kelly* (1723) 8 Mod. 115. See also, HENRY ROLLE, UN ABRIDGEMENT DES PLUSIEURS CASES ET RESOLUTION DEL COMMON LEY 2 (Crooks & Leake, 1668), vol. II, p. 22, (F) (1) "Faits" 115 (Hereinafter cited as Rolle Ab.).

[71] *Clement v. Henley* (1643) 2 Rolle Ab. 22. The right of enforcement, therefore, did not depend upon the use of the plaintiff's seal. See *Scudamore v. Vandestene* (1586) 2 Inst. 673; *Salter v. Kidgly* (1689) Carth. 76; SIMPSON, *supra* note 9, at 36.

irrelevant, and any less formal relationship was insufficient.[72]

The rigid *inter partes* rule, however, was not applied where the deed poll was concerned.[73] The deed poll was not physically split into two parts, and, therefore, it had no parties or nonparties as the indenture did. The obligee needed to show that the covenant had been addressed to him, but this requirement was not interpreted to mean being named in the deed.[74] Flexibility, rather than a policy of strict designation, remained the rule, and so it was held that undesignated persons, if deemed to be "parties interested in the subject matter," could maintain an action.[75]

Account

Originally, where A delivered money to B for the use of C and B refused to pay C, the only remedy C had was an action of account against B. It has been properly noted that C's action was successful because there was no necessity of a contract between B and C in the old action of account.[76] But perhaps too much stress has been laid upon the irrelevance of a contractual tie between the parties, while failing to call attention to the existence of a different requirement of privity. For, generally speaking, the early writers were in agreement with Edmund Wingate's pronouncement: "An action of accompt (sic) must be grounded upon privity; for without privity no action of accompt can be maintained. . . ."[77] The particular kind of privity

---

[72] The rule was strict to the point that the beneficiary of a covenant could not release the covenantor from his obligation toward him. If B had covenanted to A that he would pay £10 annually to C, then C could not discharge B from this obligation because C was a stranger. *Quick v. Ludburrow* (1616) 1 Rolle 196; VINER AB., *supra* n. 51, "Release," at 303; *Storer v. Gordon* (1814) 3 M & S 308.

[73] R.J. Bullen, "The Rights of Strangers to Contracts Under Seal," [1977] 6 Adelaide L. Rev. 119, 120.

[74] *Cooker v. Child* (1673) 2 Lev. 74; *Lowther v. Kelly* (1723) 8 Mod. 115; *Green v. Horne* (1695) 1 Salk. 197.

[75] *Sunderland Marine Ins. Co. v. Kearney* (1851), 16 Q.B. 925.

[76] JAMES B. AMES, LECTURES ON LEGAL HISTORY (Harvard University Press 1913) p. 119; W.S. HOLDSWORTH, A HISTORY OF ENGLISH LAW (Little, Brown, 1926) Vol. III, p. 425; RICHARD M. JACKSON, HISTORY OF QUASI-CONTRACT IN ENGLISH LAW (Cambridge University Press, 1936), p. 30; SIR ROBERT BROOKE, LA GRAUNDE ABRIDGEMENT (1573), pl. 91 "Dett". *But see*, C.C. Langdell, "A Brief Survey of Equity Jurisdiction," [1889] 2 Harv. L. Rev. 241, 260.

[77] WINGATE, *supra* note 20 at 175. Brooke and Coke had said the same. BROOKE, pl. 89, "ACCOMPT" *A COMMENTARY UPON LITTLETON*, vol. II, Lib. 3, Cap. 1, Sect. 259, 172a.

here, however, was that plaintiff could not recover without showing that the defendant stood in what equity might regard as a fiduciary relationship toward him. The declaration needed to state that the receipt was in fact for the plaintiff's "use," and that the defendant took the money on that basis. For this reason account could not be founded upon a wrongful receipt, such as the theft of funds by a stranger,[78] nor upon a donation. The old books said that if A bailed money to B to bail to C for A's use, and B instead donated the money to C, then A had no action against C because "there is no privity of use, but it lies against B."[79] The law did not view C as being liable since he had received the funds for his own use and not A's. The same objection was expressed another way by saying the parties lacked "privity of receipt."[80] In a sense the plaintiff in account did claim in a proprietary capacity[81] but the action did not function on a freely impersonal basis against any receiver of plaintiff's money. There was indeed a particular privity restriction.

Debt

The old books stated that "debt cannot be maintained without privitie."[82]

It will be remembered that in the 16th century the expression "privity of contract" had arisen in connection with a debt action against a lessee[83] but that it was only used in an abstract or schematic sense and was not the concrete objection raised in debt when a third person sought an action. The interior privity demanded in debt was essentially the defendant's personal receipt of a *quid pro quo* or benefit, and a typical objection was to say "there is no contract, nor did the defendant have *quid pro quo*,[84] or that "there is no privity betwixt the plaintiff and defendant, nor any contract in deed or

---

[78] *Tottenham v. Bedingfield* (1573) 3 Leon. 24.

[79] Y.B. (1401) 2 Hen. IV, 12b.

[80] Y.B. (1365) 39 Edw. III, 28.

[81] On the proprietary conception in account, see S.F.C. MILSOM, HISTORICAL FOUNDATIONS OF THE COMMON LAW, (Butterworths, 1969) p. 239.

[82] Y.B. (1490) 5 Henry VII, 12, pl. 18.

[83] See *supra* at pp. 11-12.

[84] Fitzjames C.J. in *Tatam's Case*, Y.B. (1536) 27 Hen. VIII, 24. The same formula is found in *Lady Shandois v. Simson*, (1601) Cro. Eliz. 880; *Harris v. de Bervoir*, (1625) Cro. Jac. 687; see also *Sands v. Trevilian*, (1629) 3 Cro. Car. 193.

law."[85]

The terminology is important here. The word contract, as used in these objections, did not connote a consensual agreement but was used instead to describe an informal transaction, such as a sale or a loan, that transferred property or generated a debt. A specialty or formal agreement was variously described as a grant, as an obligation, or as a covenant, but not as a contract. Assumpsit was considered to be an action upon "promises" not contracts, and contract did not begin to acquire its promissory connotation until assumpsit had expanded to take over the older actions of covenant and debt.[86] It took until the 19th century for the exact expression "privity of contract" to be developed.

A typical privity objection arose in debt where the plaintiff, at the request of the defendant, paid or performed for the benefit of a third person, for in that event the stranger received the benefit rather than the defendant who simply made the request. The defendant was not liable in debt even though he had promised to pay the plaintiff. This followed from the fact that debt possessed a "real" character. It was raised by the transaction and not by agreement.[87] The mismatch between defendant's promise and someone else's benefit arose in everyday situations: the plaintiff married a lady upon defendant's promise to pay him a sum of money; the plaintiff released his debtor because of defendant's promise to pay the debt himself; or the plaintiff stitched a gown for the defendant's maid, at defendant's request.[88] The defendant's liability in these beneficiary cases was not finally recognized until courts decided that "whatever would constitute a *quid pro quo* if rendered to the defendant himself would be none the less a *quid pro quo* though furnished to a third person, provided it was furnished at the defendant's request, and that the third person incurred no liability therefor to the plaintiff."[89] In addition to the receipt of *quid pro quo*, there is suggestion of a distinct personal limitation. The "no contract" objection may have included the thought that if defendant received *quid pro quo* from someone other than the

---

[85] *Anonymous*, (1680) Hardres 485. In Spelman's report of *Core v. May* (1537) 93 Seld. Soc. 132 (see also Dyer 20), it is said that C, the beneficiary, "was not privy to the contract."

[86] BAKER, *supra* n. 58, pp. 263-264.

[87] MILSOM, HISTORICAL FOUNDATIONS OF THE COMMON LAW, p. 224. The only exception involved the sale of goods, which became consensual to the extent that the seller could recover not only if he had actually delivered goods but also if he was willing to deliver them.

[88] AMES, *supra* n. 76, at 93; SIMPSON, *supra* n. 9, at p. 153 ff.

[89] AMES, *supra* n. 76, at pp. 93-94.

plaintiff, this was not a contract with plaintiff and accordingly not actionable by him.[90]

To this limitation an exception was made (previously admitted only in account) for the case of money or goods bailed "to the use" of a third person. It was stated in *Whorewood v. Shaw* (1602):[91] "Although no contract is between the parties, yet when money or goods are delivered upon consideration to the use of A., A, may have debt for them." Here A seems to have been recognized as a *cestuy que use* who held the legal interest of the thing bailed.[92]

Assumpsit

Even within the narrow confines of assumpsit the privity doctrine has not stood still. Meanings have changed, and the terminology has undergone a series of modifications.

The evolution of assumpsit saw the consideration doctrine absorb early interest-based and benefit-based rules, and it later witnessed the rise of a parties-only principle independent of consideration doctrine. Thus it reveals a process in which early meanings were abandoned as the action changed, and old ideas were brought out of inventory and applied to the modern law. This change too has left us with considerable terminological problems. The current expressions "consideration must move from the promisee" and "privity of contract" (meaning parties-only principle) have two separate histories. They are relatively recent creations whose paths did not cross until the 19th century. Chapter Two will be concerned with the early evolution of the first, and Chapter Four will deal with the rise of the second.

d. Marking the boundary of contract

There is a fourth distinctive function in the repertoire of privity. The doctrine has been used repeatedly as a mechanism to mark the boundary between contract and other fields of law. This function became particularly

---

[90] The difficulty was evident in the case where X delivered £100 to defendant to be delivered to plaintiff. As late as 1625, an objection was made that there never was a contract between plaintiff and defendant, nor any delivery by plaintiff to defendant. *Harris v. de Bervoir* (1625) Cro. J. 687.

[91] Yelv. 25.

[92] See the argument of Sir Robert Sawyer in *Cramlington v. Evans*, (1685) 1 Show K.B. 4, 5; *Harris v. de Bervoir* (1625), Cro. Jac. 687, and the Yearbook citations therein.

noticeable in the 19th century when privity of contract began to play a role in the fields of tort and the trust. Historically the entry of privity into the law of tort has been viewed as so anomalous (allegedly owing to the contract "fallacy," procedural blunders, or economic prejudice) that the significance of this function has been overlooked.[93] Privity's role in shaping the law of trust is less well-known,[94] but this was another vital episode which shaped the modern privity principle. The privity objection in these areas carried no writ-oriented meaning. It was through *principle* that the scope and basis of these other fields were controlled.

III. THE CONTEMPORARY CONTROVERSY

The cloudiness of its history is in good measure responsible for the inconclusive debate about the beneficiary action. The protagonists have differed sharply, but often their differences have been based upon limited enquiry, false confidence in broad deduction, and an unpersuasive tendency to assign single causes to a complex phenomenon.

According to Professor Hening's study, history showed how the rich legacy of beneficial rights recognized in debt was slowly squandered in assumpsit over the next 200 years. He spoke conclusively of the gradual but progressive "disinherison of the beneficiary," that is, the decline that took place when the substantive beneficial rights afforded by debt and account were confounded (by procedural blunders) with those of assumpsit.[95] In complete contrast, Stoljar's recent history argues that the 17th century cases in assumpsit represented a "clear and confident progression" towards recognition of the beneficiary's right in contract. The progression was interrupted, however, by the case of *Bourne v. Mason* (1669), and thenceforward the

---

[93] This question receives detailed treatment in Chapter IV, pp. 198-212.

[94] Treated below in Chap. IV, pp. 212-219.

[95] Hening's study, though promisingly entitled, deals mainly with the action of account, and submits a limited proposition which is scarcely doubtful: "It can be shown (conclusively, I submit) that *outside of assumpsit* this so-called 'monstrosity' has been the law of England for 500 years." *See* Crawford D. Hening, "History of the Beneficiary's Action in Assumpsit," in SELECT ESSAYS IN ANGLO-AMERICAN LEGAL HISTORY, ed. by Association of American Law Schools, (Little, Brown, 1909), vol. III, p. 340; a more extended version is contained in Hening, "The Limitations of the Action of Assumpsit as Affecting the Right of Action of the Beneficiary," [1904] 52 Amer. Law Reg. 764, [1905] 53 Amer. Law Reg. 112, and [1908] 56 Amer. Law. Reg. 73.

beneficiary's special position became obscured.[96] The story is a good bit more complicated and interesting than Stoljar suggests. Confident linear progressions are rare events in common law development, and here, in any event, the pertinent evidence is quite contrary to Stoljar's conclusion. Less enthusiastic observers have generally called attention to the "great contradictions" and inexplicable confusion in this period.[97]

Holdsworth's interpretation of these events was far more careful and balanced. He maintained that the restrictive doctrine "consideration must move from the promisee" received some recognition by the courts of the 17th century, but that it was not firmly grasped due to three disturbing influences. "This principle seems to us," he wrote,

> to be almost too plain for argument--on historical grounds because it is an obvious deduction from the conditions under which assumpsit lay, and on logical grounds because it is an elementary principle of contract law that only the parties to the contract can be bound by or take benefits under a contract.[98]

The three interfering ideas were: (a) the equitable conception of consideration, which raised the possibiliity that love and natural affection were sufficient to ground an action in assumpsit; (b) the holdings that a person not a party to an agreement could take the benefit thereunder in the actions of debt and account; and (c) the contemporary perception that benefit to the promisor counted equally with detriment to the promisee as a valid consideration.[99] Holdsworth's account, however, is ultimately unsatisfactory in two respects. He made the incorrect assumption that the proposition "consideration must move from the promisee" was the equivalent of a parties-only principle, so that the birth of the latter principle was erroneously put as early as the seventeenth century. The two rules are not only logically

---

[96] 1 Vent. 6, 2 Keb. 454, 457, 527. S.J. STOLJAR, A HISTORY OF CONTRACT AT COMMON LAW (Australian National University Press, 1975), p. 137.

[97] The 19th century text and note authors, for example, seemed disillusioned by the Heraclitean case law of this formative period. *See, e.g.*, JOSEPH CHITTY, A PRACTICAL TREATISE ON THE LAW OF CONTRACTS NOT UNDER SEAL, 7th Amer. ed. by Perkins, (Merriam, 1848), pp. 52a-5; Bosanquet and Puller's note to the case of *Piggott v. Thompson* (1802) 3 B. & P. 147, 148, note (a).

[98] HOLDSWORTH, *supra* n. 76, vol. VIII, at pp. 11-12.

[99] *Id.* at 12-13.

dissimilar,[100] but historically disconnected.[101] The parties-only rule was not recognized in assumpsit before the 19th century. Furthermore, the consideration maxim was not encountered in that form until the 19th century. Thus, it is not clear that either rule was recognized as early as Holdsworth claimed.[102]

The cloudy history of the modern rule has also obscured the debate among judges, critics and commentators. Lord Denning, in a series of vigorous opinions, has claimed that the rigorous English position against third party beneficiary actions was an invention of the 19th century that did not become "rooted" in English law until the year 1861. Historically, he argues, the courts of common law in the 17th and 18th centuries had repeatedly enforced promises made in favor of a sufficiently "interested" third party.[103] Another writer supports Lord Denning by saying--

In truth this [the privity limitation] is not a fundamental

---

[100] As Pollock has shown. See below, pp. 24-25.

[101] See below, Chapter IV, pp. 159 ff.

[102] SIMPSON, *supra* n. 9, pp. 476-477.

[103] See *Smith v. River Douglas Catchment Board* [1949] 2 All E.R. 179, 188. Lord Denning's thesis is also trenchantly expressed in this passage:

> "I wish to assert, as distinctively as I can, that the common law in its original setting knew no such principle. Indeed it said quite the contrary. For the two hundred years before 1861 *it was settled law* that, if a promise in a simple contract was made expressly for the benefit of a third person in such circumstances that it was intended to be enforceable by him, then the common law would enforce the promise at his instance, although he was not a party to the contract." *Drive Yourself Hire v. Strutt* [1953] 2 All E.R. 1475, 1482.

See also *Midland Silicones, Ltd. v. Scruttons, Ltd.* [1962] A.C. 446, 481-492 (dissenting opinion of Lord Denning). *Beswick v. Beswick,* [1966] Ch. 538, [1968] A.C. 58; *Jackson v. Horizon Holidays,* [1975] 1 W.L.R. 1468. Lord Denning's views have not been favorably received in the House of Lords: *Woodar Investments Development Ltd. v. Wimpey Construction U.K. Ltd.* [1980] 1 W.L.R. 277. Lord Denning has discussed his controversial views in his book THE DISCIPLINE OF THE LAW, pp. 289-291 (London 1979), and an assessment of his influence on English and Canadian contract law has been made by Professor Atiyah and Professor Waddams in LORD DENNING: THE JUDGE AND THE LAW, pp. 45-46, 457-459 (London 1984), edited by Jowell and McAuslan.

principle of our common law. As a rule it has no great
history. In fact it is a modern and largely academic rationale
for a group of cases running from *Bourne v. Mason* to
Tweddle v. Atkinson that were decided wholly on the
principle that consideration must move from the
promisee.[104]

On the other hand, several authors have said that Lord Denning's
historical case is not proven and that the early voices of authority, though
dissonant, "shouted loudest" in favor of the rule in *Tweddle v. Atkinson*.[105]
Here is an area in which historical argument is in fashion, and history is made
to yield clear answers. There are many questionable, if not false, assumptions
made by the protagonists about the pedigree of the modern rule. There is
insufficient recognition that the consideration rule and the parties-only rule
are two different rules and they have a different content and different history.
The case of *Tweddle v. Atkinson* (1861) is continually mistaken as the source
of the parties-only rule, as if the year 1861 was the benchmark for the strict
modern rule found in *Dunlop v. Selfridge*.[106] It is clearly an error to use old
privity references in 16th and 17th century cases as sign posts of the antiquity
of the parties-only rule. Such mismatched cases and concepts lack the
authority to prove or disprove the point.[107]

The Monist - Dualist Schools

The question whether privity of contract embodies a single
requirement or consists of two independent bases has become a major point
of controversy. Under the monist view the "parties-only" formulation neatly
states the full objection to the beneficiary action, because the consideration
question is subsumed. Samuels maintains that any further distinction is not
"useful" and "non-existent" because, no one can be a party to a contract and

---

[104] J. A. Andrews, "Section 56 Revisited," [1959] 23 Conveyancer and Property Lawyer 179,
188-189.

[105] (1861) 1 B. & S. 393. Ernest H. Scammel, "Privity of Contract," [1955] 8 Current Legal
Problems 131, 134-135; Note, "Privity of Contract," [1954] 70 L.Q.R. 467.

[106] [1915] A.C. 847.

[107] Reasoning flawed by this misconception will be found in Note, "Privity of Contract," [1954]
70 L.Q.R. 467.

yet a stranger to the consideration.[108]

The nonobvious premise in this statement resides in the word "contract" which the monist defines narrowly in the sense of bargain. Even when a donee beneficiary receives a promise directly, he is not regarded as a party to a "contract" but rather a party to a gratuitious promise. Thus, if B promises A and C that if A delivers 100 to him he will in turn deliver 50 to C, C cannot enforce B's promise though he was a party to it. The beneficiary cannot be party to a bargain or contract unless he himself gives consideration. As Furmston sees the issue, "If C is not a party to the bargain he is not a party to the contract."[109]   The monist, therefore, does not really dispense entirely with the issue of consideration. He only builds it into his definition of a "contract." The monist tendency, however, is not what is novel here. In previous centuries lawyers were always monist because they stated the full objection solely in terms of consideration, while suppressing a parties-only objection through the use of fiction.[110] The novel tendency in modern analysis is to invert the rule and state the objection without the use of the consideration doctrine.

The dualist view, on the other hand, openly segregates the two ideas and maintains that each independently accounts for the refusal of the beneficiary action. Thus, Scammell has said that "even if the rule of privity were reversed by the courts, few plaintiffs would be assisted, because of the rule that consideration must move from the promisee."[111] Yet this result does not necessarily follow from the rule, for *a priori* in every binding contract, consideration has in fact moved from the promisee, even when the beneficiary action is denied. Pollock pointed to this fallacy many years ago:

It is laid down in the books that consideration must move

---

[108] Gordon Samuels, "Contracts for the Benefit of Third Parties," [1968] 8 Univ. of Western Australia L. Rev. 378, 383. See also Furmston's views on consideration: "There is no difference between the doctrine of consideration and the rule that consideration must move from the promisee." He is able to state categorically, "The two rules are identical." M.P. Furmston, "Return to Dunlop v. Selfridge?" [1960] 23 Mod. L. Rev. 373, 382-383.

[109] Furmston, *supra* n. 108, at 383.

[110] See below, Chapter IV, pp. 163-164.

[111] Scammell, *supra* n. 105 (speaks of two independent rules). SIR WILLIAM ANSON, ANSON'S LAW OF CONTRACT, 25th ed. by Guest, (Oxford University Press, 1979), p. 421 (cases rest not only upon the rule that consideration must move from promisee, but also "upon the more fundamental assumption that no one who is not a party to the contract can acquire rights under it.")

from the promisee, and it is sometime supposed that infringement of this rule is the basis of the objection to allowing an action upon a promise made for his benefit. This is not the case. In such promises the beneficiary who seeks to maintain an action on the promise is not the promisee.[112]

It seems, therefore, that the differences between these two theories should not be exaggerated. The full objection at English Law has become the twofold restriction that only a contracting *party* who has furnished *consideration* may enforce a contract.[113] These requirements are overlapping and interdependent, and it makes no substantive difference whether the consideration element is directly articulated or interstitially incorporated into the very meaning of "party to a contract." The historical challenge raised by the monist/dualist formulation is to trace the rise of these independent objections and to explain how, when, and why this modern conjunction came about.[114] We will find this explanation in the three successive periods of the beneficiary action: the Formative Period, 1500-1680; the Chancery Phase, 1680-1800; and the Rise of the Parties - Only Principle, 1800-1890. These three periods, treated below in Chapters II, III and IV respectively, provide the main outline of this historical study.

---

[112] SIR FREDERICK POLLOCK, PRINCIPLES OF CONTRACT AT LAW AND IN EQUITY, 3rd Amer. ed. by Williston, (Baker Voorhis, 1906). The same observation has been seconded by German scholars. See ZWEIGERT AND KöTZ, *supra* n.1, at 134.

[113] The duality was clearly expressed in the writings of certain 19th century jurists. See E.H. Bennett, "Considerations Moving from Third Persons," 9 Harv. L. Rev. 233 (1895) ("A want of privity as to both the promise and the consideration certainly seems to be an insuperable obstacle to an action, upon the strict principles of the common law."); *Edmundson v. Penny* (1845) 1 Pa. St. 335 (Gibson C.J., "The plaintiff must unite in his person both the promise and the consideration of it in order to recover.").

[114] Clearly, the English position grew stricter when the test of privity became a dualism in the late 19th century. At that point, the roles of monist and dualist reversed. Before then, the monist viewpoint stated the privity rule only in terms of consideration: "Consideration must move from the plaintiff." The monist did not advert to a parties-only notion except as a procedural formality. See below, Chap. IV, pp. 163-164.

CHAPTER II

THE FORMATIVE PERIOD (1500-1680)*

INTRODUCTION

We have seen that questions about the privity doctrine continue to generate contemporary debate that may never be resolved. Many of these questions relate to the nature of privity and what relationship it has to consideration. Is privity a distinct doctrine or merely an aspect of the requirement of consideration?[1] Does the consideration doctrine contain the essence of the privity limitation (monist position)[2] or is there a distinct parties-only principle that extends beyond consideration-based privity (dualist position)?[3] Should the rule "consideration must move from the promisee" be

---

* This chapter is based upon my previously published essay "The History of Privity – The Formative Period," 33 Am. J. Leg. Hist. (1989).

[1] See R. Flannigan, Privity-The End of an Era (Error), 103 L.Q.R. 564, 568 (1987).

[2] Furmston's view, for example, is that "There is no difference between the doctrine of privity of contract and the rule that consideration must move from the promisee." He is able to state categorically that, "The two rules are identical ." M.P. Furmston, Return to *Dunlop v. Selfridge*?, 23 Mod. L. Rev. 373, 382-83 (1960); See also Andrews' view that "the only convincing reason for denying C a direct right of action is the fact that he is not privy to consideration for A's promise." N.H. Andrews, "Does a Third Party Beneficiary Have a Right in English Law," Legal Stud. 14, 17 (1988); *accord* Flannigan, *supra* note 1, at 568. (Two rules are "but different ways of saying the same thing. . . . [T]he 'privity' rule (that a non-party cannot sue) is just a description of the result supposedly demanded by the doctrine of consideration. The rule, then, is that a third party cannot sue on the contract because he or she has not provided consideration.")

[3] See *Dunlop v. Selfridge*, [1915] A.C. 847 per Ld. Haldane; *Midland Silicone, Ltd. v. Scruttons Ltd.* [1962] A.C. 446, 447, per Viscount Simonds; SIR. WM. ANSON, ANSON'S LAW OF CONTRACT, 421 (25th ed. by Guest O.U.P., 1979) (Cases rest not only upon the rule that consideration must move from the promisee, but also "upon the more fundamental assumption that no one who is not a party to the contract can acquire rights under it."); Scammell, "Privity of Contract," 8 Current Legal Probs. 131, 135 (two independent rules: "even if the rule of privity were reversed by the courts, few plaintiffs would be assisted, because of the rule that consideration must move from the promisee.") The dualist position was expressed in the writings of certain 19th century Americans such as E.H. Bennett, "Considerations Moving from

regarded as the equivalent of a parties-only rule, or is it a narrower rule which leaves, by its terms, some scope for an action by a non-party?[4] Other questions relate to the entrenchment of the privity doctrine in English law. Was it definitively established by the end of the 17th century,[5] the mid-19th century,[6] or not until the 20th century?[7] In establishing the modern doctrine did courts fully canvass and properly consider the early precedents or did they unwittingly ignore, invent or "legislate" the history of the privity doctrine?[8]

Third Persons," 9 Harv. L. Rev. 31 (1985) and Chief Justice Gibson of Pennsylvania in *Edmundson v. Penny*, (1885) 1 Pa. St. 335.

[4] According to the monist position the two rules are basically equivalent, but this requires the monist to read the consideration rule as if it said "consideration must move from the promisee and plaintiff must be the promisee." To illustrate, in a typical life insurance contract, the parties-only rule would conclusively block the third party beneficiary's action on the policy simply because he was a non-party. The consideration rule, however, would not have that effect by its literal terms because consideration (a promise or a premium payment) would have been provided by the promisee (the insured party) to the insurance company. The beneficiary is barred only if the rule is enlarged to say "and plaintiff must be the promisee." Flannigan, *supra* note 1, at 568, fn. 37, alludes to this problem but does not solve it.

The dualist position, on the other hand, recognizes that the consideration rule does not literally bar the beneficiary's action if the promisee has given consideration, and that the promisee will have done this in the usual case. Thus Pollock wrote: "It is laid down in the books that consideration must move from the promisee, and it is sometimes supposed that infringement of this rule is the basis of the objection to allowing an action upon a promise made for his benefit. This is not the case. In such promises the beneficiary who seeks to maintain an action on the promise is not the promisee." SIR FREDERICK POLLOCK, PRINCIPLES OF CONTRACT AT LAW AND IN EQUITY, 3rd Amer. ed. by Williston (1906). The observation has been seconded by 2 ZWEIGERT & KOTZ, AN INTRODUCTION TO COMPARATIVE LAW, 134.

[5] *See Bourne v. Mason* (1669) 1 Vent. 6, 2 Keb. 454; *Dutton v. Poole* (1680) Raym. T. 302, 2 Lev. 211, 1 Freem. 471, 3 Keb. 786, 1 Vent. 318.

[6] *Price v. Easton*, (1833) 4B. & Ad. 433; *Tweddle v. Atkinson*, (1861) 1B. & S. 393, 30 L.J.Q.B. 265, 4 Law Times 468.

[7] *Dunlop v. Selfridge* [1951] A.C. 847; *Vandepitte v. Preferred Acc. Ins. Corp. of N.Y.*, [1933] A.C. 70 (P.C. Can.).

[8] Lord Denning has championed the view that today's rigorous privity rule was an invention of the 19th century that did not become "rooted" in English law until the year 1861. See *Smith v. River Douglas Catchment Bd.* [1949] 2 All E.R. 179, 188; *Drive Yourself Hire v. Strutt*, [1953] 2 All E.R. 1475, 1482 ("the common law in its original setting knew no such principle. Indeed it said quite the contrary.") See also *Midland Silicones, Ltd. v. Scruttons, Ltd.*, [1962] A.C. 446, 481-492 (dissenting opinion); *Beswick v. Beswick*, [1966] Ch. 538, [1968] A.C. 58; *Jackson v. Horizon Holidays*, [1975] 1 W.L.R. 277. Ld. Denning discusses his controversial position in THE DISCIPLINE OF THE LAW, 289-291 (London 1979). H.A. Andrews adopts the same position in his article "Section 56 Revisited," [1959] 23 Conveyancer & Prop. Law 179, 188-189 ("In truth

Could (or should) the House of Lords recognize the error and overrule its modern pronouncements?[9] Finally, there remain questions relating to the doctrine's consistency with the various theories put forward to justify the enforcement of contracts: bargain theory, will theory, economic analysis, etc.[10]

To resolve these questions historical perspective is important, and one would naturally expect historical studies to provide essential data in point. However, this is a subject with a cloudy history. Conflicting views have been adopted on the basis of limited enquiry, broad deductions, and a tendency to attribute simple causation to complex developments. The history of the subject has not been developed with sufficient detail, scale and coherence to permit a proper evaluation of these views.

This chapter traces and analyzes the earliest phase of privity's development, "The Formative Period" (1500-1680). This period is crucial, because here we find the substantive origins of the modern doctrine. However, before descending into the historical details the reader may benefit from a brief overview of the major developments.

Preliminary Overview

This chapter deals exclusively with the common law courts and actions brought in assumpsit. Assumpsit was in its infancy, and the common law courts were more flexible about permitting a beneficiary action than at any subsequent time. The historical record yields a number of general conclusions.

First, the sheer number of actions and the liberal results were impressive. Relief was given frequently to the beneficiary, indicating that a strict privity rule did not exist before 1670.

Second, the frequency of relief is understandable because the two components of modern privity doctrine—the parties-only principle and the rule

---

this is not a fundamental principle of our common law. As a rule it has no great history. . . a modern and largely academic rationale . . . .")

[9] Some writers say that the rule is too deeply entrenched to be overruled except by Parliament. Gordon Samuels, "Contracts For the Benefit of Third Parties," (1968) 8 Univ. Of W. Australia L. Rev. 378, 381 ("evident that any doctrine of third party rights had been finally buried under the weight of unanimously adverse authority."); Scammell, *supra* n.3, at 135 ("the principle of privity is too deeply entrenched to be summarily grubbed out.")

[10] *See* Flannigan, *supra* note 1, at 582-592.

"consideration must move from the promisee—were not yet controlling. The first idea surfaced in argument and was advanced as an objection; it may even have been the basis of a few decisions.[11] But the contemporary evidence is clear that although the parties-only notion was fully grasped and repeatedly asserted, it was, more often than not, decisively rejected by the courts. Indeed, the only tangible "doctrine" to emerge on this point was the promise-in-law theory, a fiction[12] expressly conceived to permit the nonpromisee to sue. As to the consideration rule, during all but the last decade of this era, the idea competed as but one of several theories by which the beneficiary's right to sue was tested. The rule that the beneficiary must not be "a stranger to the consideration" was not set up until the end of the period (circa 1670).

Third, the successful actions in assumpsit by third party beneficiaries were not channelled into any single reasoning pattern. The prevailing criteria of the period were not truly contractual in the sense understood by the modern lawyer. Relief was justified by the judges through the creative mingling of various ideas sounding in property and tort, as well as contract.

Finally, there were basically four individual paths to privity for the beneficiary, and each of these will need to be treated in separate sections. The conditions under which relief could be granted were determined by the notions of interest, benefit, agency, and consideration.

(a) The interest theory (Section I) was typically expressed in the statement, "He that hath interest in the promise shall have the action." One rationale for permitting the beneficiary's action was that non-performance of the promise caused an injury to his interest, and he should receive compensation. Under this theory, assumpsit functioned somewhat as a tort remedy for the beneficiary's damages. Vindication of this interest in the performance of the promise was additionally conceptualized as the enforcement of a "use" created by the promise. Although these were ordinary promises that contained no express use, this implied use in favor of the beneficiary apparently placed a property foundation under the claim in assumpsit. The beneficiary's interest in the promise was thus conceived as his property.

(b) The benefit theory (Section II) asserted that "the party to whom

---

[11] *See* A.W.B. SIMPSON, A HISTORY OF THE COMMON LAW OF CONTRACT (Oxford University Press, 1979).

[12] *See* below pp. 49-50, 51-52. The promisee-in-law fiction permitted the beneficiary to declare, contrary to fact, that he was the promisee.

the benefit of a promise accrues may bring the action." This rationale was typically associated with cases in which there was a donation intended for the beneficiary, and the notion of benefit seems to have descended from the beneficiary doctrine in the older action of debt. The action was typically laid in *indebitatus assumpsit* but the relief extended beyond the limits of the concurrent action in debt. Recoveries were permitted on a bare promise even without a prior debt or duty owed to the beneficiary or any receipt of his property by the defendant. The beneficiary's pleadings would state, counterfactually, that defendant had made this promise directly to him.

(c) The agency cases (Section III) reveal that privity objections were avoided by the notion that the legal persona of the agent merged into that of his principal. Accordingly, the principal who was a nonpromisee was entitled to sue upon a promise made to his agent. Yet quite apart from that ground, there is clear evidence that the principal could be regarded by contemporaries as the third party beneficiary of a promise in his favor and should recover for that reason.

(d) The consideration theory (Section IV) emerged as the dominant test of the beneficiary action at the end of the Formative Period. The interest and benefit theories were replaced or absorbed, and relief for the beneficiary was curtailed at common law. The new consideration test was exceedingly strict. It arose in a discrete line of cases in which a creditor beneficiary sued a "substitute" debtor who had made a promise to pay off the debt of the creditor's original debtor. The creditor's action was barred whether or not he was the promisee of the substitute's promise, and whether or not he had provided consideration.

When the cases are divided into these four categories, it becomes possible to understand the evolution of the privity doctrine from its complex beginnings and to appreciate the remarkable triumph of the consideration theory over its rivals. The following sections will describe and analyze these theories and problems in further detail.

I. THE INTEREST THEORY

A. An Introduction to the Theory

The case of *Hadves v. Levit* (1632),[13] presents a clear illustration of the interest theory. In anticipation of a marriage between their children, the bride's father (the defendant) had promised the groom's father (the plaintiff) that he would pay £200 to the plaintiff's son after the marriage had taken place. The plaintiff for his part promised to consent to the marriage and to make a reciprocal grant of money to the defendant's daughter. After the wedding, the defendant failed to pay the £200 to the son, so the plaintiff brought an action in assumpsit, claiming as his damage that he was constrained, as a result of the breach of promise, to give the couple greater maintenance than otherwise would have been necessary.

The father's claim was rejected by the Court of Common Pleas.[14] Richardson, J. stated that the action should have been "more properly" brought by the son, for he was the person "in whom the interest is." He relied upon a 1580 decision concerning a woman who had a license to transport herrings to Spain. A stranger had promised the woman's father, "procure her license for me and I'll pay you £100 and £100 to your daughter." The 1580 court held that the daughter should sue for her £100 share because the action concerned her "more specially."[15] Hutton, J. now reached the same conclusion, taking the view that:

> there is a difference when the promise is to
> perform to one who is not interested in the cause
> and when he hath an interest. In the first case he
> to whom the promise is made shall have the
> action, and not he to whom the promise is to be
> performed.[16]

Hutton, J. gave the following illustration of an uninterested beneficiary:

---

[13] Het. 176.

[14] It may be that this case was not finally adjudged. Nevertheless, the grounds stated appear to be the considered view of the court, and serve as a good illustration of contemporary thinking.

[15] A more exact precedent for the court's view would have been *Levett v. Hawes* (1599) Cro. Eliz. 619, 652.

[16] *Hadves v. Levit* (1632) Het. 176.

> (1) If A. promise B. to pay J.S. $10 (upon a consideration) which is not done, B. shall have the action, and not J.S.[17]

In contrast, he gave the two following illustrations of an interested beneficiary:

> (2) If there be two joint [owners] of a horse, and the one conditions with the other to go to market to sell it, who does it and appoints the payment [by the purchaser] to be made to another [the other co-owner]; in this case he only to whom the payment is to be made [i.e., the co-owner] shall have the action.

> (3) So also if my servant, by my command, sell my horse: the money to be paid to me; I shall have the action, and not my servant, for the interest is in me.[18]

Thus, *Hadves v. Levit* stood for the proposition that the "interested" beneficiary occupied so strong and preeminent a position that even a promisee seeking an action in damages against the promisor might be nonsuited. A contemporary commentator abstracted this rule from the case:

> And so it is said, that where a Promise is made to a second person to perform something to a third person that hath an interest in the cause: In this case he to whom the Promise is to be performed, and not he to whom it is made shall have the action.[19]

The line drawn by Hutton, J. between the interested and uninterested beneficiary related to the compensatory function of assumpsit. One example he gave of an "interested" beneficiary involved the delivery and sale of the beneficiary's own property to a purchaser who promised to pay the price

---

[17] To appreciate why J.S. is uninterested in this example, we probably should assume B. is trying to make a donation to him.

[18] *See supra* note 13.

[19] TRADES-MAN'S LAWYER AND COUNTRY-MAN'S FRIEND 67 (1703). This work was an early practical commercial law text apparently intended for merchants and laymen. Its author is unknown.

directly to the beneficiary. Delivery to the purchaser was made by the beneficiary's co-owner or by his servant. Since the beneficiary, as owner, had parted with his property, his interest would consist in the damage he sustained if he did not receive the price. The promisee, his servant, was not the owner of the thing and could not be harmed by or compensated for the breach. It is evident that the 1580 case of the Spanish herrings cited by the court logically supported this reasoning.[20] His illustration of an uninterested beneficiary was completely different, for it involved a promise to pay £10 to a beneficiary who had no evident prior right to the money. The beneficiary was simply the intended recipient of a gift. If the promised performance did not occur, his patrimony would not be increased, nor would it be reduced. Hutton's distinction was close to that between a creditor and a donee beneficiary.

The application of his distinction to the facts in the *Hadves* case logically explains the decision. The father was viewed as an inappropriate plaintiff because his compensable interest appeared nominal and nebulous. When he attempted to state his loss in tangible form, he could only plead that the defendant's breach of promise made it necessary for him to pay the married couple greater maintenance than would otherwise have been necessary. This was an unconvincing allegation since the father was not under a legal obligation to provide such maintenance. The son's loss, by contrast, was concrete. He had married on the strength of the dowry promises. In taking a wife, he (or his father) had probably bargained for the stipulated sum, and he had parted with a certain freedom or foreclosed an alternative alliance, perhaps to the lady he actually preferred.[21] Such detriments associated with undertaking marriage were already recognized at common law

---

[20] There, the promise was made to the father, but it was the daughter who had parted with her license to transport herrings to Spain. It was she who was primarily damaged by the promisor's failure to pay her the money.

[21] Traditionally, the subjective wishes of an engaged couple were often subordinated to the strong economic reasons for marriage under feudal law. *See*, LAWRENCE STONE, CRISIS OF THE ARISTOCRACY, 1558-1641, Chap. XI (O.U.P. 1965); JOEL HURSTFIELD, THE QUEEN'S WARDS, 111-156 (2nd ed. 1973); Lawrence Stone has noted, however, a changing social pattern concerning matrimony in 17th century England. The traditional motives for marriage based upon economic, social or political considerations which made marriage primarily a contract between two families for the exchange of concrete benefits had given way by 1660, except in the highest ranks of the aristocracy, to a pattern in which the children of both sexes should be given the right of veto over a future spouse proposed by their parents. THE FAMILY, SEX AND MARRIAGE, 181-186 (1979 abridged).

as a form of valuable consideration.[22]

This immediately suggests that "interest" and "consideration" could easily have been regarded by the judges as similar, even identical ideas in many contexts, and it is tempting to ask whether the recovery given in *Hadves* could have been justified on the basis that the beneficiary had provided consideration to the defendant. The groom could bring the action on the father's promise not only because he was interested in the father's performance but because he himself had provided consideration for the promise by marrying the daughter. Why was this reasoning neglected? The explanation is that in 1632, the test of consideration did not regulate who might sue on a promise. Consideration was seen as a requirement associated with the validity of defendant's promise to the promisee and not as the measure of the right to recover damage for breach of promise. If the aim was primarily to determine which type of plaintiff deserved an action for compensation, the judges could not have found a more sensible or direct test than to accord the action to the "interested" beneficiary and deny it to the "uninterested" beneficiary. Certainly, however, this view was subject to change. Apparently, the possibility that the judges might reevaluate the interest test in terms of consideration was always present in the Formative Period. When this reevaluation occurred in 1669,[23] it caused the interest test to disappear.

B.   Further Illustrations

There were other cases in this period that gave recovery to the "interested" beneficiary, and each seems based upon the compensatory purpose of the action. In three cases (Nos. 3, 4, 5 below) the court expressly referred to the interest theory, while in two others (Nos. 1, 2 below) no explicit reference was made. Furthermore, in three cases (Nos. 1, 4, 5 below) the beneficiary is described as having a "use" raised in his favor.

---

[22] *See* Lord Bacon's statement in *Reynell v. Peacock* (1602) 2 Rolle 105, 106: "It would be mischievous if the one who marries in consideration of the land could not avoid the (prior) trust, because he would lose by that the advancement which perhaps he could have had through another woman, and thus the consideration he gives is valuable." *See also, Holford v. Holford* (1672) 1 Chan. Cas. 216.

[23] *Bourne v. Mason* (1669) 1 Vent. 6, 2 Keb. 454.

1.

In *Levett v. Hawes* (1599)[24] a father brought assumpsit upon a promise made directly to him that marriage money would be paid to his son. The court was of opinion that the action ought to have been brought by the son, "for the promise is made to the son's use and the ordinary covenants of marriage are with the father to stand seised to the son's use; and the use shall be changed and transferred to the son, as if it were a covenant with himself; and the damage of non-performance thereof is to the son."[25]

2.

In *Rippon v. Norton* (1602)[26] the defendant's son, Richard, assaulted and wounded the plaintiff and his son, Walter. Thereafter plaintiff complained to the justice of the peace and required surety of the peace. The defendant, however, promised that if plaintiff would not proceed further with his complaint then he, Richard's father, would guarantee that his son would keep the peace and not assail plaintiff or his son in the future. Notwithstanding the defendant's promise, his son Richard later assaulted Walter and wounded him. Plaintiff brought assumpsit and recovered a verdict of £20 for the cost of curing his son and his lost service. Relying, however, on the case of *Levett v. Hawes* (*supra*), the defendant objected in arrest of judgment that the father had no proper action. Upholding this objection the court said, "because there is not any damage to the father by the battery to the son an action lies not for the father. And although it were objected that the father was at the charge for the curing the son of his wounds, yet, because it was a thing he was not compelled unto, it is no cause why he should maintain this action." (Note: in a subsequent term the son brought his own action in assumpsit and recovered.)[27]

3.

In *Brand v. Lisley* (1610)[28] the plaintiff-beneficiary was a creditor of W for $100. W delivered certain goods to the defendant equal to and in

---

[24] Cro. Eliz. 654.

[25] *Id.*

[26] Cro. Eliz. 849.

[27] *Id.* at 881.

[28] Yelv. 164.

satisfaction of his debt to plaintiff. The plaintiff made demand upon defendant for payment and the defendant requested forbearance and promised to pay by a certain day. Plaintiff's action in assumpsit resulted in a verdict which was affirmed. The court found that the plaintiff had an interest in the goods in defendant's hands and that the defendant had received consideration. It was said "For the delivery of the goods to the defendant to satisfy the plaintiff the £100, the plaintiff has *an interest and property* in the goods, and then by the plaintiff's forbearance of the defendant for a time, the goods being due" immediately, the defendant had a benefit and *quid pro quo*.[29]

4.

In *De La Bar v. Gold* (1662)[30] the plaintiff's "agent"[31] leased a share of a ship to Wood, and Wood subleased to Gold. Wood defaulted on his rent, and plaintiff's agent, seeking payment from Wood's assets in defendant's hands, agreed to forbear in consideration of defendant's promise to pay Wood's debt. Plaintiff's suit for breach of the promised payment ended inconclusively, but Windham J. discussed recovery for plaintiff in terms of the interest theory:

"If the promise were in consideration that A. hath sold goods to B. he promiseth to C. £10, C. hath no remedy because he is but an attorney of A. to receive for his use; and A. only can have an action upon the case against B. for not paying the money to C. But if A. sells to B. and B. promiseth in consideration thereof to pay to C. £10 which A. owed C., in this case C. shall have an action because it appeareth the interest was his: . . ."[32]

5.

In *Corny & Curtis v. Collidon* (1674)[33] the defendant's mother had been taxed by the plaintiffs, the Churchwardens at Deeping, for repairs to the Church, and failing to make payment, her mother had been excommunicated at their prosecution. The daughter went to the Bishop and promised that if

---

[29] *Id.* (Emphasis supplied.)

[30] 1 Keb. 44, 63.

[31] This case is the earliest example that the writer has found in which the term "agent" is used in its representative sense.

[32] 1 Keb. 63, 64.

[33] 1 Freem. K.B. 284.

he would absolve her mother, then she (the daughter) would pay the taxes. The Bishop granted absolution, but the daughter did not pay the taxes and the Churchwardens made her a defendant and recovered a verdict. It was objected that the Churchwardens lacked an interest in the cause because they were not in office at the time of the defendant's promise. The court held per curiam in favor of plaintiffs, applying the simple brocard "He that hath interest in the promise shall have the action."[34]

C.   Beneficiary's Interest Distinct From the Promisee's Consideration

The examples set forth above suggest that common law courts in this period had conceived the notion that the consideration for the defendant's promise could be distinguished from the external interest of the beneficiary. For example, in *Rippon v. Norton* (No. 2 above), consideration did move from the beneficiary's father to the defendant.[35] Without the father's promise not to prosecute, it is not to be supposed that the defendant would have been bound *ab initio* under the action of assumpsit. Yet the beneficiary (his son) had a superior stake in the defendant's promise to guarantee the peace. It follows that the beneficial interest was a notion independent of the requirement of consideration, and formed a distinct basis for allowing the action in the nonpromisee's name. These recoveries support Corbin's statement that "the harm for which the action of assumpsit was maintained was harm that resulted from the breach (misperformance of the promisor), not harm that was incurred as an inducement of the promise. It was not a detriment given in exchange for the promise, but a detriment that was caused by non-performance of the promise."[36]

The Important Role Played by the Use

In three of the five examples, the court gave form and substance to

---

[34] *Id.* at 285.

[35] The presence of good consideration was especially noted in Yelverton's report of the case:

"Twas adjudged by Gaudy, Fenner and Yelverton that the action well lay, and the consideration precedent was sufficient for the plaintiff to maintain his action . . . and by reason of the complaint made in behalf of the son of the plaintiff, the son [of the defendant] might be in question before the justice of the peace, for that reason the consideration is good; . . ." Yelv. 1 & 2.

[36] ARTHUR L. CORBIN, CORBIN ON CONTRACTS, (West Publishing, 1951), sec. 122.

this external interest by finding that a "use" had been raised for the beneficiary, even though the defendant had made an ordinary promise in which a use was not mentioned. This implied use placed the interest in relief, making it seem like a distinct property asset that contrasted with the consideration necessary to create a binding promise. There was, of course, an inducing consideration that ran from the promisee to the promisor, but no similar consideration moved from the beneficiary, and the latter was not bound by any promise to perform.

D.   The Prevalence of the Property Connotation[37]

These early cases show that both proprietary rights and personal rights could be recognized under the broad notion of a beneficiary's interest. Where corporeal property was put into the defendant's possession to be delivered to the beneficiary, the beneficiary was treated as if he were already vested as owner. The ownership theory was even crudely applied in the case where unspecified money was placed in defendant's hands. The locus of the beneficiary's interest was not so much in the defendant's promise to deliver the money, as in his right to his own property. In some contexts it appears that the word "interest" had a meaning roughly equivalent to the modern notion of "title," and courts would often say the "interest and property" is in the beneficiary.[38] This proprietary thinking was certainly assisted by the use, an allied conception frequently mentioned when recoveries were allowed. The use had long played the same role in the debt beneficiary cases, the rule in debt being that where goods or money were bailed to A. for the use of B., B

---

[37] The following discussion uses the terms "proprietary" and "personal" in the sense described by Salmond. According to him, the essential difference is that proprietary rights are valuable, and personal rights are not. The former are those which are worth money; the latter are those which are worth none. SIR JOHN W. SALMOND, JURISPRUDENCE 264 (8th ed., Sweet & Maxwell, 1930).

[38] There were many examples in the contemporary literature in which an "interest" denoted specific property concepts. In analyzing the trust, the courts distinguished between the legal interest of the trustee and the equitable interest of the cestui. *Warmstrey v. Tanfield* (1628) 1 Eq. Ca. Abr. 46. In a sale of unappropriated fungible goods, like so many quarters of grain, judges said the contract gave no immediate "interest" to the vendee in any particular goods until delivery which, Kingsmill said, "proves that he did not have an interest in the grain at the time of the bargain . . . ." Anonymous Y.B. (1472) 11 Edw. IV, f. 6 pl. 10. It was also said that a bailee who held goods to secure a loan had a "special interest" in them (his lien) although the borrower remained the general owner. "If I borrow money and deliver plate for the security of it, the general property is in me, yet the bailee hath a special interest in it, till the money is paid." Per Manwood, C.B., *Clark's Case* (1587) 2 Leon 30. Finally, in Chancery a person's material interest in a court proceeding was determinative whether he should be joined as a party. WILFORD, TREATISE ON PLEADINGS 52-53 (1780).

could bring an action.[39] This rule was taken over in assumpsit, but it was carried a step beyond a completed bailment. A use might arise out of a simple promise, and the beneficiary of that use could enforce it with or without a bailment of his goods in assumpsit.[40]

We must be cautious, however, not to carry the proprietary theory too far. That explanation is too narrow to fit every case. A case might also involve personal interests in bodily security (*Rippon v. Norton*), and this interest would have no economic value in the absence of injury to it. Injury to this interest would have patrimonial consequence only when not indemnified; the personal interest itself was not an asset before the injury.

Nevertheless, though bearing this caveat in mind, it still seems important to note that in this stage of development there was a recurring tendency or preference to make the beneficial interest in assumpsit "sound" like a property interest. The justification for relief always appears more elementary when the defendant detains that which "belongs" to the plaintiff, and the requirement of personal privity is more easily ousted, even under modern law, to the extent that "real" promises or contracts may seem to be involved.[41] Hans Julius Wolfe has observed that the early road along trespass and assumpsit started out from granting protection to property, not promises, and that "resorting to the law of property and torts for the repayment of a loan or realizing a debtor's liability for not carrying out an agreement is the one great alternative to making the engagement itself actionable."[42]

The same resort to property took place when judges enforced

---

[39] *See Whorewood v. Shaw* (1602) Yelv. 25; *Harris v. De Bervoir* (1652) Cro. Jac. 687.

[40] *E.g.*, *Levett v. Hawes* (1599) Cro. Eliz. 652; *Corny & Curtis v. Collidon* (1674) 1 Freem. K.B. 284.

[41] In every legal system, so-called "real" contracts, such as sales and mortgages, produce rights that can be asserted against the world. Andrew Tettenborn, "Covenants, Privity of Contract and the Purchaser of Personal Property" 41 Camb. L.J. 58 (1982). Josserand has written: "La grande règle de la relativité des conventions cesse d'etre exacte dans la mésure òu les contrats sont par eux-meme productifs ou translatifs de droits réels opposables aux tiers." WEILL, LA RELATIVITE DES CONVENTIONS, 308 (Paris, 1939). An illustration is the doctrine of *Tulk v. Moxhay* (1848) 2 Ph. 744 (restrictive covenants on freehold land) and the doctrine of the *Strathcona* case [1926] A.C. 108 (notice of prior ship charter).

[42] "Debt and Assumpsit in the Light of Comparative Legal History," 1 Irish Jurist 316, 321, 326 (1966).

promises for the benefit of a third person.[43] A proprietary interest, for example, was decisive in determining whether insurance contracts could be enforced by the beneficiary. The courts of law and equity would annul policies in which the named insured held no interest. The necessity of having an "insurable interest" reflected the desire to suppress fraud and wagering[44] on such policies and to make indemnity the true object of the contract.[45] In 1690 the Chancellor annulled a life insurance policy on the ground that the insured had "no concern or interest depending" in the life of the deceased.[46] The requirement was later codified by statutes enacted in the 18th century,[47] and as a result, insurance did not emerge as a feasible third party beneficiary contract in England.[48]

---

[43] A modern observer has noted that the American judges also developed a third party beneficiary action by conceiving that the "property in the promise" belonged to the beneficiary. Anthony Jon Waters, "The Property in the Promise: A Study of the Third Party Beneficiary Rule," 98 Harv. Rev. 1111 (1985).

[44] "No longer ago, than when I first sat in the Court of King's Bench, I have heard these insurances called fraudulent . . . It may be a temptation to burn houses." Per Ld. Hardwicke, *Sadlers Co. v. Badcock* (1743) 2 Atk. 554, 556.

[45] Sir Peter King's manuscript report of *Depaiba v. Ludlow* (1719 Common Pleas) (Harv. Leg. Ms; 177 Eng. Leg. Ms. Project, J.H. Baker, Ed.), states, "the nature and form of those policies do both suppose that he who makes an insurance hath an interest in the thing insured, the end of the policy is to share the danger of the adventure between the insurer and the insured; now if he had no interest there was no danger to share or divide. . . ." *See also*, GEORGE RICHARDS, I RICHARDS ON INSURANCE 326, (5th ed. 1952 by Fredman); ENRICO BENSE, HISTOIRE DU CONTRAT D'ASSURANCE AU MOYEN AGE, 34 (Paris, 1897), "En effet, dés la première application de cette institution, on voit qu'il était neċessaire pour la validité de l'assuré, que l'assuré fut interessé a la conservation de son objet . . . cela ressort directement du language des documents qui éxigent qûe, pour assurer un navire, par example, l'on en soit copropriétaire.")

[46] *Wittingham v. Thornborough* (1690) 2 Eq. Ca. Abr. 635, Pre. Chan. 20. A far more detailed report of the case is found in a Lincoln's Inn Ms. (1684-1691) p. 67, (mf. 558, Eng. Leg. Ms. Project, Ed. J. H. Baker.)

[47] (1746) 19 Geo. II, c. 37; (1774) 14 Geo. III, c. 48.

[48] This early history left a residual impact on subsequent development. Even today, apart from statute, English law does not permit suit upon a life insurance policy by a third party beneficiary designated by the insured. *In re Englebach's Estate* [1924] 2 Ch. 348; HARDING S. HALSBURY, HALSBURY'S STATUTES OF ENGLAND, (3rd ed. by Yonge, Butterworths, 1968), vol. 22, sec. 570. It was not possible until the statute of 1867 c. 144. The American rule whereby the designated beneficiary is seen as having obtained a vested property right which can be asserted in his own name has received no recognition, save in the Married Women's Property Act., 1882, c. 75, sec. 11. For the history of the American rule and English comparisons, see William R. Vance, "The Beneficiary's Interest in a Life Insurance Policy," 31 Yale L.J. 343 (1922).

The interest conception played a similar role in the area of the assignment of debts. Though assignments of choses in action were generally forbidden on grounds of "maintenance," they were enforceable when the assignee had a "prior interest" in the debt received from the assignor;[49] for example, a debt owed to the assignor by a third person could be transferred to the assignee in discharge of a pre-existing debt between the assignor and assignee. In both the insurance and assignment contexts, the incidental evil which needed to be avoided—fraud, wagering, maintenance, etc.—caused the courts to examine carefully the interest of the plaintiff bringing the action and to deny that action when he had no proprietary stake in the defendant's promise.

E.   The Collapse of Interest Into Consideration

By the late 17th century the interest theory had practically vanished. We first hear of it in 1609, and then no more after 1703. For reasons that are not entirely clear, its career effectively ended around 1680.

There is no direct evidence to tell us why the judges stopped relying upon the interest theory, but the reasons may parallel the puzzling "breach of continuity" that contract historians have found in tracing the consideration doctrine itself.[50] By this is meant the inability to trace the steps by which that doctrine made the transition in assumpsit's movement from tort to contract. There remains an unaccountable gap between the damages in tort due for nonperformance or misperformance (detriment in the "primary" sense), and the contractual notion denoting the detriment inducing the promisor's performance (detriment in the "artificial" sense). In Professor Fifoot's words, "between the tortious and contractual aspects of assumpsit, a gulf is fixed across which no logical bridge can be built."[51] The detriment sustained by the promisee to induce the promise may be only a penny. The

---

[49] Charles Sweet, "Choses in Action," [1894] 10 L.Q.R. 303; [1895] 11 L.Q.R. 238; Winfield, "Assignment of Choses in Action in Relation to Maintenance and Champerty," [1919] 35 L.Q.R. 143; GEORGE KEETON & L.A. SHERIDAN, EQUITY, 199 (2nd ed. Professional Books 1976).

[50] The "breach of continuity" theory was first described in Sir John Salmond, "The History of Contract" [1887] 3 L.Q.R. 166, 171-178. *See also* C.H.S. FIFOOT, HISTORY AND SOURCES OF THE COMMON LAW, 397 (Stevens, 1949); and WILLARD T. BARBOUR, THE HISTORY OF CONTRACT IN EARLY ENGLISH EQUITY, 59-60 (Oxford University Press, 1914).

[51] *Ibid.*

damage caused by the promisor's nonperformance may be £1000. How was this real detriment transmuted into the inducing, artificial kind? It would not have resulted from sheer confusion.[52] The possibility of organized simulation, namely the theory that fusion came about because contracts were intentionally dressed up as torts, cannot be directly proven.[53]

In a real sense the interest theory presents a similarly baffling and perhaps historically-related problem, namely to explain how the interest of the beneficiary, seen as an external material element, melded into the artificial contractual element that induced the promise. The metamorphosis of both doctrines occurred in the second half of the 17th century. To say that its absorption into the consideration requirement was an inevitable consequence of assumpsit's movement from tort to contract is to state a plausible conclusion, but not one that is easy to prove in such abstract form. At a more concrete level, however, there were two historic events affecting the beneficiary that would have facilitated such a merger: First, during this period the common law judges lost jurisdiction over the use and the beneficiary's action could no longer be based upon the strong property footing provided by the use; second, "love and natural affection" was ruled out as the type of consideration which would found an action in assumpsit and consequently, the beneficiary of a gift could not assert an interest based upon natural consideration. The following sections examine these two events more closely.

1.   **The Nexus with the Use is Lost**

As early as 1586 there had been actions in assumpsit in which the judges construed ordinary promises for a third person's benefit as if a "use" had arisen in his favor.[54] Consequently, the use came to be a justification for letting the third party action lie, enclosing the interest conception in a container with a proprietary content.

In *Megod's Case* (1586)[55] Mounson enfeoffed two persons of land with the intent that they should convey to whomever he should thereafter sell

---

[52] SIMPSON, *supra* note 11, at 582.

[53] *See* Milsom, "Not Doing is No Trespass," [1954] 12 C.L.J. 105.

[54] *Megod's Case*, Harvard Ms. 16 at F. 388a (reprinted in SIMPSON, HISTORY OF CONTRACT, *supra* n. 11, at 638 (1975) reported in Godbolt 64; *Levett v. Hawes* (1599) Cro. Eliz. 652; *De La Bar v. Gold* (1662) 1 Keb. 44, 63; *Corny & Curtis v. Collidon* (1674) 1 Freem. K.B. 284.

[55] *See supra* note 54.

the land. Then Mounson sold the land to the plaintiff, but the feoffees did not convey. In an action of assumpsit in Common Pleas, the plaintiff recovered against the feoffees. Gawdy and Clench, JJ. held: "this is a good consideration, seeing that there is a trust placed in them that they should make an assurance to the other. And where there is a good consideration in the Chancery, on this an action on the case can lie here. And judgment entered that there was a good consideration and that the action lies well." Recoveries in 1599[56] and 1674[57] were also based upon this reasoning.

Similar reasoning was argued to the court in *Dutton v. Poole* (1680)[58] where Trinder stated:

> "For which cause affection to children is sufficient to raise a use to them out of the father's estate; and therefore the daughter had an interest in the consideration, and in the promise."

The use/interest nexus was close in two senses. The use was an external and proprietary right in the beneficiary and it too arose upon consideration. At this time, however, the common law lost jurisdiction over the use, and it became the exclusive preserve of Chancery.[59] This withdrew an important theoretical support from the interest conception. The broken connection seems especially important in light of a parallel movement in Chancery in the same decade. The Chancellor recognized that the trust beneficiary's interest in the "use upon a use" was a proprietary right.

2.   **The Hardening of Consideration Redefined the "Interest"**

The second notable dynamic began late in the reign of Elizabeth I.

---

[56] In *Levett v. Hawes* (1599) Cro. Eliz. 652, the promise of marriage money between two fathers was treated as a promise made "to the son's use." The court stated that "the ordinary covenants of marriage are with the father to stand seised to the son's use: and the use shall be changed and transferred to the son, as if it were a covenant with himself; and the damage of non-performance thereof is to the son."

[57] In *Corny & Curtis v. Collidon* (1674) 1 Freem. K.B. 284, defendant's promise to the Churchwardens to pay the taxes then owed by the defendant's mother was held enforceable by a subsequent set of officeholders. The defendant's promise was seen as "intending a use for these non-promisees," and C.J. Hale is reported as saying, "It's not necessary the consideration should always move from the parties: but in consideration of money paid by A [a] use may be raised to B. [I]t's a matter of damage to whom the promise is made."

[58] 2 Lev. 211.

[59] *See* below, notes 211, 212.

It tended to make the beneficiary's interest conform to the standard of valuable consideration. By 1588, the common law courts ruled out "natural love and affection" as consideration for an assumpsit.[60] Neither promisee nor beneficiary could succeed unless the defendant's promise was given in return for a valuable consideration, as contrasted with mere "good" or "natural" consideration. The latter variety could create and transfer a proprietary right, yet it would not sustain an action by the beneficiary on that right. An early instance of this was *Brett v. J. S.* (1600)[61] where the Court of Common Pleas stated that,

> natural affection of itself is not a sufficient consideration to ground an assumpsit, for although it be sufficient to raise an use, yet it is not sufficient to ground an action without an express *quid pro quo.*[62]

The "interest" of the beneficiary had to be revised in conformity with this relatively new distinction. If the beneficiary sacrificed his interest or gave valuable consideration, then he should have the action. It was not enough that a use had been raised in his favor out of natural love and affection. This may be shown by *Levett v. Hawes* (1599). The cestui's father had received a promise to pay the son £200 upon his marriage, and the valuable consideration, we can assume, was the marriage. Chief Justice Popham held that the father could not bring this action because,

> the action ought to have been brought by the son, and not by the father; for the promise is made to the son's use, and the ordinary covenants of marriage are with the father to stand seised to the son's use; and the use shall be changed and transferred to the son, as if it were a covenant with himself;

---

[60] *Harford v. Gardiner*, (1588) 2 Leo. 30. See the discussion in Baker, "The Origins of the 'Doctrine' of Consideration," 336, 344, in ON THE LAWS AND CUSTOMS OF ENGLAND U. of N.C. Press, (Morris Arnold, *et.al.*, eds. 1981) [hereinafter "Origins"]. *See also* SIMPSON, HISTORY OF CONTRACT, *supra* note 11, at 434-437.

[61] Cro. Eliz. 756.

[62] *Id.* The linking of *quid pro quo* to consideration was not uncommon in the early stages of *assumpsit.* Dr. Baker's study of the King's Bench rolls down to 1550 has led him to reassert the role *quid pro quo* played as a linking phrase in *assumpsit* declarations. "For over twenty years the *quid pro quo* clause dominated *assumpsit* declarations and bid fair to jostle consideration out of use." "Origins" *supra* n. 60, at 340.

and the damage for non-performance thereof is to the son.[63]

This distinction was reexamined by C. J. Hobart in 1623[64], and then put in succinct terms by Sir Francis Bacon who stated,

> "Therefore if a man covenant in consideration of blood, to stand seised to the use of his brother or son, or near kinsman, an use is well raised of this covenant without transmutation of possession, nevertheless it is true, that consideration of blood is not to ground a personal contract upon: as if I contract with my son, that in consideration of blood I will give unto him such a sum of money, this is *nudum pactum*, and no assumpsit lyeth upon it; for to subject me to an action, there needeth a consideration of benefit, but the use the law raiseth without suit or action.[65]

Bacon's emphasis upon the defendant's plight ("For to subject me to an action, there needeth a consideration of benefit") suggests that he held a policy basis in mind. From the defense point of view, a lawsuit is a grave matter involving possible arrest, imprisonment, and expense. The ground for subjecting anyone to such liability must be stronger than a promise given out of mere love, friendship and other ephemerae. The same double standard may be found in Pollexfen's argument against permitting a beneficiary to sue her brother upon his promise made to their father. Pollexfen said *arguendo* that "there is not that privity requisite to the raising of an use as is to the bringing of an action."[66] In roughly the same period, the Chancellor sharpened the same distinction because he was forced to distinguish an assignor's from an assignee's interest in a chose in action.

> That those assignments ... although they do not vest an interest, yet have so far prevailed in all courts that the grantee hath such an interest that he may sue in the name

---

[63] *Levett v. Hawes* (1599) Cro. Eliz. 652.

[64] *Buckley v. Simonds* (1623) Winch 59, 61.

[65] SIR FRANCIS BACON, THE ELEMENTS OF THE COMMON LAWES OF ENGLAND 72, 73 (1630, reprint ed., 1978), (Persona conjuncta aequiparatur interesse proprio).

[66] *Dutton v. Poole* (1680) 1 Freem. 471.

of the party, his executors or administrator.[67]

The task of explaining how a thing in action could be sometimes nonassignable due to the threat of maintenance, but at other times properly actionable by the assignee because he had an interest, fostered the recognition that the assignee's litigable interest was conceptually severable from ownership of the debt itself.[68]

It seems, then, that the relationship between two distinct levels of consideration had drawn into focus the superior interest that a promisee possessed, as opposed to that of certain beneficiaries or cestuis que use.

II. THE BENEFIT THEORY

The notion of benefit, which made its debut in assumpsit in the early 17th century, provided a broad basis for the beneficiary action.

The source of the benefit idea lies in the expression "use" or "oeps" which was taken over from the actions of debt and account. As Pollock and Maitland's research demonstrates, the word "oeps" or "use" as used in the debt and account cases simply meant a benefit, and this did not connote either the later Chancery trust, the division between equitable and legal title, or the civil law "usus".[69] Thus, Professor Hening correctly states--

> What is here contended is that in case of debt and account in the Year Books or in Rolle the word "oeps" or "use", etc. is used in the then familiar and common everyday meaning of benefit. The beneficiary recovered in debt or account, not because he was a cestui que trust, that later protegé of Chancery, but because the primary obligation known as a debt or receivership had been created for the plaintiff's benefit . . . .[70]

On the same principle, contracts made by a servant *ad opus* his master were said to be for the master's benefit, and this was sufficient to

---

[67] *Deering v. Carringdon* (1701) Viner Ab., "Assignment" (3).

[68] *Hurst v. Goddard* (1670) 1 Chan. Cas. 169.

[69] SIR FREDERICK POLLOCK AND FREDERICK MAITLAND, THE HISTORY OF ENGLISH LAW, 228-229 (2nd ed. Cambridge University Press, 1968).

[70] Hening, 53 Amer. L. Reg. 112, 125-126 (1905).

permit the master's action.[71] When this older idea was applied to the beneficiary action in assumpsit, however, it was transformed from the notion associated with quid pro quo in the action of debt. For in debt, the defendant's receipt of a benefit grounded his liability to the plaintiff, whereas under the action of assumpsit, plaintiff had to say that he had not received a benefit that the defendant had promised to confer upon him. The alleged benefit could differ sharply from the compensatory notion of "interest" because the benefit in question was frequently a gift. If the defendant merely failed to deliver a gift, then the donee's *interesse* was not in any sense really damaged. Similarly, detrimental consideration could not serve as the rationale for these recoveries because often the plaintiff was a donee-beneficiary who, absent some sort of justifiable change of position, did not incur any detriment at all. In this line of cases, the courts placed liability upon the ground that the defendant was breaching a promise by retaining to himself a benefit that only the beneficiary deserved. This meant that the benefit category was broad enough to encompass not only bargain situations in which the beneficiary was interested but gift situations in which he was not. For example, where a donor delivered a sum of money or some goods to the defendant for the use of the plaintiff-donee, and the defendant promised the donor to deliver to the plaintiff, the plaintiff could sue the defendant on this promise, though the promise had not been directed to the plaintiff,[72] and though by hypothesis, he gave no consideration and had no compensable interest.[73]

Clearly the attitude of this period toward promises of gifts contrasts with modern law, which views contracts basically in terms of commercial exchange. Our bias, however, must be recognized as a modern one. In the Formative Period there was little conflict between the doctrine of consideration and the idea of enforcing promises of gifts.[74] The 16th and 17th century cases show that gifts, marriage contracts, family agreements, etc. were enforceable in assumpsit, even though these agreements would not be viewed by modern standards as part of the world of commerce. The

---

[71] *See below* the text at notes 102 ff.

[72] *Hornsey v. Dimocke* (1672) 1 Vent. 119; *Starkey v. Mill* (1651) Style 296, Cremer Ms. p. 380; *Oldham v. Bateman* (1638) 1 Vener 335, pl. 8.

[73] *Disborne v. Denabie* (1649) Rolle Abr. 30, 31; *Rockwood's Case* (1589) Cro. Eliz. 164; *Thomas v.* (1655) Style 461.

[74] Professor Dawson in his work, GIFTS AND PROMISES, 223 (1980) even argues that it is hard to find any historical evidence of common law suspicion or hostility directed toward gifts. Rather, the judges simply adopted an attitude of indifference, unconvinced that gifts furnished serious reasons to bestir themselves.

distinction between a creditor and a donee beneficiary was not so clear in that day. Assumpsit was only a minor commercial remedy at that time. The living commercial law was essentially carried on in defeasible bonds, statutes merchant, or statutes staple. The important commercial transactions, Professor Thorne tells us, were handled by the self-executing medieval forms, and consequently "the run of commercial cases by-passed the common law courts."[75] Furthermore, it was perfectly compatible to say that in a gift situation, consideration was a requisite to bind the defendant to the promisee, but that the donee's benefit provided the rationale why he, even though a "stranger" to that promise, should be able to enforce it.

A.   Case Examples

An early application of this theory came in *Provender v. Wood* (1628).[76] The plaintiff brought assumpsit for breach of a promise made to his father to pay plaintiff £20 upon marriage to the defendant's daughter. Recovery was put by Yelverton and Richardson, J.J. upon the wide ground that "the party to whom the benefit of a promise accrews (sic), may bring his action."[77] Then in 1649, Chief Justice Rolle is reported to have said in the per curiam case of *Disborne v. Denabie*,[78] that "it matters not from whom the consideration moveth, but who hath the benefit thereby."[79] The facts were that A and B were under an obligation to pay £20 to C when he should reach the age of 21. A made B his executor, then died, and B assigned assets to D from whom he secured a promise that D would pay £20 to C when he came of age. It was held, on the benefit principle, that C, who by then was of age, could have an action "sur le case" against D, though no consideration came from C.

A third application of the theory came in the case of *Starkey v. Mill*

---

[75] Samuel E. Thorne, "Tudor Social Transformation and Legal Change," 26 N.Y.U.L. Rev. 10, 20-21 (1951); *But see,* BAKER, 94 Seld. Soc. 261 (1977), who argues that a good many assumpsit actions in the early 16th century concerned the affairs of businessmen. For a discussion about the "infinite flexibility" of the conditional bond, see, SIMPSON, *supra* note 11 at 112-113.

[76] Het. 30.

[77] *Id.*

[78] (1949) Rolle Ab. 30, 31. pl. 5.

[79] Quoted from Twisden J., *De La Bar v. Gold* (1662) 1 Keb. 63, 64 C.J. Hale repeated this statement in *Courteis v. Collingwood* (1675) 3 Keb. 434, 435.

(1651).[80] This case is briefly reported by Style; it is also abridged by Rolle, and there is a report in manuscript by Charles Cremer of Gray's Inn that gives a different and more accurate account.

1. Style's Report of Starkey v. Mill

According to Style's report, a father delivered to his son a quantity of goods worth £80 and received a promise in return that the son would pay over £20 to his sister. The sister brought an action in assumpsit against her brother for breach of his promise and recovered a verdict. It was moved in arrest of judgment that there was no consideration for the plaintiff to bring her action, there being "no debt due to [her], but only an appointment for the son to pay money to [her], in consideration of the goods given him by his father." Hales, for the plaintiff, argued that a debt had arisen in the plaintiff's favor. Chief Justice Rolle, with Jermyn and Aske, J.J. agreeing (Nicholas, J. doubting), held for the plaintiff. The Chief Justice stated that a good action lay in assumpsit:

> It is good as it is, for there is a plain contract because the goods were given for the benefit of the plaintiff, though the contract be not between [her] and the defendant, and [she] may well have an action upon the case, for hers is a promise in law made to the plaintiff, though there be not a promise in fact, and there is a debt here; and the assumpsit is good.[81]

The "promise in law" doctrine was the 17th century answer to the promisee (or parties-only) objection and this is the first reported case in which this device for overcoming the objection was applied. The objection had been a source of some controversy in the 15th and 16th century beneficiary cases, and earlier courts vacillated on the question to a degree almost inconsistent with a serious regard for *stare decisis*. The best examples of this vacillation were the suits upon marriage agreements. Here, every possible position seems to have been adopted or tried out. Some decisions held that only the promisee

---

[80] (1651) Style 296; *Starkey v. Mylne* (1651) Rolle Ab. 32. Cremer Ms. p. 105 (Grays Inn Library Ms., H-1792, Eng. Leg. Ms. Project, Ed. J. H. Baker).

[81] *Starkey v. Mill* (1651) Style 296.

(*e.g.*, the father) could maintain the action.[82]   Other cases held that the action could be brought solely by the beneficiary[83]   A third position avoided a compulsory choice of plaintiff and opted for a permissive rule under which either promisee or beneficiary could sue.[84]   Such evidence clearly suggests both the persistence of the promisee objection and the fact that it was never fully accepted as law.

2.   Cremer's Report of Starkey v. Mill

Cremer's manuscript report of *Starkey v. Mill* sheds stronger light upon the holding, the manner of declaring upon a promise in law, and other aspects of the decision. The action is clearly referred to as one in *indebitatus assumpsit*. The declaration stated that during his lifetime, the *grandfather*[85] of the plaintiff Alice and her brother the defendant, gave certain goods worth £80 to the defendant. Defendant promised that he would pay £20 to Alice after the death of grandfather. The plaintiff's declaration made it appear that she herself was a co-promisee in a three-way agreement:

> Whereas the grandfather did order and appoint that the defendant in lieu of the said goods should pay £20 to the said plaintiff after the death of the grandfather who in consideration that the said Alice at the instance of the defendant would accept of the said promise for the payment of the said £20 defendant then promised to pay after the death of the grandfather. And plaintiff averred that the grandfather died such a day and defendant was indebted to the plaintiff such the same day in the said £20 which the defendant undertook and was to pay to the plaintiff according to the special agreement between the grandfather and the plaintiff and defendant in lieu of certain goods to the

---

[82] *Archdale v. Barnard* (1608) 1 Viner 333 (Assumpsit): *Anonymous* (1682) Het. 12; *Cardinal v. Lewis* (no date) 1 Viner 335 (Assumpsit) and cited in Het. 176. *See also, Norris v. Pine* (1538), cited in 2 Levinz 211. Whether *Norris v. Pine* was ever finally adjudged or not was discussed in *Dutton v. Poole* (1680) Jones, T. 102, 103.

[83] *Levett v. Hawes* (1599) Cro. Eliz. 619; *Hadves v. Levitt* (1632) Het. 176; *Evans v. Jamney* (1640) *cited by* Twisdon, J., 1 Keb. 121, 122.

[84] *Bafield (Administratrix) v. Collard* (1647) Aleyn 1; *See also Dutton v. Poole* (1680) Raym T. 302. The court in *Taylor v. Foster* (1601) Cro. Eliz. 807, may also have subscribed to this, but Professor Simpson reads the case to mean that only the promisee was entitled to *sue*. SIMPSON, *supra* note 11, at 480, n. 3.

[85] Rather than the father, as reported by Style.

value of £80 given by the grandfather to the defendant for the payment of the same and that the defendant *Sic indebitatus assumpsit.*

That Alice was not in reality a promisee, however, emerges clearly from subsequent references to her as a "stranger" and from the discussion of the promise-in-law concept.

The manuscript report also reveals that the promise-in-law concept was a legal doctrine for some time before 1651. Style's report leaves the impression that this idea was announced for the first time by Rolle, C. J., but defendant's counsel treats it as an established doctrine in his motion in arrest of judgment:

> Lach moved in arrest of judgment that an indebitatus assumpsit generally does not lie upon a promise in law without showing a particular debt or duty out of which the promise might arise, but in our case there's not any precedent debt or duty of the plaintiff which is in the third person etc.

Hales argued that the delivery (bailment) of the goods to the defendant had created a debt to Alice and that being so, then assumpsit would lie concurrently. The Chief Justice agreed to this proposition:

> And Rolle deemed that the gift of goods here to the defendant for the payment of the £20 for the plaintiff tantamount as if he had delivered the £20 to the defendant to be paid over to the plaintiff. So he held that if A sells a horse to B to pay £20 for him to C (to whom A is indebted £20) C may have an action of debt for the £20 tho he be a Stranger.

The Chief Justice then said in dicta that he did not doubt that in a case of marriage money the beneficiary might have an action upon a promise in law:

> If two fathers agree that the father of the daughter shall pay to the son of the other father so much money for a marriage portion, the son who is a stranger shall have debt or a special action of the case upon this agreement between the two fathers.

This account amplifies our understanding of Rolle's view. The benefit rationale was, for him, not restricted to the proprietary features of an action in debt. Rather, it could even apply to a set of promises that involved no bailment of goods or money to the promisor, no prior indebtedness to the beneficiary, nor a use in favor of the beneficiary.

3. More Light from Sprat v. Agar

That the benefit rationale in fact extended this far is confirmed by the later case of *Sprat v. Agar* (1658), a leading case whose importance has been historically overlooked because of a misleading and "irrelevant"[86] report by Siderfin. Fortunately, an enlightening report of the case appears in Cremer's manuscript and the following account is based upon it.[87]

The declaration stated an action in assumpsit by Henry Sprat against the executrix of John Agar. Upon a communication of marriage between the plaintiff and the daughter of Sir Thomas Lockier, a certain John Agar had promised Sir Thomas Lockier that in consideration for his consent to the marriage, that he, John Agar, would settle certain lands after his death upon the plaintiff. Thereafter the consent was given and the marriage took place. Yet John Agar, in breach of his promise, made a will devising all his lands to his wife and heirs and made her his executrix. Plaintiff obtained a verdict and damages of £1300.

Upon defendant's motion in arrest of judgment, the court first resolved that an action could lie against John Agar's executrix upon this "collateral promise." Secondly the court resolved:

> That though the promise was made to Thomas Lockier yet because it was to the benefit of the plaintiff he may well have the action. These two points were resolved without argument. But the 3rd and principal point was whether notice ought not to be alleged given to John Agar of the consent of Thomas Lockier, which is not alleged and the marriage without consent binds not him in his promise, and *adjournatur.*

---

[86] *See* SIMPSON, *supra* note 11, at 480, n.3.

[87] *Sprat v. Agar*, Cremer Ms. p. 380. (Gray's Inn Library Ms. H-1792, Eng. Leg. Ms. Project, Ed., J.H. Baker).

This is the only "benefit" case known to the writer in which the beneficiary was permitted to enforce a purely executory agreement, that is to say, a simple promise without a prior bailment to the promisor for the plaintiff's use. It should be remembered that assumpsit had taken over the work of the older actions and there was still the difficulty of fitting old established rights of action into the new framework.[88] The holding in *Starkey v. Mill* (1651) had been modelled upon an action in debt for money bailed to the use of plaintiff. That this extension was decided in *Sprat* "without argument" is sufficient to indicate that the point was considered well-established, which corroborates Rolle's statement to that effect in 1651.

Furthermore, no other case has been found in which a question about notice was specifically linked to the beneficiary action.[89] Notice frequently arose as a privity issue in the law of assignment and the early law of agency, but here it was contended that the beneficiary should not recover because he had failed to notify the promisor that the marriage had ever in fact taken place.[90] The question of consideration came up in the course of resolving this issue. The court observed that the promisee, Thomas Lockier, would have had the right to sue the defendant because "part of the consideration moved from him," but his right to sue was now barred because the plaintiff had already sued. The implication was clear, though not stated, that the plaintiff's marriage supplied the other part of the consideration, so that his "meritorious act" might be taken to furnish an alternative ground (the other being the benefit theory) for his right of action. In the pivotal decision of *Bourne v. Mason* eleven years later, the case of *Sprat v. Agar* was fully argued and

---

[88] SIMPSON, *supra* note 11 at 482-483.

[89] Cf. *Baker v. Smith* (1651), Style 295, 303; *Crane v. Crampton* (1662) Cro. Car, 34.

[90] "Baldwin cited many cases upon the common difference, viz. where it lies in equal conusance of both parties no notice ought to be alleged otherwise when it lies in the knowledge of the plaintiff only. All which cases Allen agreed, but what he relied upon was that in this case the promise was made to Thomas Lockier, from whom the consideration arose, viz. the consent, so that Thomas Lockier might have had his action, and then notice ought to have been given which the court conceded. Then says he the action being transferred by operation of law to him that hath the benefit, the contract stands the same to the plaintiff as it should have done to Thomas Lockier if he had brought his action, and though Thomas Lockier be a stranger to the action, yet he is a party to the contract. The court: Thomas Lockier might have had this action, because part of the consideration moved from him (Contra had he been a mere agent) and a recovery by him had been a bar to an action by the plaintiff as this is a bar to an action by Thomas Lockier, but now the election is determined as to the action, and Thomas Lockier is become a mere stranger and might be a witness in this action, then he brings as a third person according to all the books, no notice is requisite for if any other can tell you as well as I, then you must ask."

reviewed, and at that time, the court reassigned the reasoning in *Sprat* to the basis that consideration had moved from the plaintiff.[91] This now reveals to us something as to how and when consideration replaced the test of benefit. In 1658, consideration had not been the reason given for the beneficiary's right to sue. His right to sue had been decided without argument on the basis of the benefit rationale. Consideration given had only been the reason why the promisee himself might have sued and why notification to the promisor would have been necessary if he had sued. But by 1669, consideration had replaced benefit as the rationale for the beneficiary's right to sue.

Beyond *Sprat v. Agar*, the remaining traces of the benefit theory become fragmentary.[92] At the turn of the 18th century, one writer fashioned the following principle:

> And so generally in all cases any one for whose use, or for whose benefit a Promise is made may have an Action for the breach of this promise, although the promise were [not?] made to him but to another.[93]

Thereafter, no further case references to the theory are made until a dictum by Butler, J. in 1787,[94] and an argument by Sergeant Le Blanc in 1797.[95]

III. THE "AGENCY" THEORY

It may seem unhistorical to categorize cases of this period under the rubric of agency. The contemporary terminology was actually a mélange of such terms as attorney, factor, deputy, servant and bailiff. The word agency, as a term of art, was to remain unknown to the common law as late as Blackstone. It was first introduced to the English scene near the close of the

---

[91] *Bourne v. Mason* (1669) 1 Vent 6.

[92] Possibly relevant is *Green v. Horn* (1693) Comb. 219, an action in covenant, where it was stated in King's Bench, "The plaintiff may take the benefit of it, though not mentioned as party; if I oblige myself to pay J.S. £100 the obligation is made to him, for whose benefit it is."

[93] TRADES-MAN'S LAWYER, *supra* n. 19, at 64. *See also, Anonymous* Style 6 (1647).

[94] "Independent of the rules which may prevail in mercantile transactions, if one person makes a promise to another for the benefit of a third, that third person may maintain an action upon it." *Marchington v. Vernon* (1787) *cited in* 1 B. & P. 98, 101, note (c).

[95] "If a promise be made to A. for the benefit of B., B. may maintain an action on that promise." *Co. of Feltmakers v. Davis* (1797) 1 B. & P. 98, 101.

Formative Period by Lord Nottingham, and from then on it was utilized frequently by 18th century chancellors.[96]   Nevertheless, the essential characteristic of modern agency—the legal power to alter the principal's legal relations with third parties—had been recognized long before, and therefore, the legal idea played a role in the Formative Period. It is true that the early bases were extremely narrow. Agency was the exception, not the rule of contractual intercourse. If the principal strayed beyond narrowly recognized bounds, he was simply a stranger to the contract. Even to apply the terms principal and agent in this period requires some sacrifice of terminological accuracy in the interest of convenience. When originally introduced, agency was simply a branch of master and servant, whereas today, master and servant is a branch of agency. Agency has come to embrace not only the field of contractual representation—the sphere of primary relevance here—but the

---

[96] The evolution of this development seems to have been as follows: (1) In the 16th century, agency was not a received term. The word servant did not even appear in its commercial sense until the time of Marlowe and Shakespeare. *e.g.*, Henry V, Act IV, scene 1. (2) Windham, J. seems to have been one of the first common law judges to use it in its representative sense. *De La Bar v. Gold* (1662) 1 Keb. 44, 63. (3) Next, there are four references to it in the Statute of Frauds (1677) 29 Car. II, c.3. (4) Chancellor Nottingham first used the term in a series of decisions in equity. *Clark v. Perrier* (1679) 2 Freem. Ch. 48; *Harvey v. Baker* (1677) 79 Seld Soc. 631; *Mellish v. African Co.* (1678) 79 Seld. Soc. 705; *Green v. Garnder* (1675) 79 Seld Soc. 170; *Fashion v. Atwood* (1679) 2 Chan. Cas 6, 36. (5) Thereafter the term generally proliferates in Chancery. *Bartlett v. Hooper* and Armstrong, (1691) James Wright's Reports (Harvard Leg. MS) (1685-1691), 22, (Eng. Leg. Ms. Project, Ed. J. H. Baker); *Brotherton v. Hatt* (1706) 2 Vern. 574; *Jennings v. Moore* (1708) 2 Vern. 609; *Gofrey v. Furzo* (1733) 3 P. Wms. 185. (6) The identification of a factor as a trustee for his principal is made in *Burdett v Willett* (1708) 2 Vern 638. (7) An undisclosed principal was held liable in *Waller v. Hendon* (1723) 2 Eq. Ca. Abr. 50. (8) By the mid-18th century, agency had achieved full currency in equity, but not at law. *Parrot v. Wells* (1690) 2 Vern. 127; *Morret v. Paske* (1740) 2 Atk. 52; *Caniel v. Adams* (1764) Amb. 495; *Lissett v. Reave* (1742) 2 Atk. 394; *Schrimshire v. Alderton* (1743) 2 Strange 1182. (9) Using an analogy to agency, Lord Hardwicke granted relief to a third party beneficiary in *Hook v. Kinnear* (1750) 3 Swans, 482. (10) As late as Blackstone, there is still at common law only the general heading of servants, although he described a special category of servant (later to be called agents) as follows:

> "There is yet a fourth species of servants, if they may be so called, being rather in a superior, a ministerial, capacity; such as stewards, factors, and bailiffs whom, however, the law considers as servants pro tempore . . . ."

SIR WILLIAM BLACKSTONE, COMMENTARIES ON THE LAWS OF ENGLAND, 427 (Chitty, ed. Lippincott, 1858). (11) The modern vogue for the word received impetus in the 19th century when Williams Dictionary (1819) distinguished itself by entering the first definition embodying its modern meaning and connotation. The concept "agent and patient", which can be found in earlier dictionaries, has an entirely different meaning.

non-contractual field of services as well.[97]

The exact role of the agency concept and its relationship to third party beneficiary contracts has proved difficult to interpret. The incautious historian is susceptible to two mistakes. He may find the state of agency notions disarmingly primitive and thus dismiss the evidence, or he may see great significance in these cases and attempt to reconceptualize the holdings on a basis that the judge of that period did not have at his disposal. In other words, he may project the modern law upon the old, and thereby remove the quotation marks from around the word before the proper time. This was the serious error of the 19th century commentators and abridgers who turned the cases inside out wherever they caught sight of an agent in the facts.[98]

In the 20th century, A. M. Finlay turned an exaggerated notion of agency into the keystone of his analysis. His notion was the "blood-relation agency theory." Finlay divided the whole of the early jurisprudence under consideration into two "parallel and quite distinct" lines of cases:

> One where the beneficiary was closely related to one of the contracting parties, and the other was not. In the latter case an action was invariably denied to the beneficiary, but in the former his claim was just as certainly looked upon with favor. In almost all of these cases there was some vague statement that the consideration and the promise to the father may well extend to the children, or the nearness of the relation gives the daughter the benefit of the consideration performed by the father etc., but it is clear that the true basis of them all was some kind of fictitious relationship that has now disappeared from our law, and which approximates more closely to agency than to anything else we know today.[99]

But Finlay simply overestimated the weight of this factor and ignored much

---

[97] FLOYD R. MECHEM, A TREATISE ON THE LAW OF AGENCY, sec. 8 (2nd ed., 1914).

[98] *See* particularly note (p), in SIR JOHN COMYNS, A DIGEST OF THE LAWS OF ENGLAND (5th ed. by Hammond; Strahan, 1822). Vol. I, p. 304. The tendency is also quite apparent in SIR EDWARD FRY, A TREATISE ON THE SPECIFIC PERFORMANCE OF CONTRACTS 41-46 (Johnson, 1858).

[99] A.M. FINLAY, CONTRACTS FOR THE BENEFIT OF THIRD PERSONS 14-15 (Sweet & Maxwell, 1939).

evidence (*see e.g.* the cases in Section I) that would have refuted his theory.

To understand the historical connection between the early principles of agency and the beneficiary action under assumpsit, we must consider six underlying features.

A.   The Status Incapacities

One seminal influence upon the evolution of contractual representation was the common law's denial of capacity to infants, married women and monks. These incapacities made it desirable, if not essential, to recognize their role as agents. Monks, for instance, were civilly dead, yet as a practical matter, monastic houses had to purchase necessaries and enter into important transactions with the secular world. This was achieved by allowing a monk to enter into contracts as agent for his sovereign.[100]   A similar agency was recognized where a wife acted on behalf of her husband. The instrumentalist theory, discussed below, was very useful in a world in which many individuals had no capacity to act on their own. It provided a partial escape from the inconveniences of personal privity.[101]

B.   The Instrumentalist Fiction

"Throughout the law of agency," says Tiffany, "we are continually met with the notion that the constituent and representative are one and the same person, and that the rights and liabilities of the constituent are not other than they would be were he actually present and acting in person."[102]   In other words, we are met by the fiction of identity of principal and agent. This was the theory expressed in the Latin *qui facit per alium facit per se*. The agent, whether he had capacity or not, was not a contracting party at all. In terms coming down to us from the Year Books, he was only "instrument and minister."[103]   A corollary of the theory was the immunity of the agent. He

---

[100] SIMPSON, *supra* note 11, at 539.

[101] The Romans had found a similar benefit in the organization of the family and in slavery. Weill writes that "Les fils de famille et les esclaves étaient en effet de merveilleux instruments d'acquisition pour le paterfamilias." LA RELATIVITE DES CONVENTIONS EN DROIT PRIVE FRANCAIS, 47 (Paris, 1939).

[102] FRANCIS B. TIFFANY, HANDBOOK OF THE LAW OF PRINCIPAL & AGENT 11 (West Publishing, 1903).

[103] Y.B. (1472) 11 Edw. IV. T. f. 6, pl. 10, per Pigot.

could neither sue nor be sued.[104] It was immaterial whether the agent had legal capacity since he was only the principal's "tool," and thus, he could be a slave, an infant or even a lunatic. This identity fiction provides an obvious explanation for the rule that the agent's authority was revoked from the moment that his principal died or became insane.[105]

C.   The Reception of Medieval Agency into Assumpsit

Contract, Professor Street once said, did not create agency principles; tort was the driving force.[106] The truth of that observation seems confirmed by examining the initial stages of development in assumpsit. The rise of assumpsit did not revolutionize or visibly hasten the growth of modern agency. We find, rather, that older rules which had been operative in debt were simply taken over bodily. The plaintiff who attempted to hold a principal liable in debt had to show that the principal had received a benefit or a *quid pro quo*. Year Book cases show that this raised an interesting privity issue.[107] It was settled that the requisite could be satisfied in one of two ways: (a) the principal had issued a particular command, namely, he had particularly directed the agent to enter into the contract;[108] or (b) the principal had received a benefit, namely, the principal had notice that he had received something to his own use.[109]

These narrow bases were then taken over as the actionable framework within assumpsit. But their narrowness made the principal's liability the exception rather than the rule. Broader doctrines of apparent authority and implied command did not yet exist. In pre-mercantilist England, the principal was not liable except for his commands or his enrichment.

The 17th century, however, brought about an expansion of liability.

---

[104] THOMAS A. STREET, FOUNDATIONS OF LEGAL LIABILITY 454 (Thompson, 1906).

[105] STOLJAR, THE LAW OF AGENCY: ITS HISTORY AND PRESENT PRINCIPLES 15 (1961).

[106] STREET, *supra* n. 104, at 454.

[107] For an illustration see the *Abbot of Hailes' Case*, Y.B. (1313-1314), 6 & 7 Ed. 11, 32.

[108] Rolle Ab., vol. I, p. 94 (S) pl. 1, 2.

[109] "A man shall not be charged by the contract of his wife or servant, if the thing comes to his use, having not notice of it. But if he commands them to buy he shall be charged though they come not to his use, or had notice thereof." WILLIAM NOY, THE PRINCIPAL GROUNDS AND MAXIMS, 151 (3rd Amer. ed. by Hening), (Rothman Reprints, 1980).

It came about with the enlargement of the notion of authority and the gradual desuetude of the "particular command" theory. Unsuited for the commercial world, the "particular command" doctrine was last reaffirmed in 1618 in *Southerne v. Howe*.[110] There seems to be no application afterwards. The text outlining it in Doctor and Student[111] received criticism in 1703, and the doctrine was disaffirmed in the Trades-Man's Lawyer.[112] A substitute distinction emerged between "general" and "special" authorization,[113] and general authority came to embrace a servant's usual and notorious duties. The changing rule signified that commercial reliance upon the appearances of authority was beginning to count more than hidden commands. Thus, it was said, "the contracts of a servant may also bind the Master, especially where the servant is known and common bailiff to his master and doth use to buy for him."[114]

For example, the merchant who gave his factor general authority to make purchases could no longer defeat the seller's action for the price simply because the factor violated a particular command and mistakenly purchased the wrong type of goods. In that instance, liability was justified by saying "Let the Master take heed what factor he makes."[115] On the other hand, the master was not bound when the world was on notice as to any absence of authority, as where,

> If a man-servant that keepeth his shop, or who is accustomed to sell for him, shall give away his goods, he shall have trespass against the donee.[116]

The example presumably ties together issues of authority, notice, and reliance, and the relationship to the overall question of privity is important. The servant had no authority to donate; the donee apparently could not have been deceived by the appearances of authority; and the master had no notice. In that event, the master was a stranger to the transaction.

---

[110] 2 Rolle 5, 26.

[111] CHRISTOPHER ST. GERMAN, DOCTOR AND STUDENT, (ed. by Plucknett & Barton; Selden Society, 1974), Dial. II, ch. 42.

[112] TRADES-MAN'S LAWYER, *supra* n. 19, at 17.

[113] *Id.*

[114] NOY, *supra* n. 109, at 94.

[115] *Petties v. Soam* (1601) Goulds. 139.

[116] NOY, *supra* n. 109, at 152.

By 1623 the sphere of the principal's liability was still expanding without abandoning the instrumentalist theory, but at the same time, the move was tempered by the corollary that the principal's right to enforce contracts would be similarly advanced. In *Seignor v. Wolmers* (1624),[117] the plaintiff sent his servant to compose a debt with the defendant, and the defendant finally promised the servant that he would pay an agreed amount to the master. The court dismissed the objection that the master could not sue because he had not received the promise. Dodderidge, J. said that the master and servant constituted a single person for the purposes of assumpsit.

> An assumpsit to the servant for the master is good to the
> master: an assumpsit by appointment of the master of the
> servant shall bind the master, and is his assumpsit.[118]

Then Dodderidge, J. added a thought that went a long way toward making agency contracts reciprocally enforceable. He said:

> for whatever comes within the compass of the servants
> service, I shall be chargeable with, and likewise shall have
> the advantage of the same.[119]

His phrase "the compass of the servants service" was a precocious manner of recasting the understood scope of the master's liability, and represented the direct forerunner of the doctrine later developed by Chief Justice Holt.

D.   The Fiction as a Solution to Privity

The orthodox view today is that agency is a recognized "exception" to the privity requirements of modern contract.[120] In the Formative Period, however, agency was not viewed in this manner. By merging the principal and agent into the same plaintiff or defendant, the instrumentalist theory freed the principal's suit in assumpsit from two objections which otherwise might have been effective: (a) The promisee (or parties only) objection—the agent was

---

[117] *Seignor v. Wolmers* (1624) Godbolt 360.

[118] *Id.* at 361.

[119] *Id.*

[120] GEOFFREY C. CHESHIRE AND C.H.S. FIFOOT, LAW OF CONTRACT, 387 (5th ed. Butterworths, 1960); F. E. Dowrick, "A *Jus Quaesitum Tertio* by Contract," 19 Mod. L. Rev. 374 (1956).

promisee, yet his principal is plaintiff. (b) The consideration objection—the consideration was supplied by the agent with his own money or goods, yet it is the principal bringing the action. Without the instrumentalist fiction, the principal's suit in his own name should have been more difficult, since the defendant would object that "plaintiff is not the promisee" or "plaintiff is a stranger to the consideration."

The case of *Sadler v. Paine* (1582)[121] illustrates how these objections fared in the 16th century. The plaintiff's uncle, whose name was Ducket, dealt with the defendant, and the uncle obtained from the defendant a promise to reconvey certain land back to the plaintiff (previously this land had been conveyed to defendant) upon payment of £50. The defense raised the promisee and the consideration objections.[122] But Baron Shute, with Chief Baron Manwood agreeing and Clench dissenting, got around these objections by using the agency principle. The Baron is reported as saying:

> It seems to me to the contrary, that qui per alium facit per seipsum *(sic)* facere videtur: and although the agreement for the reassurance was between Ducket [the uncle] and Paine the defendant, still it is alleged in the court that it was done at the request of the plaintiff and that will be understood to be his act: ... all will be understood by the agreement of the plaintiff where it is done by another; when if all had been agreed between the plaintiff and defendant and the defendant says to Ducket, do you wish to give your promise for him? and he says . . . everything is done in the behalf of the plaintiff.[123]

Baron Shute was clearly following the instrumental or ministerial theory of agency. Through a prior particular command the agent came fully within the persona of the principal. In a substantive sense the unification of their personalities dissolved the promisee and consideration objections, yet procedurally, it remained somewhat unclear how the matter should be pleaded.

---

[121] Sav. 24.

[122] Presumably, the point about consideration was that the promised £50 was to be paid by the "agent" Ducket and, therefore, did not move from the plaintiff.

[123] *Sadler v. Paine*, (1528) Sav. 24.

Tatam's Case (1536)[124] was a much-cited Year Book precedent in which a husband was permitted to sue in assumpsit upon a promise given to his wife in his absence. The husband pleaded the assumpsit, as if upon a promise made to himself directly, and without any averment of particular command, and the court held this good. He had approved or ratified the agreement the wife had entered into in his stead. Would it have been possible to plead that the promise had in fact been made to the wife and not to the plaintiff? The principal's allegation that he was the promisee was understood to be pure fiction,[125] but it was apparently an important technicality, for disregard of it in the 16th century would have been a fatal mistake. That seems to have been the lesson of *Jordan v. Jordan* in 1595.[126] The debtor promised the plaintiff's attorney that if the attorney would forbear arresting him, he would appear in Queen's Bench on the day of the writ or else would pay the debt before. The defendant neither appeared nor paid, and upon being sued, he moved in arrest of judgment that the plaintiff had declared upon a promise made to his attorney and not to himself, "and for this cause principally it was held to be ill, and adjudged for defendant."[127] *Jordan's Case* may be seen as insisting on the technical view that the plaintiff must plead as if he was in fact the promisee, and perhaps this view rested upon the related idea that a single promise should not give rise to more than one action in assumpsit.

By 1628, however, the judges of King's Bench had clearly relaxed the strictness of the pleading. In *Legat's Case*,[128] a debtor's promise to pay was made to plaintiff's "attorney," and plaintiff declared that the promise had been made to himself. The court found this to be well-pleaded, but said it could also have been pleaded as a promise received by the attorney.[129] We have already referred to the vacillation by the judges on this same question in the marriage money cases.[130]

---

[124] Y. B. 27 Hen. VIII, 24 pl. 3. As to the confused dating of this case, see FIFOOT, HISTORY AND SOURCES OF THE COMMON LAW, 353 n. 58; and SIMPSON, HISTORY, *supra* n. 11, at 266 n.1.

[125] SIR HENRY FINCH, NOMOTECHNIA 66 (Society of Stationers, 1613).

[126] Cro. Eliz. 369.

[127] *Id.*

[128] (1628) Latch 206.

[129] "que fuit bien l'un voy, ou l'auter." Latch 206.

[130] *See supra* pp. 50-54.

E.   The Principal Assimilated as Third Party Beneficiary

As noted above, the instrumentalist fiction provided a particular reason why agency was not yet viewed as an exception to privity requirements. There was, in addition, a more general reason. The beneficiary action, as we have seen, worked well to compensate the interested third party plaintiff. Even if contemporary agency theory had not followed the instrumentalist approach, there was far less of a burning need to devise any exception to the rules of assumpsit. It was not difficult to envision the principal as an interested third party beneficiary and there is considerable evidence that contemporaries perceived the principal in this light. Consider Hutton, J.'s view in *Hadves v. Levit* (1632). His operative principle was that, "there is a difference when the promise is to perform to one who is not interested in the cause, and when he hath an interest." Then he drew contrasting examples, the last of which was "If my servant by my command, sell my horse: the money to be paid to me; I shall have the action, and not my servant, for the interest is in me."[131] Note that he brought the master into privity of contract with the purchaser, not on an agency theory, but on the elastic basis of interest. As a lawyer of his times, and certainly not ignorant of the instrumentalist fiction, he believed that cases dealing with servants should be classified, in principle, with the marriage money case before him. By a similar mode of thought his colleague, Richardson J., could "put the case" of *Iorning v. Iorning* (1595), where the debtor promised the creditor's servant during the trial on his indebtedness, "Leave the suite *(sic)* and I'll pay your master." It was accordingly held that "the master shall have the action upon the case."[132]   The court, in addition, cited *Tatam's Case* (1536) and *Core's Case* (1537), the latter involving merchant and factor, and the former concerning a promise to a wife who acted on behalf of her husband. The same thought process was evident when the author of the Trades-Man's Lawyer, in 1703, attempted to explain "how a promise may be made to another person for my use, upon a good consideration." He adopted this bold rule:

> Anyone to whose use, or for whose benefit a promise is made may have an action for the breach of promise, although the promise were not made to him but to another.[133]

---

[131] Het. 176.

[132] *Iorning v. Iorning* (1595), cited Het. 176.

[133] TRADES-MAN'S LAWYER, *supra* n. 19, at 64.

This general principle is of interest in itself as reflecting the impression left by the cases upon a contemporary lawyer. His supporting examples, however, hold our immediate interest, because he reveals himself as one who still attempts to integrate the "agency" line of cases into the third party beneficiary cases. Thus, he drew his general rule from cases dealing with bailment,[134] marriage agreements,[135] promises to raise marital portions,[136] and tort actions against a master;[137] and with these he interspersed five "agency" cases brought in assumpsit.[138]

More than a half-century later, Comyns' Digest (1762-67) provided fourteen examples to demonstrate a similar proposition, and at that point, only two were agency cases.[139] Perhaps this was a signal that agency as an exception had begun to grow in strength.

F.   The Evolution of Agency into an "Exception"

It was not until the late 18th or early 19th century that agency came to be formally viewed as any kind of exception to contractual privity. In the course of time, the instrumentalist theory had become riddled with exceptions and anomalies. Wigmore has described how the particular command rule gave way to the more commercially expedient rule of implied command, and broadened further into the scope of employment rule. Applying general economic and social analysis to account for the growth of vicarious liability, he pointed out that in the final stage, it was not only the command rule which disappeared, but much of the fiction about identity as well.[140] There had also been great growth in the numbers and types of professional middlemen who usually possessed an independent interest of their own in the contracts they arranged (*e.g.*, del credere agents, factors' commissions). Their personal

---

[134] *Bell v. Chaplain* (1664) Style 6.

[135] *Anonymous* (1674) Style 6.

[136] *Dutton v. Poole* (1680) 2 Lev. 211.

[137] Y.B. (1492) II Edw. Iv, 6; *Sands v. Child, Franklin and Leach* (1694) 3 Lev. 351.

[138] These citations are to *Legat's Case* (1628) Latch 206; *Tatam's Case* (1536) Y. B. 27 Hen. VIII, f. 24 pl. 3; *Core's Case* (1537) 1 Dyer 20a; *Seignor & Wolmer's Case* (1624) Goldbolt 360; there is an additional citation to the master servant illustration given in *Hadves v. Levit* (1632) Het. 176.

[139] COMYNS, *supra* n. 98, at 156 (E).

[140] John H. Wigmore, "Responsibility for Tortious Acts: Its History", 7 Harv. L. Rev. 383, 393 (1894).

interest made it expedient to allow them to sue and be sued. Furthermore, when the principal's claim came to be subject to the defenses assertable by the defendant against the agent, as in the case of undisclosed agency, their antagonistic interests made separate identities more desirable. The doctrine of the undisclosed principal, dating from 1723, is quite inconsistent with a privity principle which says that only the parties to a contract may sue upon it. Some authors have called it anomalous, unsound, and unknown to every legal system except that of England and America.[141]

Thus, the straight line once found in agency's past became a triangle, and a new challenge was posed to the privity requirements of assumpsit. It is not surprising that one of the first places that one finds the modern formula "consideration must move from the promisee" turns out to be from an early 19th century action recognizing a shipping agent's right to sue the carrier for goods lost in transit.[142] Agency was too dynamic to be restrained by the narrow consideration question; it became regarded as an exception to it.

Why did this "exception" evolve so slowly? Three reasons ought to be mentioned. First, it is said to have been the dragline effect caused by the criminal-law form of the trespassory action. The Statute of Westminster forbade "punishing" one man for another's wrongs, and thus, for a long time the criminal tone of the action (*e.g.*, the plea of "not guilty") must have made vicarious liability difficult to engraft upon the master's status.[143] If vicarious liability was slow to attach, this correspondingly delayed contractual enforcement. It would otherwise have been manifestly unreasonable to say that the master, as defendant, could not be liable except by some combination of notice, use, and authority, but when donning the plaintiff's hat, he could

---

[141] STOLJAR, LAW OF AGENCY, *supra* note 105, at 203; P.S. ATIYAH, AN INTRODUCTION TO THE LAW OF CONTRACT 234 (2nd ed. 1971); Pollock, Notes 3 L.Q.R. 358, 359 (1887).

[142] In *Joseph v. Knox* (1813) 3 Camp. 320, a case recognizing the plaintiff-agent's right to hold a shipper liable for the loss of goods to be sent overseas to his principal, Lord Ellenborough said, at 321, "There is privity of contract established by these parties by means of the bill of lading . . . To the plaintiffs, therefore, from whom the consideration moves, and to whom the promise was made, the defendant is liable . . . He cannot say to the shippers they have no interest in the goods and are not damnified by his breach of contract. I think the plaintiffs are entitled to recover the value of the goods, and they will hold the sum recovered as trustees for the real owner."

[143] Statute of Westminster II, (1285) 13 Edward I, c. 35; 2 POLLOCK AND MAITLAND, *supra* n. 69, at 531, ("Throughout the Year Books men are 'punished' for trespasses, and, when we are to be told that an action of trespass will not lie against the master, we are told that the master is not to be 'punished' for his servant's trespasses – quia quis pro alieno facto non est puniendus.")

simply capitalize upon the fictional allegation that the defendant had dealt directly with him, Because the liability aspect carved out rules in the form of exceptions to a prohibition, it probably served to depress rather than to stimulate conceptual growth. Might it not be among the many policy reasons canvassed for Chief Justice Holt's employer liability doctrine, that as a legal purist, he had recognized, and was then rectifying, an asymmetrical unfairness between enforcement and liability that existed both in contract and tort?

The second reason may well have been the unclear location of title as between the principal and factor. As for money passed between master and servant or merchant and factor, it had always been thought that the ownership of it was impossible to trace, and therefore, the servant, factor, or any bailee, received title upon delivery.[144] As to specific goods, however, it became clear toward the end of the 17th century that the bailor, merchant or consignor really retained in himself title to the goods, even though he gave possession to his factor or consignee.[145] The courts of equity spearheaded this transition by splitting the incidents of ownership, recognizing an equitable title left in the principal, and treating the factor as a constructive trustee.[146] Our modern system of direct agency could hardly have developed until this internal transition had taken place.

Third, as we have noted before, throughout the 17th century, agency operated within a legal context that enabled the courts to envision the principal as a contract beneficiary. It was not until about 1680 that the consideration objection, and not until the 19th century that the parties only objection, became forces serious enough to disturb this picture. Prior to that time, therefore, there was hardly a tendency to distinguish the beneficiary from the principal, much less to speak of an exception to the privity requirement.

Furthermore, it was not until the 19th century that agency became (in

---

[144] *Core's Case* (1537) 1 Dyer 20a; *Anonymous* (1563) 3 Leon. 38. In the latter case it is said in King's Bench that if A delivers money to B to buy cattle, A cannot have an action for the money. The money by the delivery is "to" the bailee B. A can only have an account.

[145] *Moore v. Moore* (1612) 1 Bulst. 169; *Clark's Case* (1587) 2 Leon 30, 89. In NOMOTECHNIA, *supra* n. 125, Finch was clear that in bailment "to keep", the bailment was revocable and the bailor could retake the goods without request, because "the property" was not out of the bailor. But on a bailment "to employ," he said nothing directly about the location of title, probably because the law was unsettled.

[146] *Burdett v. Willet* (1708) 2 Vern. 638; *Whitcomb v. Jacob* (1711) 1 Salk. 160; *Godfrey v. Furzo* (1933) 3 P. Wms 185; *Scott v. Surman* (1742) Willes 400.

Stoljar's phrase) a significant, single subject.[147]   The first treatise on the subject was written in 1813, followed by Joseph Story's treatise in 1839.[148] In the meantime, agency's slow parturition from assumpsit had this important reciprocal consequence for the beneficiary action.   Trade pressures argued strongly and consistently for expanded relief on the master's or principal's contracts, but the inchoate state of agency required and enabled integrating his case into a broader general theory that had to be kept more flexible and liberal than it probably otherwise would have been.   If the exception had been recognized earlier, the door to third party actions at common law just might have closed sooner than it did.

---

[147] STOLJAR, LAW OF AGENCY, *supra* note 105, at 15.

[148] SAMUEL LIVERMORE, LAW OF PRINCIPAL AND AGENT, (2 vols. Baltimore, 1813); JOSEPH STORY, COMMENTARIES ON THE LAW OF AGENCY, (Boston, 1839).

IV. THE CONSIDERATION THEORY

It becomes clear from a study of the theories of interest, benefit, and agency that the consideration doctrine in this period was not, at first, the dominant factor regulating beneficiary suits. The importance of consideration does not stand in relief until one nears the end of this period and even then it emerges only within a specific line of cases that we shall call the substitute-debtor cases. Encountering the new importance of consideration in one kind of case suggests that as we dig deeper we shall uncover the original context and reasons for the modern restriction. The task is to understand how this narrow context was enlarged at the expense of the other theories.

A.   The Substitute-Debtor Fact Situation

The specific cases in question concern what may be described as the substitution of one debtor in place of another. To illustrate in accordance with the case of *Bourne v. Mason* (1669), suppose that debtor A owes £100 to the creditor, and at the same time debtor B owes debtor A £100. Instead of wasting motion, the two debtors then and there exchange promises that their mutual debt will be discharged and satisfied upon debtor B's payment of £100 directly to the creditor. Could the creditor sue to enforce B's promise to A? In the case of *Bourne v. Mason*, the creditor was refused an action upon such a promise, but not simply because the promise had not been made to him.[149] The chief ground was that the creditor had furnished no consideration, either by forbearance on collection of the debt, or by discharging the original debtor, A, and accepting B in his place. In the court's words, "here the plaintiff did nothing of trouble to himself or benefit to the defendant, but is a meer stranger to the consideration."[150]

It must be noted further, however, that the plaintiff's relationship to the consideration was but one part of this objection. A complementary issue was the defendant's relationship to the consideration. For example, the creditor's action was also denied if the substitute debtor was a volunteer who was not originally indebted to another. In *Clypsam v. Morris* (1669)[151] a volunteer came to the creditor and promised to pay off a debt owed to the creditor by a third party, and the creditor agreed to forbear for a fortnight.

---

[149] This ground, though omitted in Ventris's report, appears to have been of importance in Keble's report, at 528.

[150] *Bourne v. Mason* (1669) 1 Vent. 6, 7.

[151] 2 Keb. 401, 443, 453.

Here, although the plaintiff was a promisee and his forbearance involved detriment to himself,[152] the court would not grant recovery since consideration did not move to the *defendant* personally. Twisden, J. stressed that the defendant was not obliged *ab initio* to pay the debt. Of what benefit was forbearance to him when he was not originally a debtor to anyone? It was a case where the defendant, not the plaintiff, was a stranger to the consideration.

Now in these substitute-debtor cases, the consideration requirement was of a different order and stringency than elsewhere encountered. In *Bourne*, the consideration moved to the promisor from the promisee, yet it was objected that nothing moved from the plaintiff. In *Clypsam*, it moved from the plaintiff creditor (the promisee), but not to the defendant, who stood to gain nothing by it. The operative rule to be deduced, therefore, cannot have been simply that consideration must move from the promisee, or from the plaintiff, for such a rule would not have blocked the beneficiary.

The results become more intelligible, however, when treated as cases in which courts silently imposed new policing tasks upon the consideration requirement. There were two sensitive issues to which the judges may have reacted. Firstly, the agreement in *Bourne* was the equivalent of a forbidden assignment of a chose in action, that is, it amounted to the assignment of the burden of an obligation from one debtor to another.[153] Enforcement of such a transaction would have placed in question the rule that an obligor may not revoke or discharge his own obligation without the concurrence of the obligee.[154] Second, a creditor was not permitted to hold a substitute debtor liable in assumpsit unless he had promised to discharge his original debtor, for otherwise he acquired two debtors and there was a danger of double recoveries or double liabilities.[155] The court's decision to formulate the objection to recovery in terms of consideration masks both issues. The consideration doctrine was not the root of the matter, but was rather a proxy mechanism to deal with these residual problems. To pursue this point further we should examine the background of the substitute debtor problem.

---

[152] Indeed, the Chief Justice thought such forbearance was sufficient detriment and inclined for the plaintiff. 2 Keb. 401.

[153] Common law views on prohibited assignments are discussed below in Chapter III. See pp. 145-152.

[154] *Hurford v. Pile* (1616) Cro. Jac. 483.

[155] *See below* pp. 71-72.

B.   Some Background to Bourne v. Mason

Several centuries before the Formative Period, when promises were not yet enforceable by assumpsit, debts could not be substituted or shifted informally by parole agreement or novation. In an action in debt in 1431, a court had said, "Notwithstanding that all three [parties] are in agreement and that he shall pay the debt for the other, nonetheless the other is not discharged of his debt by anything at all."[156] A creditor desiring to discharge his debtor on a simple debt needed to enter into an accord and satisfaction with him.[157] Other than through an accord and satisfaction, the informal substitution of one debtor for another was impossible due to the absence of a promissory remedy to bind the second debtor, or to discharge the first. Feelings of unfairness prevented the courts from granting an action in debt against the substitute debtor, when at the same time the original debtor remained undischarged. It was felt that one *quid pro quo* could not create two distinct debts, and "the same money cannot be lent to two."[158]

With the advent of assumpsit, however, a discharge could be accomplished through an express promise. There were cases reflecting that the creditor's simple promise to accept a substitute operated *ipso facto* as an implied discharge of the original debtor. In 1624, for example, a creditor's promise to forbear suing the original debtor was judicially construed to mean an absolute forbearance never to sue him. It was said that if the creditor attempted to sue his original debtor, he would be "chargeable in an action upon the case for it is an implied promise in the plaintiff that he should forbear his suit totally."[159] Without at least an implied promise of discharge, both plaintiff's and defendant's promise lacked consideration.[160]

In 1650 the court, growing more technical, abandoned the approach of discharge by implication of law, and ruled that the plaintiff had to plead the

---

[156] Y.B. (1433) 11 Hen. VI, 43 (30).

[157] SIMPSON, *supra* note 11, at 104. An executory accord was not a bar to an action of debt, nor was an accord a defense to a debt due by bond. A formal contract could only be varied formally.

[158] *Marriott v. Lister* (1762) 2 Wils, K.B. 141, 142; *Butcher v. Andrews* (1692) 1 Salk. 23.

[159] *Mapes v. Sidney* (1624) Cro. Jac. 683, 684. Both Chief Justice Hobart and Keeling, however, argued contrariwise that the plaintiff should not lose his original debtor unless plaintiff had expressly promised that he would not resort to him. *Id. Clypsam v. Morris* (1669) 2 Keb. 401.

[160] *Body v. A* (1587) Goulds. 49.

discharge of the first debtor or else the consideration was bad. Thus, Chief Justice Rolle said in *Newcomin v. Leigh:*

> He doth not say that he will discharge Cooper, and so Newcomin may sue Cooper notwithstanding the assumpsit; for though it may be it was the intention of the parties to discharge Cooper, yet it appears not so by the words of the assumpsit set forth. . . .[161]

More vacillation was evident in 1671, when the courts relaxed the technical need to set forth in the pleadings an agreement to discharge, just so long as the evidence showed that there was in fact such an agreement.[162] It seems, therefore, that though the required manner of pleading the discharge periodically changed over the years, the substantive rule continued to be that the creditor could not hold the substitute debtor liable in assumpsit unless he had promised to discharge his original debtor.[163]

C.   The Danger of Double Recovery

The tie-in between discharge and consideration is indispensable in understanding the true difficulty in *Bourne v. Mason.* Ventris' report bases the court's rejection of the creditor's action upon a lack of consideration; yet, since consideration did move from the promisee, the blank conclusion does not illuminate why the court denied the action. A deeper difficulty was the absence of any discharge by the creditor, and consequently, the possibility of a double recovery or a double liability, a danger that could at least be kept in check by the consideration objection. The subsidiary problem came to the surface in Keble's report of the case, where it was said *per curiam*, "the action lieth not by the plaintiff in regard the defendant doth not promise to discharge

---

[161] (1650) Style 249. A clearer report of this case is found in Cremer's Ms. under the name *Necomb v. Lee* (1650) p. 37, Case No. 65 (Gray's Inn Ms, Eng. Leg. Ms. Project, Ed. J.H. Baker). The facts there stated were that Cowper bought fish from plaintiff and requested the defendant to pay the debt to plaintiff within six months. The defendant promised that in consideration if plaintiff would accept him as his debtor and would forbear him for six months, he would pay. The Court said, "it is not good consideration. When Lee who is not debtor promise payment in consideration of forbearance of him, yet it is no benefit for Lee, nor to Cowper who is not spared nor discharged by this promise of the defendant." *Accord, Johnson v. Walker* (1651) p. 46 *Ibid.* The same view was taken in *Abbot v. Moor* (1670) 2 Keb. 543, 557, and was repeated in Keble's report of *Bourne v. Mason* at p. 287: "and albeit the colloquim were inter omnes partes, and the promise made to the plaintiff Bourne himself, yet judgment staid."

[162] *Oble v. Dittersfield* (1672) 1 Vent. 153; *Davison v. Haslip* (1672) 1 Vent. 152.

[163] *Roe v. Haugh* (1698) 1 Salk. 29.

the plaintiff, and he is a stranger to the plaintiff, the promise being made to one Patty he to whom the promise was made must bring the action, and the plaintiff hath still remedy against him (his original debtor). But *adjournatur.*"[164]

Since the creditor was not the promisee of anyone concerned, he could not have promised to discharge his original debtor.[165] To allow him to sue upon a promise in his favor which lay solely between his undischarged debtor and the substitute would pose the serious risk that he might also attempt a second recovery against his original debtor.[166] Even if the creditor received a promise from the substitute, the danger did not abate so long as the original debtor had not been released.[167] It was, of course, possible for courts to deem the original debtor discharged by implication of law, but that could be thought to permit something rather dangerous. An obligor could discharge his own obligation by simply transferring it to a substitute. Expressed another way, it would be the assignment of the burden of a contract. By vetoing relief with the simple stamp "no consideration," the courts avoided and buried these problems.

---

[164] 2 Keb. 527, 528. (Emphasis supplied).

[165] SIMPSON, *supra* note 11 at 479, has taken the view that plaintiff was a promisee, but this seems to be contrary to both Keble's and Ventris' reports of the case.

[166] It has been said that this danger hardly existed in fact, and that no sensible jury would have permitted the double recovery. STOLJAR, *supra* note 105, at 137. This is not persuasive from a psychological point of view. The danger existed, and was expressed as a fear because the judges found no law on the subject; there was little control over what juries might do, and to a system unpersuaded that creditor beneficiaries should have such actions, even potential dangers are enough.

[167] *Forth v. Stanton* (1669), 1 Wms. Saund. 210, 2 Keb. 465, 1 Lev. 262; Cf., *Russel v. Haddock* (1667) 1 Lev. 188. The same danger was used as a ground to deny a shipping agent the right to sue the carrier, even though the agent was the promisee. *Dawes v. Peck* (1800) 8 T.R. 330.

D.   The Early Synthesis of Two Privity Objections

An interesting feature of this analysis is that the consideration and promisee objection give the appearance of being synthesized. The reasoning perhaps looked to the common lawyers like a continuous circle. Where the plaintiff was not the promisee, he would not have discharged his debtor. And not having discharged his debtor, how could he have given consideration?[168] Perhaps such logic was the first step toward the view favored by some modern writers whereby the nonpromisee must always be regarded as a stranger to the consideration. It is otherwise difficult to explain why there was not one successful action against a substitute debtor in which the plaintiff was a nonpromisee, even though recoveries by nonpromisees in other lines of cases were fairly common.[169] This contrast between the substitute debtor cases and other decisions ignoring the same promisee (or parties-only) objection suggests that while the objection was argued and known long before 1669, it did not become established and authoritatively linked to the consideration doctrine before then.

One learned author has stated that all talk of a rule that only the parties to a contract can sue upon it is obviously modern, that an amalgamation of the consideration and promisee objections did not take place

---

[168] An earlier example of this circular relationship was *Howlett v. Hallet* (1599) Rolle Ab. 27, pl. 51. *See also Ritley v. Dennet* (1607) Rolle Ab. 30, 31.

[169] The following list collects most of the successful actions by nonpromisees. *Courteis v. Collingwood* (1675) 3 Keb. 434; *Hadves v. Levit* (1632) Het. 176; *Dutton v. Poole* (1680) Raym T. 302; *Hornsey v. Dimocke* (1672) 1 Vent. 119; *Rippon v. Norton* (1601) (2nd case) Cro. Eliz. 881; *Gilbert v. Ruddeard* (1608) 3 Dy. 272a; *Provender v. Wood* (1628) Het. 30; *Bafield v. Collard* (1647) Aleyn 1; *Oldham v. Bateman* (1639) 1 Viner 335, pl. 8; *Rookwood's Case* (1589) Cro. Eliz. 164; *Body v. A.* (1587) Goulds. 49; *Starkey v. Mill* (1651) Style 296; *Disbourne v. Denabie* (1649) Rolle Ab. 30, 31; *Thomas v.* (1655) Style 461; *Levett v. Hawes* (1599) Cro. Eliz. 619; *Evans v. Jamney* (1649) cited in 1 Keb. 121, 122. For example, in *Megod's Case* (1586) reported in SIMPSON, *supra* note 11, at 638 Mounson enfeoffed two persons of land with the intent that they were to convey, and plaintiff brought assumpsit. Whether the plaintiff, who had not dealt with the defendants, should recover was discussed in terms of consideration. The defendants insisted that the consideration for their promise did not flow between themselves and the plaintiff. Counsel argued "that the action did not lie, seeing that there was no consideration as between plaintiff and defendants, but this was solely between the said Mounson and the defendants." Counsel's argument was in reality the promisee objection redefined in terms of consideration, but it was completely ignored by Clench and Gawdy, J.J. who were satisfied simply to say that good consideration existed for the promise given to Mounson, the feoffor:

"The action lies well . . . this is a good consideration, seeing that there is a trust placed in them that they should make assurance to the other. And where there is good consideration in the Chancery on this an action on the case can lie here."

until the 19th century. He concluded, "it is quite incorrect to suppose that the 19th century principle is contained, as is often said, in *Bourne v. Mason*."[170] Yet, another view of the evidence may be that although a "parties-only" rule was not expressly formulated in *Bourne* (or in any other substitute-debtor case), it may have logically resulted anyway as a consequence of the circular relationship between discharge and consideration.

V. 1670-1680: THE TRIUMPH OF CONSIDERATION AND THE DEMISE OF THE BENEFICIARY ACTION

A. The New Matrix

The decisive turning point came about when the rival theories were all absorbed into the consideration doctrine. Somewhere between the decision in *Bourne v. Mason* (1669), and that of *Dutton v. Poole* (1680), we encounter a new assumption. The *Bourne* decision marked the first time a court compared the inconsistent results being reached under the divergent lines of cases and theories. A novel effort was then made to synthesize these holdings. The all-important assumption was made that consideration should be the matrix or master-concept against which past divergences must be explained. The counter assumption, that benefit or interest should be the basic model for the third party action, was evidently too remote to be entertained. The new assumption rested upon the supremacy of the consideration doctrine, and the feasibility of reconciling all lines of cases to it.

This reconciliation takes place in *Bourne v. Mason* (1669). There was simply no earlier case that attempted to take a comprehensive view. In the course of refusing to grant an action to the creditor beneficiary on the ground of lack of consideration, this court showed that the consideration doctrine could explain away contrasting results in the donation cases without reversing them. The incongruity posed by *Sprat v. Agar* (1658)[171], a marriage-money case, could now be fitted into a wider scheme, and so the court explained that the recovery in that case was based upon consideration, the "meritorious act" of marriage performed by the beneficiary himself.[172] The new rationale, although far-removed from the actual holding which had been based on the benefit theory, acquired a certain credence coming from Twisden, J., who had

---

[170] SIMPSON, *supra* n. 11, at 476.

[171] 2 Sid. 115; Cremer Ms. p. 380 (Gray's Inn Library Ms., H-1792).

[172] Discussed *supra* pp. 52-54.

been counsel for the plaintiff Sprat.[173]   The judges also reevaluated the holding in the *Physicians Case*,[174] where a physician had performed a cure in consideration of a sum of money to be paid to his daughter. In discussion of this case, the court now reassigned the daughter's recovery to the new ground that "the nearness of the relation gives the daughter the benefit of the consideration."[175] This precise phraseology would later become the leitmotif of *Dutton v. Poole*.[176]

In addition to these cases, a wide range of precedents was argued to the court.[177]   In the process of reconciling these cases, the court in effect relegated the donation cases into a *sui generis* category that was incapable of growth or expansion. The rationale to enforce a gift became a corollary of consideration. This was a breakthrough for the consideration doctrine, and the decision in *Bourne v. Mason* quickly acquired a reputation for having established the framework of the future.[178]

B.   Dutton v. Poole (1680)

The terms of the reconciliation were tested and applied eleven years later in an action in assumpsit brought by a donee beneficiary. This was the famous decision of the Exchequer Chamber in *Dutton v. Poole*. Grizil's father was about to cut down a stand of oak trees to raise a dowry for her in her forthcoming marriage to Sir Ralph Dutton. Her brother, who was to be the future heir of the land, interceded and prevailed upon the father not to disfigure the land by cutting the oaks. In consideration, he promised the father that he would pay Grizil £1000 after her marriage. After the marriage her father died, and she and her husband brought assumpsit for non-payment of the sum. Suit was not brought in the father's name by his executrix

---

[173] This fact is noted in 2 Keb. 457, 458.

[174] Cited at large in 1 Vent. 6.

[175] *Id.* at 7.

[176] The idea of "extending" consideration to a near-relation was certainly well known in connection with uses. *Bould v. Sir Henry Winston* (1608) Cro. Jac. 168. However, *Dutton v. Poole* may have marked the first occasion on which it was suggested that such "extended" consideration was good and sufficient in assumpsit.

[177] *See* the authorities in 2 Keb. 527.

[178] As to the scope of which counsel, in *Lowther v. Kelly* (1723) 8 Mod. 115, 116, could broadly declare: "It was laid down as a rule that no person shall recover upon an agreement but he who is party or privy to the consideration thereof."

(Grizil's mother) because she was apparently the only witness to the defendant's promise,[179] and being the executrix (and an interested party), she would have otherwise been disqualified from testifying.[180]   Thus, it was expedient to bring suit in the beneficiary's name, and representing the defendant was counselor Holt (as he then was), who objected that Grizil was "neither privy nor interested in the consideration" and that the promise had been made not to her but to her father.[181]   Nevertheless, in the Kings Bench, the court held for the plaintiff and the Exchequer Chamber affirmed, although regrettably we have no report of this last court's opinion.

Now the great difference between this case and any previous gift case of the 17th century was the assumption that the beneficiary's action must satisfy the consideration test or it would not lie. The noteworthy aspect of the decision was the unprecedented display of consideration theory that burst forth from counsel and the Court of Kings Bench in support of Grizil's action. Justice Wilde found that Grizil's marriage could be viewed as a "meritorious act"[182] given for her brother's promise; Chief Justice Scroggs stated that the natural love and affection of the father was a consideration that extended to the daughter.[183]   One report (Ventris') explains the justification given for this vicarious extension as being the "nearness of relation between Father and Child."[184]   Yet in another report we are told that the court ultimately rested upon actual benefit and detriment: "and so judgement was given for the plaintiff, for the son hath the Benefit by having the Wood; and the daughter hath lost her portion by this means."[185]

To add to this rich collection, we also know that in his argument for plaintiff, Trinder tried out four distinct theories of relief:

    (1)   pure benefit, a test recognized in previous gift cases,
    (2)   natural affection (which Scroggs, C. J. evidently
           favored),

---

[179] 3 Keb. 786.

[180] *Anonymous* (1675) 1 Mod. 107.

[181] The quoted phrase is found in Levinz' report at p. 211.

[182] 1 Freem. 471.

[183] 2 Lev. 211, 212.

[184] 1 Vent. 318, 332, at 333. See the discussion of the *Physician's Case, supra,* at note 74 & 75.

[185] 2 Lev. 211, 212.

(3) plaintiff's "interest" arising from a "use" in her favor, and
(4) the promisor's benefit and the beneficiary's detriment.[186]

In the end, the theory favored by the court of Kings Bench was apparently that natural consideration "extended" to a close relation. At least this has become the orthodox understanding as to why the beneficiary recovered.[187] But if this be so, then the case has perhaps received a mistaken emphasis. The claims of legal historians[188] that *Dutton v. Poole* was an exceptional and anomalous result for its day are wide of the mark. The case and its result, seen as a donee's action in assumpsit, had been commonplace at common law in the 17th century. It is not necessary to review the theories and cases once again. One refutation of any other characterization is simply to look at the weakness of the authorities relied upon by defendant's counsel. Three out of the four precedents relied upon by Holt before the Kings Bench had recognized a beneficiary's action upon a promise not received by him, and as to the fourth case, which was favorable to the defendant, two judges now said it had been wrongly decided.[189] In the Exchequer Chamber, counsel cited five cases, but only one was clearly in

---

[186] These theories have been interpolated from various passages in Trinder's argument. 2 Lev. 211, 121. These are set out below, in their natural sequence in the report, with numerals added to correspond to those in the text:

1) "if a man deliver goods or money to H. to pay B., B. may have an action, because he is to have the benefit of the promise,"

2) "and the father is obliged by natural affection to provide for his children;"

3) "for which cause affection to children is sufficient to raise a use to them out of the father's estate; and therefore the daughter had an interest in the consideration, and in the promise,"

4) "And the son had a benefit by this agreement, for by this means he hath the Wood, and the daughter is without a portion. . . ."

[187] 2 Street 153. The report of the Exchequer Chamber's affirmance is a single line in Raymond T. 302, 303, which dispatched the promisee objection. It stated, "the action is maintainable by the party to whom the promise was made, or to the *cestuy que use,* the promise was indifferently."

[188] For such a conclusion, *see* Scammel, [1955] 8 Current Legal Problems 131, 134; 2 Street 153; Note, [1954] 70 L.Q.R. 467, 468.

[189] The first three cases cited by Holt were *Rippon v. Norton, Hawes v. Leader (sic),* and *Starkey v. Milner (sic).* The fourth case was *Norris v. Pine* and the doubts were expressed by Scroggs, C. J. and Jones, J. *See,* 2 Lev. 211, 212.

his favor while two were clearly opposed.[190] Furthermore, beneficiaries were obtaining the same results upon similar promises in Chancery in decrees innocent of any reference to natural or valuable consideration.[191]

Thus, the exceptional fact about this case was surely not the result, but only the new assumption, and the new corollary of consideration devised for a gift beneficiary. From older cases it was known that natural consideration could suffice to raise and vest a use,[192] but this sort of consideration had not yet been held adequate to sustain assumpsit on a use thus established. *Dutton v. Poole* probably was the first case of assumpsit to go so far. The reasons given largely undermined the claims of donees and beneficiaries. It may also have eliminated the line between the internal and external interest conception, by making internal consideration the future determinant of the beneficiary's privity. Through the cases of *Bourne* and *Dutton*, a new position was forged. The latter was not an exception to the former, but actually a deepening of the assumption upon which it rested.

C.   The Abrupt Demise Of the Beneficiary Action After 1680

There must have been, however, greater significance to the legal events between 1670-1680 than the narrow doctrines we have so far mentioned. When we take our stand at common law in 1680 and look to the future, the significant thing is that we see nothing. The next one-hundred years at common law are practically devoid of similar actions in assumpsit. The beneficiary's action had been guillotined sometime in this decade. Only one case of importance arose later -- *Crow v. Rogers* (1724)[193] -- and it was a creditor beneficiary action quite similar to *Bourne v. Mason*. A person named Hardy was indebted to both the plaintiff and the defendant and thus,

> upon a discourse between this Hardy and the defendant it was agreed that the defendant should pay the plaintiff's debt of £70 and that Hardy should make the defendant a title to

---

[190] The favorable case was *Archdale v. Barnard* (1608), unreported except in 1 Viner 333 (Assumpsit). The cases opposed were *Rippon v. Norton* and *Levet v. Hawes*.

[191] *E.g., Chamberlaine v. Chamberlaine* (1678) 2 Freem. 34; *Cassy v. Fitton* (1679) 79 Seld. Soc. 729: *Thynn v. Thynn* (1684) 1 Vern. 296.

[192] *Sharrington v. Strotton* (1565) Plowden 298; *Calthorpe's Case* (1574) 1 Dyer 334b; *Collard v. Collard* (1594) Popham 47.

[193] 1 Strange 592.

a house.[194]

The plaintiff brought assumpsit on defendant's promise (to Hardy) but the court held, in a two-line opinion and "without much debate," that the plaintiff was "a stranger to the consideration" and gave judgment for the defendant.[195] Outside of this case, if we take into account some scattered dicta by Lord Holt,[196] Buller, J.,[197] and Lord Mansfield,[198] as well as several decisions of indirect bearing reached under the Statute of Frauds,[199] this brings the trail at common law to an abrupt end. There are no more recoveries, nor more actions than those referred to. It is a strong possibility that most of the beneficiary actions were channelled into Chancery, where the consideration doctrine was in the process of being received and notions of privity would have been less restrictive.[200] Yet, the sheer magnitude and swiftness of this shift cannot be altogether explained by, or attributed to, the power of single cases like *Bourne v. Mason* or *Dutton v. Poole*, particularly as this is thought to be a period without hardened notions of *stare decisis*. It ought to be recognized that the latter case overruled no prior decision, it laid down no new restrictions on the beneficiary's action, and above all, it granted the beneficiary a recovery. Thus, if one were in the position of the contemporary lawyer, blind-folded from the light of subsequent history, it would have been impossible to discover clear signals or clues from any isolated examination of this landmark case that would have unmistakably presaged an irrevocable turn to Chancery. Clearly, there must be other conspiring causes, and these will be addressed below.

D.   Four Possible Explanations

There were, in fact, four major events during this decade that may help explain the abrupt demise of the beneficiary action.

---

[194] *Ibid.*

[195] Only the cases of *Bourne v. Mason* and *Dutton v. Poole* were cited by the defendant and plaintiff respectively in support of their position. The earlier jurisprudence was apparently considered either irrelevant or superseded.

[196] *Yard v. Eland* (1669) 1 Ld. Raym. 368, 369.

[197] *Marchington v. Vernon* (1787), cited in 1 B. & P. 98, 101, n. (c).

[198] *Martyn v. Hind* (1776) 2 Cowp. 437, 443: "As to the case of *Dutton v. Poole*, . . . it is a matter of surprise, how a doubt could have arisen in that case."

[199] *Fish v. Hutchinson* (1759) 2 Wils. K.B. 94; *Buckmyr v. Darnall* (1705) 2 Ld. Raym. 1085.

[200] *See e.g.,* the failure of the privity defense in *Harvey v. Baker* (1677) 79 Seld. Soc, 631.

First, the Statute of Frauds of 1677,[201] to a considerable extent, had the effect of drying up three sources of third party actions in assumpsit. The Statute now required a writing in six categories of contracts, and the first three were: (1) an executor's promise to answer damages out of his own estate; (2) a promise to pay the debt of a third person; and (3) contracts in consideration of marriage. These were three important kinds of beneficiary contracts. The requirement of a writing would have discouraged some contract-making in the first place, reduced the number of actions brought in the second place, and would tend to encourage important contracts to be formalized under seal. For example, the simple promise of marriage-money would most likely reappear as a contract under seal enforceable through an action of covenant, and this alone would represent a significant subtraction from the normal caseload of assumpsit. No other reason accounts as persuasively for the fact that there was not one marriage-money case reported at common law between 1680 and 1860.[202] Further, the Statute also said that all grants and assignments by parole of any trust or "confidence" were null and void.[203] This formality would have made it difficult for common law judges to continue to find implied uses in a parole promise. Perhaps the Statute snapped the link which the judges had forged between implied uses and the interest theory. At the same time that formalities were weighing down the common law, the Chancery trust was expressly exempt from the Statute. Clearly, the more open channel of relief on a simple contract was a suit in Chancery upon a trust theory.

Second, several vital policy decisions regarding assignments and negotiable instruments counterbalanced any inconvenience in the common

---

[201] (1677) 29 Car. II, c. 3.

[202] This check upon the flow of marriage-money cases fits with Professor Thorne's hypothesis that the cases out of which the modern law of contract grew were not the important transactions which would have been handled by penal bonds and recognizances. These were the fringe transactions brought in assumpsit due to the insignificance of the sums involved or the inexperience of the parties. "The hypothesis is best supported," said Thorne, "by the marriage settlements that play their part in the evolution of the informal contract. Transactions such as these were by no means new: lands, often of immense value, and money had for centuries been assured by parents on the married couple, using the standard procedures of bonds and counter-bonds, simultaneous fines, or feoffments of condition. No instruments are more common in family archives. The settlements litigated in the common law courts of the 16th and 17th centuries, on the other hand, seem without exception to be concerned only with small estates and to mirror only unsophisticated suitors and their parents acting in the absence of legal, or even of reasonably informed, advice." Samuel E. Thorne, "Tudor Social Transformation and Legal Change," [1951] 26 N.Y.U.L. Rev. 10, 21.

[203] (1677) 29 Car. II, c. 3. sec. IX.

law's hardening position toward the beneficiary action. In the 1670's, the prohibition against assignments of debts was noticeably relaxed, and these transactions began to shed the presumption of maintenance. This matter will need to be developed in greater detail in chapter III.[204]

Furthermore, in the 16th and 17th centuries negotiable instruments were assimilated into the action of assumpsit. Bills of exchange had surpassed their original function of paying debts in distant places and of avoiding the risks of transporting actual money, and had developed into a perfectly flexible "paper currency." This created a clear exception to the prohibition associated with the transfer and assignment of debts, whether the debts of merchants or any contracting party.[205] Promissory notes, which came in as a later convention, were at first denied enforcement in assumpsit because they had no tradition within the custom of merchants.[206] By an act of parliament in 1704, however, notes were put on the same footing with bills.

Third, there developed a new gravitational pull from Chancery. It is true that for a long time equity had entertained a non-material notion of consideration, a tolerance for direct actions against third parties,[207] and according to Barbour, may have been enforcing third party beneficiary contracts for over 200 years.[208] Yet, it was not until the period at hand that the modern trust conception emerged. The coincidence between the rise of the trust and the sharp decline of the beneficiary action in assumpsit was strikingly close. By Nottingham's chancellorship (1672-1683) the "use upon a use" was enforceable, and the personal nature of the cestui's interest was transformed into a real right, and out of this union the modern trust was born. This instrument was now distinctly advantaged to protect the third party interest, and strategically exempted from the coverage of the Statute of Frauds. The historical timing of its birth may have aborted the confused trends that we have traced in assumpsit, and absorbed the beneficiary action into Equity's domain.

---

[204] The leading case of the period in question is *Carrington v. Harway* (1665) 1 Keb. 803.

[205] This important fact was described by Treby J. in *Bromwich v. Lloyd* (1697) 2 Lut, 1582, 1585.

[206] *Buller v. Crips*, (K.B. 1704) 6 Mod. 29, 1 Salk 130. *See* Gilmore, "The Commercial Doctrine of Good Faith Purchase," 63 Yale L. J. 1057 (1954).

[207] *E.g., Chamberlain v. Chamberlain* (1678) 2 Freem. 34; *Pollard v. Downes* (1683) 2 Chan. Cas. 121.

[208] BARBOUR, *supra* n. 50, at 164-165.

Fourth, the trust became regarded by the late 17th century as the exclusive preserve of Chancery, so that an action for breach of a trust promise could not be brought in assumpsit. At an earlier date there had been no jurisdictional objection to such an action. The judges of King's Bench had once held in *Megod's Case* in 1586[209] that an action in assumpsit lay against feoffees of land who refused to convey lands to the purchaser designated by the feoffees. It was reasoned that the trust is good consideration in Chancery and therefore should also be regarded as good consideration under the action of assumpsit. Reference may also be made to the opinion of Lord Chief Justice Hobart who thought that a cestui should be able to bring an action of assumpsit against his trustee and recover damages for a breach of trust.[210] Another view, however, finally carried the day. The Chief Justice of Common Pleas, Lord North, said in a case in the Exchequer Chamber,

> That no Action on the Case will lie for a breach of Trust, because the determination of the principal thing, viz, the Trust, does not belong to the Common Law, but to the Court of Chancery.[211]

The common law judges might take notice of a trust, but they lacked the authority to give a remedy for its breach.[212] Assumpsit and trust were accordingly severed jurisdictionally on the ground of basic competence; there was now an objection to any attempt to link together the enforcement of a use in favor of a beneficiary by an action in assumpsit. It is not surprising, therefore, to find that *Dutton v. Poole* (1680) was the last case prior to this jurisdictional split in which it was seriously argued that the beneficiary's "interest" arising from a "use" in her favor, entitled her to recover at common law in assumpsit.[213] Beneficial "interests" were actionable before 1680 either because they were uses, or were analogized to uses, and the disappearance of

---

[209] SIMPSON, *supra* note 11, at 632; Godbolt, 64.

[210] *Jevon v. Bush* (1685) 1 Vern. 342: *see also* 1 Eq. Ca. Abr. 384 (D); *Megod's Case* (1586) Godbolt 64, and reprinted in SIMPSON, *supra* note 11, at 638 held that an action on the case would lie for a feoffee's failure to transfer property subject to a use.

[211] *Barnardiston v. Soame*, Vol. 6 State Trials, 1064, at 1098 (1674).

[212] "Trusts are properly at this day judged by the judges, though the jurisdiction be in another court to execute and perform them; . . ." Serj. Maynard *arguendo* in *Barns v. Freeman* (1668) Carter 195, 197. "Even the courts at law take Notice of Trusts," argument in *Bladen v. Earle of Pembroke* (1690) Nels. 164, 165 relying on Chief Justice Hale's views in *Lawrence v. Beverleigh* (1671) 2 Keb. 841.

[213] *See supra* pp. 77-78.

both notions from assumpsit after 1680 was a serious blow.

Though there are possibly other factors to be considered,[214] the above reasons, together with the privity limitation recently established in assumpsit, mainly account for this remedial shift into Chancery.

In conclusion, during the 16th and 17th century, the beneficiary suing in assumpsit succeeded as in no other period. The period ended, however, with the formation of a solid privity limitation based upon the consideration doctrine. Contemporaries may not have easily appreciated that such a significant event had occurred. The triumph of consideration over its rival alternatives was not heralded by decisive rulings or contemporary fanfares. Rather, it was evidenced by an abrupt decline after 1680, and a quiet burial in the long hiatus that followed.

---

[214] (1) Between 1670-1680, the action of *indebitatus assumpsit* was extended into a quasi-contractual remedy. The first case of this nature was decided in 1678. Now that this remedy was, for these purposes, unconstrained by consideration or personal dealings between the parties, it may well have reduced the need for some third party action to be brought in special assumpsit.

(2) One should consider the extraordinary efforts of Chief Justice Holt whose tenure on King's Bench comes just after this period. Holt was both a conservative and purist, and he resisted vigorously all attempts to extend assumpsit to plaintiffs who were not promisees. For a dramatic example, see his refusal to treat promissory notes as enforceable by assumpsit in *Clerke v. Martin* (1703) 2 Ld. Raym. 757, which caused a great outcry from the Lombard Street merchants who thereafter secured an act of Parliament overruling the judgment. (1704) 3, 4 Anne c. 9. On his opposition to the extension of the action into quasi-contract, *see Thorp v. How* (1702) Bull. N.P. 130; *City of York v. Toun* (1700) 5 Mod. 444; *Ward v. Evans* (1702) 2 Ld. Raym. 928.

(3) The jurisdictional rivalry between common law and equity, as personified in the beginning of the century by Coke and Ellesmere's confrontation and continuing thereafter. Scroggs, C. J. possibly revealed awareness of this in *Dutton v. Poole*, when he stated his determination to bend over backwards to retain common law jurisdiction of the case. He said the court would not put the plaintiff in the position of having to go into Chancery if the suit "in anyway agrees with the rules of law." 1 Freem. 471. This rivalry of course cut both ways, with both sets of tribunals seeking to aggrandize their jurisdiction.

CHAPTER III

THE CHANCERY PHASE (1680-1800)

INTRODUCTION

The beneficiary action in equity did not suddenly spring to life in the late 17th century. There is an earlier history to be told in which the *cestui que use* and the beneficiary of a simple promise were given relief by the Chancellors.[1] But we have little knowledge of these developments. For present purposes the year 1680 is taken as a point of departure, but not as an arbitrary one. As we have already seen, it marked the termination of beneficiary recoveries in assumpsit, but in Chancery it opened a remarkably creative era encompassing the work of such resourceful Chancellors as Lord Nottingham and Lord Hardwicke. During this period, Chancery recognized and refined the trust, received the common law doctrine of consideration into contract, produced new agency principles and increased the assignability of promises. These developments created a new path for the third party beneficiary action, but they were also part of the founding of modern equity.

At one time, however, the great writers on English contract paid little attention to the logical tie between the promise in favor of a third person at common law and the existence of equivalents and counterparts in Chancery. Though Chancery had long been enforcing third party promises, the leading common law authors had been asserting rather dogmatically that two parties

---

[1] Barbour's study of 15th century petitions, for example, would indicate that beneficiaries who were not parties or promisees regularly petitioned for relief on marriage contracts. See Sir Wm. Drury's petition, Bundle XV, No. 20a, p. 189. Barbour also makes reference to beneficiary actions on assignments and surety agreements. The actual disposition of these cases, however, is not known. WILLARD T. BARBOUR, THE HISTORY OF CONTRACT IN EARLY ENGLISH EQUITY, (Oxford University Press, 1914) p. 126.

could not by contract confer rights upon a third person not a party thereto.[2] This neglect of Chancery's work ended with Professor Corbin's pathbreaking essay in 1930 in the Law Quarterly Review.[3] For Corbin, formal differences in terminology, procedure, remedy, fiction, or formula were an insufficient reason to ignore the fundamental fact that the Chancellor had recognized the beneficiary's right to recover. The test of a legal right, he wrote, was simply the existence of some judicial remedy to secure that right, and that test must be applied to the Chancellor's decree. If the beneficiary was allowed to enforce a promise exchanged between contracting parties, he must be viewed as having acquired a legal right whether the Chancellor conferred upon him the name of *cestui que trust*, assignee, or any other name.[4] Thus, he said, "The definition and classification of such fundamental terms as right and duty depend upon results reached and not upon formalities of the procedure used . . . ."[5] The realism and functionalism of this approach brought into the open the advanced state of beneficiary relief in Chancery. This seems elementary today; yet all who study this subject are conscious of the liberating effect of Corbin's insight.

The common law judge and the Chancellor must have been governed by very different notions of privity of contract. We sense that the Chancellor's view was far broader and more flexible, and the writ of subpoena was not fettered by the same objections that applied to the action of assumpsit. Neither privity of contract nor consideration were original doctrines in equity. Each was *received* from the common law, and the extent of this reception was quite minimal in 1680.[6]

The general purpose of this chapter is to examine the main institutions and doctrines of Chancery dealing with third party contractual rights, and to explain the significantly wider conception of contractual duty held by the Chancellor. In this way more specific insights can be offered than

---

[2] *E.g.*, SIR WILLIAM ANSON, ANSON'S LAW OF CONTRACT, 25th ed. by Guest (Oxford University Press, 1979) p. 411: "No one but the parties to a contract can be bound by it or entitled under it." SIR JOHN SALMOND AND PERCY H. WINFIELD, PRINCIPLES OF THE LAW OF CONTRACTS 78 (Sweet & Maxwell, 1927): "No man can enforce a contract to which he is not a party even though he has a direct interest in the performance of it."

[3] Arthur L. Corbin, "Contracts for the Benefit of Third Persons," [1930] 46 L.Q.R. 12.

[4] "If there is no judicial remedy, direct or indirect, there is no right. If there is a judicial remedy, whether it be direct or indirect, there is a right," *Id.* at 14.

[5] *Id.* at 15.

[6] See below pp. 88-110.

the highly abstract explanations given by apologists of the ethical and proocooual ochoolo of thought.[7]

The Chancellor's wider conception can be explained on the basis of higher and stronger ethical principles. The Chancellor pursued the ideal of ensuring the enforcement of all promises, including those to benefit third parties. Professor Atiyah has suggested that promise-based liability was, before 1770, generally subordinated to the role played by benefit-based and reliance-based liability.[8] This suggestion does not necessarily weaken the findings of the present research. Ethical impulse supplied the dynamic for a lower privity barrier in Equity. As noted below in connection with Professor Atiyah's views,[9] the principle of Conscience explains better than reliance or enrichment principles why the Chancellor gave more frequent relief to the third party beneficiary. Conscience-based duties looked primarily at the defendant, not at his privity with another. The Conscience Principle focused unilaterally and inwardly rather than relationally and outwardly. Since Conscience was concerned with the preservation of the defendant's soul, the beneficiary's claim would deserve recognition not only because he had relied or because the defendant would be otherwise enriched, but because the promisor *ought* to perform. Thus, whereas common-law privity suggested that personal obligations are closed circles, the equitable view accommodated the beneficiary within a triangle.

The classic triangle was the trust, an institution in which substance was generally elevated over form (the beneficial rights of the *cestui* prevailed over the seisin of the feoffee). The Chancellor's ethical values were undoubtedly in sympathy with the feoffor's reliance or confidence in the feoffee, and could not easily witness the spectacle of unjustly enriched feoffees prospering through default on their own promises. He reinforced the substance of obligations by making the duty of subsequent transferees depend upon the state of their conscience, and so regarded what a man knew or noticed as the equivalent to what he had promised. In this sense knowledge and notice were as efficacious to conscience-based duties as consideration was to assumpsit.

---

[7] For a lucid treatment of this debated issue, see generally, WILLIAM W. BILLSON, EQUITY IN ITS RELATIONS TO COMMON LAW (Boston Book Co., 1917).

[8] P.S. ATIYAH, THE RISE AND FALL OF FREEDOM OF CONTRACT 158-162 (Clarendon Press, 1979).

[9] See below at pp. 96-98.

The complementary processual explanation argues that the Chancellor possessed certain procedural efficiencies, particularly discovery, compulsion and general flexibility. The basic privity problem, Williston argued, was caused by the insufficient elasticity of common law remedies. These remedies contemplated two sides to a case and could not deal with more, while equity could successively deal with any number of conflicting interests.[10] Another way of putting this was that the common law required an election between narrow writs or causes of action, whereas the Chancellors had always tried to judge according to the substantial merits of the case.[11]

Furthermore, until the Statute of Elizabeth (1562-63)[12] made compulsory process available generally, witnesses could not be compelled to testify in courts of law as to what was received or promised under a contract; and down to the 19th century, a testimonial privilege in favor of parties litigant in general (and of contractual parties in particular) prevented the compelled disclosure of promissory evidence from the parties.[13] The inability at law to compel a party opponent to testify as a witness or to produce writings in his possession also made it difficult to administer any test based upon *bona fides*.[14] In Chancery, on the other hand, it had been the plaintiff's right ever since the 14th century, by writ of subpoena and bill of discovery, to compel testimonial and documentary evidence from the defendant and other witnesses.[15] Also, Chancery followed the doctrine of the dependency of promises and thus a defendant in a suit for specific performance could raise defenses between himself and the third party beneficiary.[16] The common law, on the other hand, followed the doctrine of independent promises and it was not well equipped to deal with defenses and unfulfilled conditions that the defendant might raise to bear the beneficiary's suit. Also noteworthy was

---

[10] Samuel Williston, "Contracts for the Benefit of A Third Person," [1902] 15 Harv. L. Rev. 767, 773.

[11] W.S. HOLDSWORTH, A HISTORY OF ENGLISH LAW, vol. IX, (Little, Brown, 1926) p. 373.

[12] 5 Eliz. I, c.9, sec. 12.

[13] JOHN H. WIGMORE, WIGMORE ON EVIDENCE, vol. Viii, 3rd ed. (Little, Brown, 1940) secs. 2218, 2219.

[14] William M. McGovern, "The Enforcement of Informal Contracts in the later Middle Ages," [1971] 59 Calif. L. Rev. 1145, 1180.

[15] WIGMORE, *supra* n. 13, secs. 2190, 2218.

[16] William M. MGovern, "Dependent Promises in the History of Leases and Other Contracts," 52 Tul.L.Rev. 659, 674 (1978).

Chancery's policy of conserving procedural energies and expenses. The maxim was that "Equity prevents a multiplicity of suits."[17] In terms of third party beneficiary contract, this consideration meant that where D became liable to X on an obligation to render X's performance to P, it was simply wasteful to make P sue X and X sue D in order to obtain enforcement of D's promise, when one action, P vs. D, would be the most efficient and speedy.[18]

The ethical and processual explanations, however, would have to be borne in mind in every category of case in Chancery, not just those involving third party beneficiaries. The focus of the following chapter is upon particular themes which shaped third party beneficiary cases. The discussion is organized into three broad topics: the doctrine of consideration, the growth and development of the trust, and the contract of assignment. Before discussing these in some detail, it will first be convenient to give a general outline of the main argument.

(a)   *Consideration*   A prime factor influencing all development of contractual principle and third party actions is the comparatively late reception of the common law's doctrine of valuable consideration. Not until the early 18th century did the Chancellor fully embrace the view that all enforceable contracts in Chancery required consideration. In the course of this reception, however, the Chancellor developed a two-tier doctrine of consideration that served at one level to recognize a wide circle of beneficiaries on family agreements and settlements, and at another level to restrict the circle of beneficiaries upon commercial and business agreements. That this reception of valuable consideration took place nearly 150 years after the same doctrine attached in assumpsit raises the possibility that this lengthy "breathing period" was significant in producing a more advanced beneficial action. During this period, the Chancellor was free from the issue of whether the plaintiff-beneficiary or the defendant had received or given valuable consideration. When at last valuable consideration did become a serious doctrine in Chancery in the 18th century, the die had already been cast in favor of the beneficiary, particularly the family beneficiary. The family beneficiary's action would have been eliminated by the incoming doctrine of valuable consideration, and it became expedient to establish a double standard, that is, a two-tier doctrine of consideration.

---

[17] RICHARD FRANCIS, MAXIMS OF EQUITY (1727); (reprint ed., Garland Publishing, 1978) p. 35.

[18] An example of this thinking is to be found in *Harvey v. Baker* (1677) 79 Seld. Soc. 631.

(b)   *The Trust*   The essential nature of the *cestui's* enforceable right gradually changed from a primarily contractual to a proprietary basis. This change in "fundamentals" was directly in step with the gradual relaxation of certain restraints that fettered the use down to the 17th century.   The Chancellor's conception of the *cestui's* interest evolved from the highly personal notion of "confidence," which at first was too personal even to be beneficiary's asserted against the trustee's heir, to a later reconceptualization recognizing the trust asset as the beneficiary's own property. Despite this new dimension, the trust remained the functional equivalent of a promissory remedy, though immune from the standard objections requiring personal privity. As the turning point in this change occurred around 1670-1680, this, too, may have been a contributing cause to the advantage enjoyed by the beneficiary action in Chancery, and to the frequent resort to the trust.

(c)   *Assignments in Equity*   Although different in appearance, the contract of assignment also functioned as a third party beneficiary contract.   The evolution of assignment in equity should be seen as the growth from a general prohibition into a freely permitted contractual agreement enforcing debts between legal strangers.   In the common law, the assignee was treated only as an agent enforcing the rights of his assignor for his assignor, but in equity, a contractual link between the assignee and the debtor was forged by developing the notion of notice, by dispensing with fictional agency, and by requiring valuable consideration.

I. THE DELAYED TRANSITION TO CONSIDERATION

From the late 17th century through the middle of the 18th century, the courts of equity were in the process of absorbing the doctrine of valuable consideration as it was understood in the common law action of assumpsit. Interchange between the two English systems was not by any means completely novel. The effect of independent sets of tribunals upon the growth of consideration ideas was like the respiratory action of two lungs in the same atmosphere.   Yet this interchange complicates the task of sorting out the origin and the historical sequence in which the doctrine of valuable consideration took shape. It was a remarkably gradual assimilation that was not effectively internalized until 150 years after the rise of the same doctrine in assumpsit. Not until the 18th century did the Chancellor purport to follow a general rule that all contracts require consideration,[19] and not until the 19th century did he acknowledge a consideration barrier to the beneficiary

---

[19] *Mitchell v. Reynolds* (1711) I P. Wms. 181, 193, discussed below at p. 104.

action.[20]

Perhaps the clearest steps were these: equity knew something called "consideration" (in the sense of *causa*) even before the common lawyers had domesticated the term; somewhat later equity developed another doctrine of consideration within the context of enforcing uses, well before there was an action of assumpsit and well before the technical notion of valuable consideration could be conceived and applied at law and exported to Chancery. To avoid confusion, it is necessary to distinguish three strains of this doctrine, all bearing the same title, which have obtained in Chancery at various times: the civilian doctrine of cause (or consideration), the doctrine of consideration administered in the law of uses, and finally, valuable consideration specifically associated with the action of assumpsit.

The earliest test known to Equity for the enforcement of promises was probably the canonist notion of *causa*. We lack direct evidence for this assertion, but the balance of historical probabilities seems weighted in its favor.[21] The word "consideration" was frequently used as a synonym for *causa* to explain why nude contracts and naked promises were not enforced. Thus, as the Doctor explained to the Student,

> But yf hys promise be so naked that there is no maner of consyderacyon why yt shoulde be made than I thynke hym not bounde to perfourme it for it is to suppose that there wa som errour in the makyng of the promyse.[22]

By the late 15th century, the second doctrine called "equitable" consideration developed in connection with the creation, vesting, and revocation of uses. This variety embraced at least three forms of consideration: the payment of money, marriage, and natural love and affection (near relation).[23] The role played by this doctrine was to rebut the

---

[20] See below, p. 194.

[21] A.W.B. SIMPSON, A HISTORY OF THE COMMON LAW OF CONTRACT, (Oxford University Press, 1975) pp. 396-402.

[22] CHRISTOPHER ST. GERMAN, DOCTOR & STUDENT, ed. by Plucknett & Barton (London, 1974) Dial. II, Ch. XXIV. Canon law sources employed two theories. one contrasted *nude* with *vested* pacts or promises, and another contrasted *cause* with *causeless* agreements. Professor Simpson, in History of Contract, *supra* n. 21 at 384, indicates that these tests were fused into the general theory of cause.

[23] A.W.B. SIMPSON, AN INTRODUCTION TO THE HISTORY OF LAND LAW, 169 (Oxford University Press, 1961); *Cf.* HOLDSWORTH, *supra* n.11 vol. 322.

so-called resulting use, which was an equitable presumption arising when the feoffee gave no value to the feoffor.[24] The absence of consideration for a conveyance would cause the use to result back to the feoffor, but a conveyance for consideration would pass the use to the feoffee. For these purposes, past consideration would not pass a use.[25] Natural love and affection, though not at first admitted as an acceptable form of consideration[26] was deemed sufficient to create and vest a use as early as 1504.[27] This view was settled by the case of *Sharrington v. Strotton* (1566).[28] The practical effect was to enable the courts to give effect to family settlements of landed property, frequently in connection with marriage, which was itself deemed a good consideration for this purpose.[29]

Despite the word "equitable" in the title, it is not probable that this doctrine originated in Chancery. That title was not current in the 15th and 16th centuries and there is no evidence that the detailed rules were initially worked out by the Chancellors.[30] Rather, due to the statute 1 Rich. III c. 1 (1484),[31] which gave common-law courts an extensive jurisdiction and familiarity with uses well before the Statute of Uses (1535), it was apparently the common lawyers who formulated and built up the rules and principles about consideration in the law of uses.[32] Thus despite the Chancery origins suggested by its name, the "equitable" doctrine of consideration has not been

---

[24] SIMPSON, HISTORY OF LAND LAW, *supra* n. 23, at 167.

[25] *Ibid*, p. 168.

[26] SIR ROBERT BROOKE, LA GRAUNDE ABRIDGEMENT 54 (Feffements al Use") (1573). *Hunt v. Bate*, (1568) Dyer 272.

[27] SIMPSON, HISTORY OF CONTRACT, *supra* n. 21, at 341. *The Duke of Buckingham's Case* Y.B. (1504) 20 Hen. VII, M.P. 10, pl. 20.

[28] Plowden 298.

[29] See *Collard v. Collard* (1594) Popham 47.

[30] SIMPSON, HISTORY OF CONTRACT, *supra* n. 21, at 327 (1975). D.E.C. Yale, "The Revival of Equitable Estates in the 17th century," [1957] C.L.J. 72.

[31] This Act provided that the *cestui que use* could make legal conveyances of the land held to his use, and the conveyance would bind himself, his heirs and the feoffee to uses. *See* SIMPSON, HISTORY OF LAND LAW, *supra* n. 23, at 173-74 (1961).

[32] SIMPSON, HISTORY OF CONTRACT, *supra* n.21, at 327. Dr. Baker asserts that as a result of this jurisdiction the common-law courts ultimately did more than a Court of Conscience could have done to assimilate the position of *cestuy que* use to that of common-law tenant in fee. In his view the statute of 1484 was probably the ultimate source of the theory that the use was a "common-law institution," 94 Seld. Soc. 196 (1977).

demonstrably linked to the canonist doctrines of the early chancellors.[33] After it became clear that this doctrine as to uses differed in important respects from the consideration doctrine that later arose in assumpsit -- i.e. it applied only to uses, and the consideration of natural love and affection proved unacceptable in assumpsit[34] -- the word equitable may have been subsequently added as a means of distinguishing the two doctrines. This distinction would not have been clear much before the 18th century, however, for as late as *Dutton v. Poole* (1680) the earlier doctrine remained an unspecified "disturbing influence" upon the action of assumpsit.[35]

Therefore, when another consideration doctrine attached to the action of assumpsit between 1535-1585,[36] plainly it was not simply the "equitable" doctrine that had penetrated through. To enforce promises under assumpsit, the judges by 1588 were generally insistent upon something more tangibly valuable than affinity, love or friendship.[37] They developed instead, from what model or source one cannot be sure, that peculiar notion of valuable consideration, either of a detriment or benefit, that has been the distinctive feature of English contract. Some historians contend that the proximate inspiration for this development was a concept indigenous within common law, perhaps deriving from the influential notion of *quid pro quo*, or springing instead from the trespassory notion of detriment in the writ of assumpsit.[38]

---

[33] *See* J.L. Barton, 27 U. Tor. L.J. 373, 378-379. Dr. Baker, in his essay "Origins of the 'doctrine' of Consideration, 1535-1585," found in the collected essays ON THE LAWS AND CUSTOMS OF ENGLAND, 336 (1981), edited by Arnold, et al., states categorically that "the law of uses was the creation of the common-law courts, not (as so many have assumed) of canonist chancellors." (at p. 351.). *But see* HOLDSWORTH, vol. V, *supra* n.11, at 322.

[34] *Hartford v. Gardiner*, (1587) 2 Leon. 30 ("Love is not a consideration upon which an action can be grounded."); *Brett v. J.S.* (1600) Cro. Eliz. 756. For further details, see above, p. 52.

[35] HOLDSWORTH, *supra* n. 11 vol. VIII, at 12. According to Dr. Baker, "It was probably not until late in Elizabeth I's reign that it occurred to anyone that there might be two doctrines," "Origins" *supra* n.33, at 336-337. SIMPSON, HISTORY OF CONTRACT, *supra* n.21, at 279.

[36] Historians more or less agree that this is the critical period. Baker, "Origins" *supra* n.33, at 336-337. SIMPSON, HISTORY OF CONTRACT, *supra* n. 21, at 279.

[37] *Hartford v. Gardiner* (1587) 2 Leon. 30: "Neither love nor friendship will ground an assumpsit to pay money." *See also*, *Brett v. J.S.* (1600) Cro. Eliz. 765. The rule that consideration had to be something of value was established by 1580. Baker, "Origins" *supra* n. 33, at 343.

[38] Several recent studies of consideration doctrine, Baker, "Origins" *supra* n.33, at 336 ff., Ibbetson "Assumpsit and Debt in the Early 16th Century," (1982) Cambridge L. J. 142, have given new foundation to the older view that consideration was an indigenous English development, but upon reasons that depart from the traditional lines of argument. (For the

A contrary viewpoint--which might be called the "*ab extra*" school of thought--holds that the real antecedent was the projective analogical force of equitable consideration with which the judges were already familiar.[39] An interesting contemporaneous event, at least in terms of chronological coincidence, was that the rise of consideration within assumpsit corresponds closely with the fall of *laesio fidei* petitions in the ecclesiastical courts.[40]

These theories as to sources and origins have not been resolved, but they at least suggest for present purposes that during the prologue to the Chancery phase of the beneficiary problem, both law and equity possessed parallel doctrines, of somewhat related pedigree, that played leading parts in the vesting of uses, as opposed to the bringing of assumpsit.

A.   The Gradual Reception by the Chancellor   (1550-1800)

Having made reference to the interrelated growth of these ideas in the common law, we are now in a position to trace the subsequent reception of valuable consideration by Chancery. The transition to this contractual doctrine will be made clear by examining three periods during the years 1550-1800. It will be important to note that in the final stage, the Chancellor had

---

older debt-based theory, see OLIVER W. HOLMES, THE COMMON LAW (Little, Brown, 1881), p. 258 ff.; for the detriment hypothesis, see James B. Ames, "The History of Assumpsit", [1888] Harv. L. Rev. 1, and "Parol Contracts Prior to Assumpsit", [1884] 8 Harv. L. Rev. 252. Professor Baker's examination of the King's Bench roll down to 1550 indicates among other things that the origins of the "in consideration" clause lie in various linking phrases that were inserted between the recital of the bargain and the assumpsit in order to explain the undertaking. The most common of these was a kind of "*quid pro quo* clause", and only later did the phrase "in consideration" come into use, first alternatively, and finally, as the prevailing mode. Reviewing the other possible sources critically, such as the civilian notion of *causa* and the detriment hypothesis of Ames, Mr. Baker has found a continuous link between consideration and the notion of reciprocity in the *quid pro quo* formula that is lacking in the other sources. Mr. Ibbetson argues that consideration originally meant the exchange received by the promisor – the same principle as *quid pro quo* – and in the mid-16th century the exchange idea was essentially grafted onto the earlier, delictual notion of injurious reliance. *Supra* at 153-154.

[39] Sir John Salmond first speculated that consideration had been received *ab extra* the common law, JURISPRUDENCE, 8th ed. (Sweet & Maxwell, 1930) at 264. Simpson, pp. 327 and ff., and pp. 375 ff. has endorsed that view with research plausibly suggesting the specific point of entry to have been the equitable doctrine of consideration applied in the law of uses of land. For accounts of the remoter ancestry in the medieval Canon Law, see Paul Vinogradoff, "Reason and Conscience in 16th Century Jurisprudence," 24 L.Q.R. 273 (1908); J.L. Barton, "The Early History of Consideration," 85 L.Q.R. 372 (1969).

[40] R.H. Helmohz, "Assumpsit and Fidei Laesio," [1975] 91 L.Q.R. 406.

fully interwoven two doctrines of consideration to be used in contract analysis, and his doctrines were arranged in an hierarchical way. Down to 1800 the "stranger to the consideration" rule, and the various common-law authorities on which it was based, were not yet part of the reception, and this factor helps to explain the free use of trust and assignment notions in aid of the beneficiary action. The Chancellor dealt with the family or donee beneficiary with a freedom that the common law had not known.

(i) First Period, 1550-1630.

In the first period in Chancery, roughly 1550-1630, consideration hardly played any discernible role. Except for a few terse references,[41] we have no reliable proof that it is being used in Chancery as the test for enforcing promises generally.[42] In 1616, for example, the Chancellor enforced a promise at the instance of a third party beneficiary, but there was no mention of a consideration issue.[43] We should recall, in any event, that if the term was used in this period, it probably only carried the connotation of *causa* or motive. Equity was then holding to the canon-law notion of *causa*, as a consequence of which all promises were enforced in principle, except those without good cause. In this period, the Chancellor subscribed to the canonicist notion of *causa fidei laesionis*, whereby it was deemed a sin to violate one's sworn promise.[44] The promise of the defendant, supported in most cases by his part performance, was the allegation on which the bills relied.[45]

---

[41] *Anonymous* (1602) Cary 21; *Perriman v. Gorges* (1627-28) Nels. 3; *Alexander v. Cresheld* (16310 Tothill 21.

[42] The language was then consideration-free, as we see in a statement of 1525 from the Diversity of Courts: "A man shall have remedy in Chancery for covenants made without specialty, if the party have sufficient witness to prove the Covenants, and yet he is without remedy at the common law." Quoted in Oliver W. Holmes, "Early English Equity," [1885] 1 L.Q.R. 162, 171.

[43] *Plaile v. Plaile* (1611) Tothill 163.

[44] The defendant was commonly said to have acted "to the grave danger of his soul and the pernicious example of many others." Helmholz, *supra* n. 40, at 423.

[45] SIR DUNCAN KERLY, AN HISTORICAL SKETCH OF THE EQUITABLE JURISDICTION OF THE COURT OF CHANCERY (Cambridge University Press, 1890), p. 86 and following.

(ii) Transition 1630-1700.

A second period follows between 1630-1700. The period is marked by an increase in the number of references to the doctrine, but a general rule that all contracts in equity require consideration is still missing. Indeed, promises in favor of donee beneficiaries can be enforced without reliance upon any consideration rule.

A number of cases in equity of the late 17th century closely resembled the famous case of *Dutton v. Poole*. They provide an illuminating contrast to the preoccupation with consideration theory in that decision. Although these cases have been styled by historians as "equitable assumpsits,"[46] the relief afforded to the beneficiary was strikingly non-technical. They were innocent of any reference to the trust, to the action of assumpsit, and equally significant, the Chancellor did not refer to consideration, promisees or privity.[47]

A typical example is *Chamberlain v. Chamberlain*.[48] The father, foreseeing that there would be insufficient estate to pay a personal legacy to his younger son (the plaintiff) was about to alter his will when his oldest son (the defendant) prevailed upon him not to do so. The elder son promised that he would pay the legacy even if there were inadequate assets. Nevertheless the plaintiff was forced to sue his brother for payment of the legacy. Chancellor Nottingham decreed the defendant to pay it according to his promise to his father without any regard to assets.

Another example is *Oldham v. Litchford* (1705),[49] in which the defendant's testator was making his will and would have inserted a gift of an annuity of £40 per annum in plaintiff's favor (a nephew of the testator's wife). The annuity was to maintain the plaintiff's education at Cambridge. But defendant prevailed upon the testator by promising that if he would not put this provision in the will, that "as he was a Christian," the defendant would

---

[46] *See* C.C. LANGDELL, A BRIEF SURVEY OF EQUITY JURISDICTION, 2nd ed. (The Harvard Law Review Association, 1908). p. 99 *et seq.*

[47] See *Chamberlaine v. Chamberlaine* (1678) 2 Freem. 34; *Cassy v. Fitton* (1679) 79 Seld. Soc. 729; *Barrow v. Greenough* (1796) 3 Ves. Jun. 152. The case of *Thynn v. Thynn* (1684) 1 Vern. 296, is slightly exceptional in that the son's promise was to be an executor, but only in trust for his mother.

[48] 79 Seld. Soc. 632; (1678) 2 Freem. 34.

[49] 2 Freem. 284, 2 Eq. Ca. Abr. 44.

take care to see it paid. The court decreed that the defendant must pay plaintiff the annuity, and made particular reference to the case of *Dutton v. Poole*.

These two cases are illustrations of apparent gifts intended for third party beneficiaries. In the circumstances, the promise was inevitably of a type that the testator himself was powerless to enforce, since the promise was not to be performed until after his death. Often the testator's executor, who theoretically could enforce the promise on the testator's behalf, might himself be the recalcitrant promisor. As a practical matter, the only party living who may wish to bring such a suit in many instances would be the beneficiary. But, unlike the case of *Dutton v. Poole* at common law, the consideration issue was not debated by the parties or the court of Chancery. It was handled as a simple case of breach of promise, for as Lord Nottingham said in one case of this type, it was "the constant course of this court to make such decrees upon promises that the testator would not alter his will."[50]

It would be possible to argue that the Chancellor's silence about consideration may be explained by the fact that the beneficiary appears to be kin-related. Arguably, as the court would frequently say later on in the 18th century, it is not necessary to be so "curious" about the consideration when the plaintiff is within it. This hardly seems convincing, however, for in several cases the beneficiary is not related at all to the donor.[51] Actually, at this time the consideration justification is simply not a test of contractual enforcement. In the late 17th century, equity had not fully "received" the doctrine in the law of contract. It would be several generations before the rule recognizing the beneficiary "within" good consideration is announced. The Chancellor was not being technical, but simply preventing fraud and enforcing, in accordance with conscience, promises that *ought* to be enforced.

Promises in a Forum of Conscience

With reference to the cases just discussed, Professor Atiyah presents a wholly different view from the conscience-based explanation outlined

---

[50] *Chamberlaine v. Chamberlaine* (1678) 2 Freem. 34.

[51] *E.g., Drakeford v. Wilks* (1747) 3 Atk. 539 ("intimate friend"); *Chamberlain v. Agar* (1813) 2 V. & B. 259 (housekeeper); *Oldham v. Litchford* (1705) 2 Freem. 285 (nephew of testator's wife).

above.[52] He takes the view that these cases were the forerunners of "secret trusts" or alternatively that they concerned the duty of an executor to pay legacies. Professor Atiyah argues that the Chancellor enforced a duty to carry out the testator's will not primarily because of the promise made by the defendant but *because the promisor was already under some pre-existing duty (as a trustee or as an executor), of which the promise was but evidence.* The promise contained in trust situations, he argues, was relatively insignificant compared to more basic reasons for enforcement -- the prevention of unjust enrichment and detrimental reliance.[53] If the trustee's duty was not enforced, he would enrich himself by retaining the property, and *the settlor would have detrimentally relied by not altering his will.* Thus, an express promise made by the trustee was not the source of his liability, but merely "evidence" of the circumstances under which the property had been transferred.[54] As to the basis of an executor's obligation to pay legacies, the learned author writes:

> The executor is liable, not because he promised, but because he received assets earmarked for a legacy. The promise is evidence of that fact; but it is not the promise which creates the obligation.[55]

The historical validity of this provocative thesis is not easily verified. Indeed, it is presented in a form in which it may be in principle incapable of historical proof or disproof, and thus be beyond historical investigation. In the first place, Professor Atiyah has carefully noted that he does not claim that his view was consciously appreciated by contemporaries or that it ever attained expression at a doctrinal level.[56] For example, he acknowledges that enforcement of the trust has never been "openly" based in Chancery upon enrichment and reliance ideas,[57] though he claims that the background

---

[52] ATIYAH RISE AND FALL, *supra* n.8 at 139-146, 156-162 (Oxford University Press, 1979). *See also,* P.S. ATIYAH, PROMISES, MORALS AND LAW, pp. 184 and ff. (Oxford University, Press 1981).

[53] ATIYAH, RISE AND FALL OF FREEDOM OF CONTRACT, *supra* n. 8, at 156. Professor Atiyah conjectures that, as an historical matter the trust "antedated" the Age of Promises and so it became a part of Chancery doctrine that escaped "contamination" by the common-law action of assumpsit and presumably its doctrine of consideration as well.

[54] *Ibid.* p. 157.

[55] *Ibid.* p. 162.

[56] *Ibid.* p. 146.

[57] *Ibid.* p. 156.

influence of these ideas was considerable.

It is impossible to measure the extent of this background influence. In the cases discussed above, the Chancellor did not mention enrichment, reliance, or the receipt of assets as the ground of relief. Instead he maintained that the defendant's fraud, strengthened by the promise he had made, created the liability.[58] Or, as he put it in *Chamberlaine v. Chamberlaine* (1678),[59] the liability rested upon the defendant's breach of promise and it was "the constant course of this court to make such decrees upon promises that the testator would not alter his will." The cases are not presented in the reports as instances in which the promise itself was insignificant or secondary, nor as instances of trusts or as executor liability. Rather, it is emphasized that the promise was a claim on the conscience of the defendant.[60] It is difficult to imagine that basic and pervasive ideas such as unjust enrichment and reliance were ever without some effect in reinforcing the result or the stated ground.[61] But since they were not articulated as doctrine in this period, their historical influence is unproven, unless we simply assume *a priori* that the lawyers in earlier centuries thought in the same way as we do.

Indeed, the thesis that promises played merely an evidentiary role overlooks or underestimates the primary principle of decision that obtained in Chancery--the principle of Conscience--and accordingly underestimates the strong tie between that principle and keeping one's word.[62]

---

[58] *Oldham v. Litchford*, (1705) 2 Freem. 285; *Thynn v. Thynn*, (1684) 1 Vern. 296; *Reech v. Kennegal*, (1748) 1 Ves. Sen. 123.

[59] 2 Freem. 34, 52.

[60] See also the statements of the Chancellors in *Drakeford v. Wilks*, (1747) 3 Atk. 539; *Barrow v. Greenough* (1796) 3 Ves. Jun. 152.

[61] Dr. Baker has argued that reliance is an age-old principle of morality that may be a major factor in cases of promissory liability even though unexpressed in the reports. *See* 94 Seld. Soc. 295 (1977).

[62] For a full discussion of the principle of Conscience *see*, W.J. JONES, THE ELIZABETHAN COURT OF CHANCERY, 424 (Oxford University Press, 1967). Paul Vinogradoff, "Reason and Conscience in the Sixteenth Century Jurisprudence," 24 L.Q.R. 373 (1908); C.K. ALLEN, LAW IN THE MAKING, p. 406 and ff. (7th ed. 1964); SIMPSON, HISTORY OF CONTRACT, *supra* n. 21, at 398 and ff. In the time of Henry VIII some common lawyers also linked the idea of keeping promises to the principle of Conscience: "the personage of a justice and royal officer is to execute justice according to your conscience, and (as I have said before) the strongest thing which is against justice is to break a covenant with a faithful promise." *Manley's Case* (1544) T. 36 Hen. 8, Gellf. 35n. (Sjt. Saunders), quoted in 94

As Professor Simpson has noted, Conscience did not connote, though it may have included, a principle of preventing injurious reliance. Conscience was not so much concerned with the injury of the petitioner as it was with preventing the respondent from endangering his soul through unconscionable behavior.[63] Barbour's early cases show that reliance is mentioned in the petition *in the form of the facts themselves* but the basis of the relief sought is always *"reason and good conscience."*[64] The animating interest of this "cathartic jurisdiction" was "the overburdened state of the conscience of the defendant."[65] Two doctrines concerning promises and trusts emerged: first, promises should be enforced even if certain legal formalities were not complied with, and second, transactions based on confidence should be protected.[66] Breach of confidence, rather than expressing the reliance principle,[67] goes back to the *laesio fidei* which ecclesiastical courts had claimed as their special province.[68]

We do not necessarily escape from the substantive importance of the promise simply by recasting the cases along the lines of unjust enrichment or injurious reliance. Good conscience is offended by violations of both principles. Unjust enrichment and causing false reliance are primarily elements of contractual *morality*. For example, the main factor that would have made a trustee's enrichment "unjust" was not the fact that he was treating property as his own (the legal ownership was in fact his) but rather that he was doing so in breach of a promise he had made to hold it to the use of someone else.[69] Furthermore, protecting the reliance interest would not serve, in every case, as an adequate ground for liability. Since the Chancellor enforced trusts established in favor of a third party who did not even know of

---

Seld Soc. 258 (1977).

[63] SIMPSON, HISTORY OF CONTRACT, *supra* n.21, at 398: "It connoted what we now call the moral law *as it applied to particular individuals for the avoidance of peril to the soul through mortal sin.*" (Emphasis in original).

[64] See esp. p. 135. Barbour, *supra* n.1.

[65] W.J. JONES, THE ELIZABETHAN COURT OF CHANCERY, 424 (Oxford University Press, 1967).

[66] Vinogradoff, *supra* n.62, at 379.

[67] See Atiyah, *supra* n.8 at 156.

[68] Vinogradoff, *supra* n.62 at 379.

[69] By Nottingham's day it would have been thought *unjust* for the additional reason that an equitable property interest was now clearly recognized to be vested in the cestui que trust.

the trust,[70] here the protection of his reliance interest would not have been mentioned because it would not have been factual. Moreover, historically, the first rulings stating that the beneficiary's reliance might cause the trustee to be liable were not rendered until the 19th century, and then only in the special context of creditor trusts.[71] As we shall see in the next chapter, these creditor trusts became subject to a "parties-only" objection, and the creditor beneficiary was treated for certain purposes as a stranger to the agreement.[72] Before that principle was received, however, the beneficiary recovered without proof of his reliance upon the promise.

How long the Conscience principle remained in full vigor is difficult to say, but it was certainly neither wholly supplanted nor eviscerated in the period under discussion. This is not to say that the normal principle applied by the early Chancellors had not changed somewhat, for it surely had.[73] There was indeed an important shift in meaning during Lord Nottingham's time. Chancellor Nottingham himself drew attention to a growing difference between the wider commands of Conscience in days past and the narrower principle he followed.[74] The narrowing resulted from Nottingham's inclination to objectify Conscience -- to leave private conscience to private judgment and to base his decisions upon the "royal conscience" or what was

---

[70] *Bale v. Newton* (1687) 1 Vern. 464; *Bill v. Cureton*, (1853) 2 My. & K. 502; *Fletcher v. Fletcher*, (1844) 4 Hare 67.

[71] *Hill v. Gomme*, (1839) 5 My. & Cr. 250, 1 Beavan 540; *Action v. Woodgate*, (1833) 2 My. & K. 492; *Kirwan v. Daniel*, (1847) 5 Hare 493; *Scott v. Porcher*, (1817) 3 Mer. 652. George Spence articulated this reliance doctrine as follows: "If, by reason of the expectations held out to the stranger to the contract, under the contract, his condition in life has been changed, to the knowledge and by the instrumentality of the parties, then the stipulation may be forced by such stranger: not, however, so much in virtue of any original efficacy in the contract between the stranger and the contracting parties, but that the stranger would suffer a positive injury if the contract were not performed, so that a direct equity arises . . . by reason of their acts in relation to him." THE EQUITABLE JURISDICTION OF THE COURT OF CHANCERY, 281 (Spence & Norton, 1850).

[72] SIR EDWARD FRY, A TREATISE ON THE SPECIFIC PERFORMANCE OF CONTRACTS, 41-46 (1858); SPENCE, *supra* n. 71, at 51-59.

[73] On this "shift" from Conscience to equity, see the account by J.H. BAKER, AN INTRODUCTION TO ENGLISH LEGAL HISTORY, 89-95 (2nd ed. Butterworths, 1979).

[74] D.E.C. YALE, LORD NOTTINGHAM'S CHANCERY CASES, Selden Soc. Vol. 73, p. XXXVII and ff. (Quaritch, 1957).

called the general conscience of the realm.[75] As precedents and doctrines became more fully developed, the moral principle was in turn systematized and steadily lost its reputation for undifferentiated discretion.[76]

Conscience and Consideration Converging

Following the Restoration, an interesting tendency became observable. At this time the concept of valuable consideration, long the mainspring of the actions of assumpsit, began to make a more general appearance in the enforcement of agreements. The period marks the incipiency of a rule that no contract is enforceable in equity without valuable, or at least good, consideration.[77] But the rule was not yet fully settled, and cases are still found in which the Chancellor decreed specific performance of *written* promises, though he could find no type of consideration to support the agreement.[78] Equity did not enforce a *parole* agreement unless there had been part performance.[79]

---

[75] *See* particularly the views expressed in *Cook v. Fountain*, 3 Swans App. 585 at 600: "With such a conscience as is only *naturalis et interna* this court has nothing to do; the conscience by which I am to proceed is merely *civilis and politica* . . . .," and *Honywood v. Bennett*, (1675) Case 307, Vol. 73 *Nottingham's Chancery Cases*, p. 214 (S.S. 1954): "I said, if this note were voluntary and without consideration, though it did bind the son in honour and private conscience, with which I had nothing to do, it could not bind him in legal and regular equity . . . ."

[76] ALLEN, *supra* n. 62, at 409.

[77] *E.g., Pickering v. Keeling* (1640) 1 Ch. R. 147: "Annuity granted without a valuable consideration not relieved here."

[78] See, *e.g., Beard v. Nutthall* (1686) 1 Vern. 427; *Frank v. Frank* (1667) 1 Chan. Cas. 84; *Wentworth v. Deverginy* (1696) Prec. Ch. 69; *cf., Parker v. Palmer* (1663) 1 Chan. Cas. 42.

[79] EDWARD B. SUGDEN, A CONCISE AND PRACTICAL TREATISE OF THE LAW OF VENDORS & PURCHASERS OF ESTATES, 13th ed. (Sweet, 1857) pp. 152-153; George P. Costigan, "The Date and Authorship of the Statute of Frauds," [1913] 26 Harv. L. Rec. 329, 344. This was the rule long before the Statute of Frauds. It has been asserted that Equity "invented" the doctrine of part performance very soon after the passage of the Statute of Frauds. *See* ATIYAH, RISE AND FALL, *supra* n. 8, at 207, relying on SIMPSON, HISTORY OF CONTRACT, *supra* n.21, at 615 *et seq.* It is clear from Chancery cases, however, that the doctrine predates the statute. Thus in *Powel v. Crompton* (1650-58) it was said, "*Paroll agreement never executed in part is not relievable in Chancery, although in that case an Action upon the case to recover damages doth lye at law.*" Reports in Chancery 1650-1658 (in manuscript) p. 15 (Lincoln's Inn Library Ms., Eng. Legal Ms. Project, mf. 962, J.H. Baker editor). *Accord, Bishoppe v. Sthratfield* (1650-58), *Ibid.* See further, YALE, *supra* n. 73; GEORGE KEETON AND L.A. SHERIDAN, EQUITY, 54 (2nd ed. Professional Books, 1969). Moreover, a much similar doctrine had been applied for centuries all over Western Europe and the English version could well be descended from romano-canonical sources and not as a reflex to the Statute of Frauds. The history is fully researched by Arthur Von Mehren, "The French Civil Code and

In the treatment of family agreements, however, the Chancellor began to insist that the beneficiary must show "good" consideration to be entitled to relief. This elastic notion actually meant that any family settlement could be enforced by a blood-related beneficiary through any series of contemplated conditions. A nexus by blood with the parties to the agreement was seen as the beneficiary's link to the consideration. The beneficiary was said to be "within" the sphere of the consideration even when he had not performed an act, forborne a right or relied to his detriment. It did not matter that he was not living at the time of the agreement. In 1676, a child of a second marriage enforced a settlement concluded prior to his father's first marriage. The consideration paid on the first marriage extended to the second, even though this defeated the subsequently arising claim of a *bona fide* purchaser.[80]

As to the progress of valuable consideration in this era, the doctrine must have been well-known to the law-trained Chancellors sitting upon the woolsack who had judicially applied it in many cases under the statutes passed in Elizabeth's reign for the protection of creditors and purchasers.[81] But the significant event of the later 17th century was the expansion of this limited application. In one of the earliest of these decisions, we observe the imported product applied to a third party's promise: "and though the Surety had no Advantage yet the Obligee had parted with his Money, and Loss is as good a Consideration for a Promise, as Benefit or Profit.[82]

Lord Nottingham was the figure who mediated the passage of this doctrine into the contract law of Chancery. More than his immediate contemporaries, he borrowed from the technical doctrine found in assumpsit. A decision by his immediate predecessor, Lord Keeper Bridgman, for example, exemplified the old-fashioned kind of doctrine that might have been penned by St. German more than a century before. In sustaining a plea of lack of consideration to enforce a creditor's promise, Bridgman decreed that the promise was *nudum pactum* and without consideration, "for the Release [of money] was no more than what by Law and Conscience ought to be."[83]

Contract," 15 La. L. Rev. 687 (1955) and see further the authorities in note 69, Chap. IV.

[80] *Jenkins v. Kemis* (1676) 1 Lev. 150, 237 1 Chan. Cas. 103. *Accord, Jthell v. Beane* (1748) 1 Ves. Sen. 215.

[81] See (1376) 50 Edw. III, c. 6; (1488) 3 Hen. VII, c. 4, as extended by (1571) 13 Eliz., c. 5 and (1585) 27 Eliz., c. 4.

[82] *Underwood v. Staney* (1666) 1 Chan. Cas. 77, 78.

[83] *Stukeley v. Cooke* (1671) Nelson 81, 3 Ch. R. 71.

By contrast, Lord Nottingham, in many cases involving business bargains and commercial agreements, held to a hardened conception, and characteristically he made a search for detriment to the promisee or benefit to the promisor.[84]

Thus, in *Hatchett v. Bindon* (1677),[85] Lord Nottingham refused for lack of consideration to enforce Bindon's promise to pay his brother Isaac's debts, even where the bill was brought against Bindon by Isaac's administrator, to whom the promise was addressed. Lord Nottingham's analysis of possible consideration for the promise allows us to observe a structured search for benefit or detriment:

> 1. There was no kind of consideration nor could be, for the plaintiff was no administrator at the time of the supposed agreement.
>
> 2. The plaintiff's promise to John Bindon to indemnify him from Isaac's creditors was no consideration neither. For how could that indemnity be valuable to him who was no way liable to Isaac's creditors . . .?
>
> 3. The letting of John Bindon into the trade was no consideration from Hatchett [the administrator] for Bindon was in it before and Hatchett could not keep him out.
>
> 4. There was no execution of this agreement by the delivery of £300 worth of goods, for they were delivered long before the agreement and have been paid since.

Again, in *Honywood v. Bennett* (1675),[86] Lord Nottingham refused to enforce a son's written promise to his father's creditors to pay all debts.

> I said, if this note were voluntary and without consideration, though it did bind the son in honor and private conscience, with which I had nothing to do, it could not bind him in legal and regular equity, but if the father settled anything on the son in consideration of this note or forbore to cut off

---

[84] Lord Coke's classic statement was that "every consideration that doth charge the defendant in an assumpsit must be to the benefit of the defendant or the charge of the plaintiff, and no case can be put out of this rule." *Stone v. Wythipol* (1588) Cro. Eliz. 126, 1 Leon. 113.

[85] 79 Seld. Soc. 565.

[86] 73 Seld. Soc. 214.

anything which he might otherwise have cut off if he had not
rested on this note, then I would hold that son to a strict
performance.[87]

From the above passages and other sources,[88] one perceives that a
far more technical doctrine had made its mark by the late 17th century. The
doctrine of valuable consideration had considerably qualified the tenderness
of Conscience and narrowed the range of promises that were enforceable.
Yet, in this transitional period, the question whether or not to enforce an
agreement lacking consideration was still left in some measure to the
Chancellor's discretion.[89] Depending on the circumstances, the Chancellor
would sometimes enforce promises without consideration.[90] In the next
century, Chancellors oblivious to the earlier freedom they enjoyed would state
categorically, "The Court has never yet executed a voluntary agreement."[91]

(iii)   Reception 1700-1800.

The third period (1700-1800) witnessed the deepening reception of
the reception and the Chancellor's innovation of a two-tier variation upon the
consideration doctrine. Perhaps the first Chancellor to elevate consideration
into a general rule of contract was Lord Parker. His view in *Mitchell v.
Reynolds* (1711) was that "[e]very contract must have a consideration either
expressed as in Assumpsits or implied as in bonds and covenants.[92] The
universal terms of this formulation--"every contract"--is of cardinal importance.
Earlier Chancellors had clearly enforced agreements that lacked any
foundation in consideration, but now no agreement lying within a Chancellor's
jurisdiction could be exempt from the rule. The new position was backed up
by decrees which explicitly declared that voluntary agreements would not be

[87] *Ibid.*

[88] See *Ayloffe v. Thomson* (1673) 73 Seld. Soc. 10; *Mowbray v. Bacon* (1680) 79 Seld. Soc. 852.

[89] *Bold v. Corbett* (1698) Prec. Ch. 84.

[90] *Beard v. Nutthall* (1686) 1 Vern. 427; *Frank v. Frank* (1667) 1 Chan. Cas. 84; *Wentworth v. Deverginy* (1696) Prec. Ch. 69; *Bold v. Corbett* (1698) Prec. Ch. 84.

[91] *Colman v. Sarrel* (1789) 1 Ves. Jun. 50, 55; *Wycherley v. Wycherley* (1763) 2 Eden. 175. *Randal v. Randal* (1728) 2 P. Wms. 464; *Brownsmith v. Gilborne* (1727) 2 Strange 738. The discretion wielded in the past had been so totally forgotten that in the last-cited case, Lord Chancellor King declared that no case could be shown which had decreed the specific performance of a voluntary agreement.

[92] 1 P. Wms. 181, 193.

carried into execution.[93]   Furthermore, Lord Parker's explicit reference to common law "assumpsits" and "covenants" leaves little doubt as to the immediate source or inspiration for this development.   The analogy to the action of assumpsit was repeated in the 1720 decision in *Oldfield v. Appleyard* (1720),[94] in which a gratuitous promise to be *surety* on *a marriage settlement* was made to a woman about to be married.   The Chancellor found,

> . . . there was sufficient Consideration for this Promise of Mr. A; *viz.* the Marriage; and such a Consideration is good at Law; for tho no Profit accrues to the Promisor, yet the other Party, without this Promise, would be liable to a Loss or Damage, and that is a sufficient Consideration to support an Assumpsit at Common Law.[95]

Throughout the 18th century, successive Chancellors laid down similar rules with the same common-law model in mind.   Thus, Lord Macclesfield stated in 1721, "a court of Equity will support and execute a contract made upon a good and sufficient consideration."[96]   In the treatise entitled the *Grounds and Rudiments of Law and Equity* (1749), the author wrote, "For the rule is that Agreements and Contracts must be on good consideration or mutual recompence."[97]

The meridian was reached in Lord Hardwicke's time.   In *Reech v. Kennegal* (1748),[98] he refused to hold an executor personally liable upon a promise he made to pay a legacy to the testator's nephew.[99]   The executor's promise had been made in the course of "an occasional conversation with

---

[93] *Anonymous* (1702) 12 Mod. 603; *Brownsmith v. Gilborne* (1727) 2 Strange 738.

[94] 2 Eq. Ca. Abr. 390.

[95] *Id.* at 391.

[96] *Frederick v. Frederick* (1721) Strange 455, 457.

[97] ANONYMOUS, THE GROUNDS AND RUDIMENTS OF LAW AND EQUITY (1749), p. 18 and Sir Geoffrey Gilbert in his TREATISE OF EQUITY (3rd ed. 1792) stated: "Equity is remedial only to those who come in upon an actual consideration" §2, p. 38. Compare Lord Northington's statement in 1758 that "any proposal made with reciprocal consideration, and accepted, and *on one part executed*, is, in my opinion, a conclusive agreement, and ought to be specifically executed." *Griffith v. Sheffield* (1758) 1 Eden. 73, 76 & 77.

[98] 1 Ves. Sen. 123.

[99] The nephew was not provided for by the will, but the legacy was in accord with the testator's stated wishes, and the executor had promised the testator before his death that he would pay it.

strangers" and Lord Hardwicke called it a "loose" promise for which there was "no consideration arising." Patterning his refusal to enforce this promise upon common law, he stated,

> At law if an executor promises to pay a debt of his testator, a consideration must be alleged; as of assets come to his hands; or of forbearance; or if admission of assets is implied by the promise; otherwise it will be but *nudum pactum*, and not personally binding upon the executor.[100]

Moreover, in *Penn v. Lord Baltimore* (1750), he found that the settling of property boundaries was good consideration for enforcing an agreement. He observed, "it is true, the court never decrees specifically without a consideration: but this is not without consideration; for though nothing valuable is given on the face of the articles as consideration, the settling boundaries, and peace and quiet is a mutual consideration on each side..." [101] In *Tomlinson v. Gill* (1756),[102] Lord Hardwicke found a distinct consideration to bind a parole promise in favor of creditors.

At this time, the phrase "valuable consideration" was comparatively new in Chancery;[103] a rule making consideration a prerequisite to a decree of specific performance does not pre-date the 18th century.[104] This linkage, however, now made consideration a more imperative requirement in equity than in the common law, *since equity disregarded the distinction between specialty and parole agreements.* Thus, neither system would enforce a simple contract without consideration, but now equity alone refused to enforce an agreement under seal without consideration.[105] To Salmond this greater reliance upon consideration doctrine reflected that the source of consideration was originally in equity,[106] but it may not prove so much since the link to specific performance occurred several centuries later.

---

[100] *Reech v. Kennegal* (1748) 1 Ves. Sen. 123, 126.

[101] 1 Ves. Sen. 444, 450.

[102] Amb. 330.

[103] Bailey, pp. 571-572.

[104] See above p. 105, 110.

[105] P.V. Smith "On the Effects of the Contemplated Fusion of Law and Equity on the English Law of Contract", 4 Papers of the Juridical Society (1871-73).

[106] Sir John Salmond, "The History of Contract," in SELECT ESSAYS IN ANGLO-AMERICAN LEGAL HISTORY, vol. III, (Little, Brown, 1909) p. 320 *et seq.*

B. The Chancellor's Two-Tier Theory

The Chancellors professed in their decrees that considerations were of two kinds, good (or meritorious) and valuable;[107] and it was clear that their respective spheres of application were linked to one another. We see this in the interlocking formulations stated by learned writers and judges.

Spence could say that good consideration was a sufficient equivalent for any benefit that may move from one connected by ties of blood, though it was not sufficient to support an action of assumpsit, nor to support a gift against the statutes passed for the protection of creditors and purchasers.[108] In a similar vein, Fonblanque wrote that a gift given upon good consideration ought to prevail, unless it were to break in upon the legal rights of others. If an indebted man conveyed property to the use of his wife and children, the conveyance could not stand up against the debts, but would come within the statute.[109] Upon this principle the Chancellor decreed that where a trust of a plantation was set up for natural children, but the plantation was later sold to a purchaser, the children were not entitled to specific relief against the purchaser, although they could obtain relief out of the assets of the settlor.[110]

The two-tier analysis dictated whether a deed could be revoked. It was held in 1739 that a voluntary deed executed in favor of the covenantor's children could not be subsequently revoked by a will. "As this is a provision for children," Lord Hardwicke stated, "there is a kind of consideration for it, and it ought to take place (sic) of all other voluntary settlements, and therefore of the will, but not of the debts and other settlements for valuable consideration."[111] Similar reasoning governed the creation of resulting trusts.[112] It was true that "trust results to the Party from whom the

---

[107] JOHN J. POWELL, ESSAY UPON THE LAW OF CONTRACTS AND AGREEMENTS (Chamberlain & Rice, 1790), vol. I, p. 361.

[108] SPENCE, *supra* n. 71, at 87.

[109] HENRY BALLOW, A TREATISE OF EQUITY, ed. by Fonblanque, (1793); reprint ed., Garland Publishing, 1979), vol. I, p. 261 "note (a)".

[110] *Williamson v. Codrington* (1750) 1 Ves. Sen. 511.

[111] *Bolton v. Bolton* (1739) 3 Swans. 482.

[112] Vide, *City of London v. Garway* (1706) 2 Vern. 571; *Randall v. Bookey* (1701) 2 Vern. 425; *Lloyd v. Spillet* (1740) Barn. C. 384, 2 Atk. 148.

Consideration moves,"[113] but an advancement came about instead where the moving consideration of the donor was love and natural affection toward the donor's child. Thus, Lord Nottingham's distinction: "a purchase in the name of a stranger is a trust . . . but "a purchase in the name of a son is no trust, for the consideration is apparent."[114] Finally, this two-tier analysis related in some degree to the controversy whether consideration was required in equity to make a valid assignment.[115] A chose in action assigned to a stranger must be upon valuable consideration,[116] except when the assignee was a near relation.[117]

These rules are testimony that good consideration was essentially the basis of enforcing family gifts and settlements, and that such agreements were placed on a level below transactions for valuable consideration. One could say that the word valuable was the Chancellor's coded message for the priority enjoyed by bargainees and purchasers over the family beneficiary. The bifurcated doctrine classified and ranked the superior and inferior equities of each party. If purchasers and creditors were not implicated, or if family beneficiaries competed solely among themselves, then the plaintiff needed only be "within" or "under" the consideration of the agreement."[118] As we have noted before, such consideration did not need to be valuable, nor move from the plaintiff in any real sense, and plaintiff was not required to be the promisee. Children of the marriage and collateral relations of their parents were able to enforce marriage articles making provision for them.[119] However, the non-related beneficiary, the "stranger" whose deficiency was lack of blood-relationship, was not within the consideration, and so could not be given a remedy. The Chancellor's talk of good consideration was essentially form, not substance. In wielding this double standard, he was in reality decreeing specific performance only to the intended beneficiary who fell within a circle of consanguineous relationship.

---

[113] *Pelly v. Maddin* (1706) 2 Eq. Ca. Abr. 744, 21 Viner Ab. 498, pl. 15.

[114] *Grey v. Grey* (1677) 2 Swans. 594, 597; *cf.*, *Elliot v. Elliot* (1677) 79 Seld. Soc. 566. See also, *Dyer v. Dyer* (1788) 2 Cox 92.

[115] See below, p. 151.

[116] *Bates v. Dandy* (1741) 2 Atk. 207. *Cf.*, *Lord Carteret v. Paschal* (1733) 3 P. Wms. 197.

[117] See *e.g.*, *Ashcomb's Case* (1674) 1 Chan. Cas. 232.

[118] Ld. Hardwicke, in *Stephens v. Trueman* (1747) 1 Ves. Sen. 73.

[119] *Osgood v. Strode* (1724) 2 P. Wms. 245; *Vernon v. Vernon* (1731) 2 P. Wms. 594; *Goring v. Nash* (1744) 3 Atk. 186; *Stephens v. Trueman* (1747) 1 Ves. Sen. 73.

As it became clearer in the 18th century that equity's doctrine was two-tiered or hierarchical, the Chancellors began to use more descriptive language. Lord Hardwicke, for example, did this in various ways. His most acute expression was that consideration fell into the first and the second degree: a purchaser claiming under consideration of the first degree would, therefore, prevail over an advanced child claiming under the second degree.[120] Another of his expressions was to contrast the "strict measure" of valuable consideration with the other lenient form.[121] He also frequently used the metaphor of weighing or balancing one type of consideration against the other, and valuable consideration clearly outweighed the lighter natural consideration.[122]

C.   Conclusion

Referring to "good consideration," Roscoe Pound once wrote that "in any consistent account of the requisites of a legal transaction producing an obligation in equity it must be held an anomaly."[123]   Pound assumed that when the Chancellors used the word consideration in contract, they meant common law consideration. He noted six "anomalous" circumstances in which equity gave relief to volunteers, despite the lack of common law consideration.

However, to characterize good consideration as anomalous distorts actual history in favor of analytical theory. There is no better method of confusing English law than by disregarding its chronology. The historical priority or original primacy of good consideration lasted through the 17th and into the 18th century, and was finally challenged by a late reception of common law consideration. Eventually valuable consideration ousted its

---

[120] "This is a claim by an heir at law against the act of his ancestor, done for what this Court calls a valuable consideration in the second degree, by way of provision or advancement for younger child . . . it is a consideration and only made so in the second degree, where the question is with a creditor who is a purchaser." Lord Hardwicke, *Wright v. Wright* (1749) 1 Ves. Sen. 409, 410 & 412.

[121] *Goring v. Nash* (1744) 3 Atk. 186.

[122] "The court does not weigh considerations of this kind." Per Lord Hardwicke, *Stephens v. Trueman* (1747) 1 Ves. Sen. 73. His successor, Lord Northington, spoke in a similar vein: "The court will . . . attend to slight considerations for confirming family settlement . . . they will not weigh the value of the consideration. They consider the ease and comfort and security of families as a sufficient consideration." *Wycherley v. Wycherley* (1763) 2 Eden. 175.

[123] Roscoe Pound, "Consideration in Equity," [1919] 13 Illinois L. Rev. 667, 671.

competitor "good consideration" in Chancery.[124]   Yet as late as 1747, Lord Hardwicke could state that the "strict measure" of common law consideration was "not the rule of this Court."[125]   This chronology was of cardinal importance to equity's attitude toward third party beneficiary contracts. If the technical issue in assumpsit was that the beneficiary who gave no consideration could not show that he had sustained damage, then the reception of the consideration doctrine posed a logical anomaly for the Chancellor. Whereas the common-law judge looked primarily to the promisee or plaintiff to see whether he had given consideration, the Chancellor examined the position of the promisor to see whether he had made a promise which in reason and in conscience he ought to perform.[126]   The imported doctrine, therefore, carried with it a technical basis irrelevant to the remedy of specific performance.   From this standpoint, the anomaly was not the exceptional instances discussed by Pound, but the imported rule itself.

II. THE EVOLUTION OF THE TRUST

Since the trust includes an agreement closely analogous to a beneficiary contract, its evolution and development form an important chapter in an account of third party beneficiary actions. Modern research has placed the approximate origins of the passive trust (the "use upon a use") in the second half of the 16th Century.[127]   In light of this research, it was not long after *Tyrell's Case* (1557),[128] (which Reeves had said "did drive uses back into the courts of equity")[129] that the Chancellor declared that the "use upon a use" had not been executed by the Statute of Uses and would be enforced

---

[124] Stanley J. Bailey, "Assignments of Debts in England from the Twelfth to the Twentieth Century," 47 L.Q.R. 516 (1931); 48 L.Q.R. 547, 572 (1932).

[125] *Goring v. Nash* (1744) 3 Atk. 186, 188.

[126] BARBOUR, *supra* n. 1, at 166.

[127] J.L. Barton, "The Statute of Uses and the Trust of Freeholds," 82 L.Q.R. 215-221 (1966); S.F.C. MILSOM, HISTORICAL FOUNDATIONS OF THE COMMON LAW 2535-29 (2nd ed. 1981).   J.H. Baker, "The Use Upon a Use in Equity 1558-1625," 93 L.Q.R. 33 (1977). The decision in *Katharine, Duchess of Suffolk v. Herenden* (1560) (unreported Ms. published in Baker, *supra* at p. 36) would indicate that the use upon the use was continuously recognized since 1560.

[128] 2 Dyer 155a; Anon. (1577) 1 And. 37; Anon. (1563) Moore K.B. 45.

[129] JOHN REEVES, HISTORY OF ENGLISH LAW, ed. by Finlason, (Reeves & Turner, 1869), vol. III, p. 548.

in Chancery.[130]   The results of this recognition were well known and appreciated by the turn of the century.[131] Henry Sherfield stated in his 1624 reading upon the Statute of Wills that the *true* name given to the use upon a use had become "trust and confidence" and that this "upstart" institution had fully established itself in Chancery.[132] Sherfield's statement shows that ten years before *Sandbach v. Dalston* (1634)[133] the passive trust was an accepted fact. In 1676 Lord Nottingham, apparently summarizing doctrine worked out by predecessors, stated clearly: "If an use be limited upon an use, though the second use be not good in law nor executed by statute, it amounts to a declaration of trust and may be executed in Chancery."[134]

During Lord Nottingham's tenure (1673-1682) an internal shift took place within the trust whereby the beneficiary was recognized as the equitable owner of the trust property. The degree to which this proprietary shift influenced the parallel story of the beneficiary action at common law cannot be exactly specified. Yet chronology suggests that this internal change was instrumental in the abrupt termination of the beneficiary claims in assumpsit that occurred at roughly the same time. From the beneficiary's point of view, the trust now issued forth not only personal rights against the trustee, but certain real rights against the trust assets which remained effective even after transfer or the interposition of third party rights. The trust beneficiary's acquisition of an equitable property right threw into the background the old

---

[130] This then left various kinds of uses which the statute did not execute: (1) uses of property other than freehold, (2) active uses, (3) a use in favor of a purpose rather than a person (e.g. charitable uses) and (4) the use upon a use. BAKER, INTRODUCTION TO ENGLISH LEGAL HISTORY, *supra* n. 73, at 242.

[131] MILSOM, FOUNDATIONS OF THE COMMON LAW, *supra* n. 127, at 239.

[132] "And this upstart hath as great a place in the Court of Chancery as uses ever had; . . . ." Baker, "Use upon Use," *supra* n. 126, at 36-37; See also *Megod's Case* (1586) Godbolt 64, Ms. report in SIMPSON, HISTORY OF CONTRACT, *supra* n. 21, at 638 (1975) where a conveyance of land to feoffees to convey to whomever the feoffor would subsequently sell the land was called a "trust" and a good consideration in Chancery.

[133] Tothill 188, but far more accurately reported as *Morris v. Darston* (1635) Nels. 30, and as to which see J. E. Strathdene, "Sambach v. Dalston: An Unnoticed Report," (1958) 74 L.Q.R. 550. See also the case of *Warmstrey v. Tanfield* (1628) 1 Eq. Ca. Abr. 46, 1 Chan. Rep. 29 as evidence of Chancery's recognition in 1628.

[134] *Grubb v. Gwillim* (1676), 73 Seld. Soc. 347. See also *Symson v. Turner* (1700) 1 Eq. Ca. ABr. 383. for Ld. Nottingham's distinction between the use and the trust, by which he explained why the trust survived the Statute of Uses, see D.E.C. Yale, "The Revival of Equitable Estates in the Seventeenth Century" [1957] Camb. L. J. 72; MILSOM, HISTORICAL FOUNDATIONS OF THE COMMON LAW, *supra* n. 127, at 236.

common-law objection about lack of personal privity with the defendant, and when the Chancellor resorted to the constructive trust, the possibility of such an objection was eviscerated further.

This internal transformation produced in Chancery what the common law failed to achieve in assumpsit during the Formative Period. It was seen that the common law had attempted to work out a proprietary conception of the beneficiary's action. Some cases spoke as if the beneficiary had a real "interest" in the thing promised. This notion failed to withstand the consideration doctrine, and within a short time the beneficiary action itself was rejected in assumpsit. Furthermore, there were arguments in favor of making uses actionable under assumpsit. This was the significance of calling the plaintiff in *Dutton v. Poole* a "*cestui*." However, this viewpoint also came to nothing, perhaps because valuable consideration was obviously missing, and also because uses were thought to lie outside of the common law's jurisdiction.

No contemporary lawyer or judge ever flatly attributed the long hiatus at law after 1680 to the ground that the trust was the better answer to these issues. Obviously, that could not have been the main thrust behind its initial recognition or its later transformation. It was an older institution that had developed for independent reasons--fear of forfeitures during war, avoidance of feudal incidents, ecclesiastical evasion of the Statute of Mortmain,[135] the nondevisability of land, *etc.* The ability to overcome the shortcomings of assumpsit was undoubtedly just a byproduct. But if by 1680 the trust bestowed some proprietary rights upon the beneficiary, required no valuable consideration for enforcement, lay squarely within the Chancellor's jurisdiction, and was in fact the functional equivalent of a promissory remedy, then it was an institution that effectively responded to many rejected arguments and inchoate ideas floated at common law. Such intersections seem to be more than historical coincidence without causal probability. Perhaps the common lawyers were impressed with the realization that the task of reconciling the beneficiary action to the action of assumpsit would denature assumpsit and produce unnecessary tampering with settled requirements. They may have recognized that despite its veneer of feudal terminology, the trust was better designed to enforce these rights.

A. The Original Conception of the Use

In medieval common law the use amounted to an unenforceable

---

[135] Statute of Mortmain, 7 Edw. 1, c. 1.

moral obligation. The use was a confidence which was, according to Fitzherbert, "*rien en ley*."[136] A confidence was an imaginary notion detached from judicial reality. It soared from the legal imagination,[137] and counted for naught. The feoffee to uses was still deemed the absolute owner, just as if no use had been agreed to. In case the *cestui* was permitted to enter the land, his possession was as precarious as a tenant at the sufferance of the feoffee. If he was ousted from possession, he could be sued for the profits he had enjoyed, and he had no defense by the common law.[138] By virtue of his occupation of the land, if it was adverse, he was a trespasser.[139] If damage was done to the land by third parties while he was in possession, an action could only be brought in the feoffee's name.[140] The policy of complete non-recognition of the *cestui's* rights was settled as early as 1465.[141]

But although the use had been turned away like an orphan by the common law, the Chancellor assumed the position of legal guardian as early as the 14th century.[142] The use was an everyday fact that was difficult to ignore. More than half the lands in England were enfeoffed to uses, and it was recognized that "they overshadow all the possessions of the whole realm"[143] and had become a principle of the social system.[144] There were

[136] ANTHONY FITZHERBERT, LE NOVEL NATURA BREVIUM (1588).

[137] See *e.g.*, C.J. ANDERSON: N'AD ESSE NEC ESSENTIA, mes est solement imagination." And Blackstone's description: "This child of the imagination." SIR WILLIAM BLACKSTONE, COMMENTARIES ON THE LAWS OF ENGLAND, vol. II, p. 331 (Tippincott, 1858).

[138] *Daelamere v. Barnard* (1567) Plowden 346.

[139] Y.B. (1500) 15 Hen. VII, 2.

[140] BROOKE, *supra* n. 26, at 23; Y.B. (1490) 5 Hen. VII, 5.

[141] B.F. Brown has put the date of the law's refusal of recognition in the reign of Edward III (1322-1377) while Reeves placed it in the reign of Henry VI (1422-1461), *supra* n. 129, at 548. However, the evidence seems best to support Spence's view that it occurred in the reign of Edward IV; See, SPENCE, *supra* n. 71, at 442 and Y.B. (1465) 4 Edw. IV, 8.

[142] The exact date is conjectural and contradicted by some authorities. SPENCE, *supra* n. 70, at 345, says that subpoenas commenced in Henry V's reign (1413-1422), but the following authorities would place it earlier: Vavisor, *arguendo* in Keil. 42 (1502) assigns it to the time of Edward III (1327-1377); and Milsom puts it at the end of the 14th century. HISTORICAL FOUNDATIONS OF THE COMMON LAW, *supra* n. 127, at 182. Helmholz's analysis of the records of ecclesiastical courts of the late 14th century shows that these courts also enforced uses under the Canon Law. "The Early Enforcement of Uses," *supra* n.40.

[143] Periam J., *Chudleigh's Case* (1589-95), (sub. nom. *Dillon v. Fraine*) 1 Co. Rep. 120a, Popham 70, at p. 75.

strong ethical reasons to provide the *cestui* some remedy. Trusts contained promises that men ought in conscience to fulfill. There was reliance and detriment consideration by the feoffor who parted with land rights and possession. To deny all remedy to the *cestui* was to sanction the spectacle of feoffees to uses enriching themselves unjustly. Furthermore, the common law already offered certain remedies in account and debt against a fiduciary who had received chattels or money and failed to deliver them to a third person.[145] The Chancellor finally decreed a remedy.[146]

This brings us to several preliminary observations about the nature of the use in Chancery. Conceptually, even though the use was *sui generis*, there always was some link between the beneficiary of a contract at common law and the *cestui que trust*. It has become conventional to say that the use or trust falls on both sides of the traditional division between estates and contracts, and between rights *in rem* and *in personam*.[147] This is not to say that it fell precisely midway between the two categories, because one aspect or the other, in particular stages of history, was often more dominant than the other. Thus, Pound said that,

> It is as if the chancellor were riding two horses, one a property theory, the other a contract theory. In general, by a little skilful shifting of his weight from one foot to the other and some shrewd balancing, he manages well. But at times he must, for the moment, shift definitely to the one or

---

[144] SPENCE, *supra* n. 71, at 458.

[145] JAMES B. AMES, LECTURES ON LEGAL HISTORY 238 (Harvard University Press, 1913).

[146] An old poem summed up the history--

> But formerly, if they proved false,
> there could be no redress,
> Till subpoenas out of Chancery,
> Did bring them to confess; and,
> by purging of their consciences,
> Made them execute the trust,
> account, dispose, convey, defend,
> Or whatever else was just.

The poem is entitled "On Conveyances at Common Law, and by the Statute of Uses," printed in WILLIAM SAMPSON, SAMPSON'S DISCOURSE UPON THE HISTORY OF LAW (Gales & Seaton, 1826), pp. 193-198.

[147] HOLDSWORTH, *supra* n. 11, at 433.

the other, and when both feet are on the property theory our analysis is at fault.[148]

These equestrian shifts explain the qualification that the use in *its first stage* was more like a contract than an estate.[149]   Did this mean that the *cestui*'s rights enforced by subpoena were derived from the promissory feature of creating the confidence, rather than in the conveyance of the estate? Let us analyze the transaction.

In the trust, ownership was riven into two separate elements: (i) the formal and (ii) the substantial or beneficial. One ordinary way of creating a use was upon a conveyance of land with livery of seisin between A and B. This part of the transaction undoubtedly created a legal estate in B. But there was, in addition, the promise B made to stand seised to the use of C. Although the Chancellor may have characterized the overall transaction as a conveyance, the latter part of it had the characteristics of a personal agreement between the feoffor and feoffee for the benefit of the *cestui*. The conveyance transferred the formal ownership, together with the burdens of ownership, so that the burdens of feudal incidents fell upon B; whereas the promise was an assurance to shift only the benefits of ownership (use, profits and enjoyment) to the beneficiary C. Thus, the purpose of the trust paralleled the purpose behind a third party beneficiary contract. Apart from an obvious jurisdictional impediment and the intransmissibility of assumpsit in earlier law,[150] there should have been no objection in principle to the use of assumpsit to enforce the feoffee's promise.[151]   Moreover, the promissory element within the trust emerged in silhouette when trusts were created without transmutation of possession; in such a case, it was the mere promise of the titleholder which created the trust.[152]   To the modern lawyer this would seem to be in substance a contract, that is, it may be under seal, or upon a common law consideration, or it may be a gratuitous promise. As the

---

[148] Pound, *supra* n. 123, at 681.

[149] BILLSON, supra n. 7, at 173; FREDERICK W. MAITLAND, EQUITY, ed. by Chaytor & Whittaker, (Cambridge University Press, 1909), p. 28.

[150] By the time enforcement was needed, the feoffor was often dead, particularly where the feoffment was to the use of his last will. Thus, the intransmissibility of assumpsit would have been an impediment in the beginning up until the 17th century. Simpson, pp. 565-573.

[151] In *Megod's Case* (1586) Goldbolt 64, reprinted in Simpson, p. 638, both Gawdy J. and Wray C.J. said that the action upon the case would lie where the feoffee had breached the trust and not conveyed the property to the *cestui* as had been intended.

[152] Pound, *supra* n. 123 at 669.

‚promise might concern trust assets other than land, such as chattels, choses in action, or even another promise, the similarities to contract could seem to vastly outweigh any resemblance to an estate. Indeed, Maitland thought it was "impossible so to define a contract that the definition shall not cover three quarters of all the trusts that are created."[153] Similarly, Pollock noted that the relation of a trustee to his *cestui que trust* is closely analogous to that of a debtor to his creditor.[154] The question arises, however, why did the judges not recognize it under the action of assumpsit, and why did the Chancellor himself decline to describe or enforce it as an agreement or promise?

B. Maitland's Historical Analysis

In his penetrating analysis, Maitland suggested three reasons-- historical, doctrinal, and teleological--to explain why the use or trust was not treated openly as a "contract," even though it plainly contained an agreement.[155]

Historically, the surrounding social problems emerged at a period far ahead of the state of the legal arts. When uses were being developed in the 13th and 14th centuries as a circumvention of the burdens of feudal land tenure, the promissory aspect of the transaction could not have been directly enforced except by a covenant under seal. The action of assumpsit had not yet evolved, and the common law was centuries away from enforcing the "simple contract." However by the 16th century, when assumpsit had made its entrance on the stage, the common law courts had missed their opportunity once and for all.[156] The Chancellor was already "in possession" of the use,

---

[153] MAITLAND, EQUITY, *supra* n. 149, at 54. But resemblance should not be exaggerated to mean an exact correlation to common law contract. Even a married woman or an infant could be bound by a use, though neither had contractual capacity. A corporation had capacity to contract but could not be bound by a use owing to the absence of a personal conscience. Valuable consideration was not necessary to raise a use. Billson, *supra* n. 7, at 173.

[154] SIR FREDERICK POLLOCK, PRINCIPLES OF CONTRACT 193, 1st Amer. ed. (Clarke, 1881).

[155] For the sake of convenience, a considerable number of Maitland's points have been reduced into three and then captioned in language which Maitland did not, and would not, have used.

[156] The argument has been made that assumpsit would not have been practical because it would not afford specific performance. THEODORE F.T. PLUCKNETT, A CONCISE HISTORY OF THE COMMON LAW 576 at n.5, 5th ed. (Little, Brown 1956). But that seems an unconvincing explanation as to why no actions were brought in assumpsit once it became available. Surely, as between the choice of no remedy or an inadequate one, feoffors would have gladly attempted to receive damages. Indeed if proof were needed of that fact it would be that

and was equipped with more efficient and flexible procedures to enforce it. The use had grown through jurisdictional isolation into an exclusive remedy.

Doctrinally, to have called the arrangement a contract would not have fulfilled the expectation of the feoffor. He would have only an "inalienable" chose in action (a promise). The landowner did not mean to exchange ownership of land for "the (inalienable) benefit of a promise." Moreover, the remedy was not for the landowner *qua* landowner anyway, but to protect the third party beneficiary (whom Maitland called the "destinatory"). Visualizing triangular obligations of this kind ran counter to the traditional view that contracts were only bilateral.

Teleologically, and most persuasively, to have stated the matter in contractual terms would have defeated the original purpose of employing uses, for that purpose could only be served in giving *no* legal effect to them. The Chancellor was not free to create new interests in land and could not say that the *cestui que use* was really the owner. The contract mode would have called attention to the creation of legal rights. Then it would have followed that the feoffor/*cestui* was actually *attempting to make a will*,[157] and on his death, relief, wardships and other feudal incidents must follow. Since the use or trust was essentially a circumvention of the law, the Chancellor naturally took common law interests as his model. The underlying purpose was better cloaked by making the use appear as nearly like a right *in rem* as possible, *i.e.*, as an "immaterialized piece of land."

The thesis so far developed indicates that the use in its initial stage was analogous to contract, and that the Chancellor in fact followed this analogy, even though he had good reason to disguise his thinking. The correctness of this interpretation can be tested by tracing the steps by which the *cestui*'s "privity" with the trustee was later enlarged and rationalized. As

---

sometimes the Chancellor only offered damages due to the circumstances. Thus, in a case of 1453 it is reported, "If I enfeoff a man to perform my last will and he enfeoffs another, I cannot have a subpoena against the second because he is a stranger, but I shall have a subpoena against my feoffor and recover in damages for the value of the land." FITZHERBERT, *supra* n. 136, "Subpoena," 19. The same difficulty arose if the breach of confidence had been brought as a tort, such as deceit. If A enfeoffed B to A's use, but B "wrongfully and deceitfully" sold in fee to C, a remedy for damages may have been available. See *e.g.*, *Doige's Case* (1442) Y.B. 20 Hen. VI, pl. 4, f.34. But was there damage to anything A actually owned? The fact that A's ownership could not be admitted—Maitland's teleological argument—seems to be the most persuasive explanation of the absence of tort or contract actions.

[157] Prior to a statute of 1540, an Englishman had no power to give freehold land by his will, unless some local custom authorized him to do so.

attempts were made to widen the *cestui*'s rights, the Chancellor began to experience difficulty with his underlying contractual model. It was ultimately necessary for him to grant the beneficiary a type of property right recognized solely in equity.

C. Beneficial Rights Under the Early Contract Model

Today the trust is binding on everyone coming to the land, except the *bona fide* purchaser of the legal estate for value and without notice. But this was not so at the beginning. Originally, Chancery proceeded upon the premise that the *cestui* had enforceable rights solely through and against the feoffee. A case of 1468 stated: "So if my feoffee dies, and the land descend to his heir, I have no remedy against him."[158] The transmission of the estate to the heir was thought to destroy the vital personal link; the essence of the original obligation was confidence and trust reposed in the feoffee as a person. The *cestui* had a claim only upon the conscience of the feoffee, not upon the land itself. It followed that the feoffee's obligation was personal and intransmissible, because neither the feoffor nor the *cestui* had placed confidence in (or perhaps knew) the feoffee's substitute, his heir. The same reason prevented the liability of a good faith transferee, because if a second feoffee had no notice of the existence of the use, then he was not a party to that confidence.[159] The only remedy was to sue the feoffee who had broken the confidence. Furthermore, the right was not only unenforceable against any successor to the legal title, but it was so devoid of the characteristics of ownership and estate that it could neither be inherited from the *cestui* nor assigned to another.[160]

The extension that brought the heir "in privity" was accomplished by the late 15th century.[161] The ground of the extension may have been a

---

[158] Y.B. (1468) 8 Edw. IV, 6; See Cary, 12. This remained the position through the remainder of Edward IV's reign. See Y.B. (1482-83) 22 Edw. IV, 6.

[159] FITZHERBERT, *supra* n. 136, "Subpoena," 19.

[160] BILLSON, *supra* n. 7, at 179.

[161] Some sources assert that the heir was first made liable in the reign of Henry IV, and with the approval of Sir John Fortescue. SPENCE, *supra* n. 71, at 446; Vavisor, *arguendo* Keil. 42 (1502); Ld. Mansfield, in *Burgess v. Wheate* (1759) 1 Blackst. W. 123. See also J.L. Barton, "The Medieval Use" (1965) 81 L.Q.R. 562, 570. However, the tenure of the Chief Justice on King's Bench was from 1442-1452, and if the matter was so advised by him, it was apparently unsettled later by different advice, as cases in the reign of Edward IV seem to show. See Y.B. (1468) 8 Edward IV, 6: Y.B. (1482) 22 Edward IV, 6.

presumptive intimacy and knowledge of the affairs of his own ancestor. Undoubtedly, there was some desire to prevent the heir's unjust enrichment, but by fastening upon a presumption of notice, the Chancellor had chosen a legal device linked to the heir's prior knowledge and consent, and ultimately to his conscience.[162]

The beneficiary's rights were further expanded when the subpoena was extended against alienees who had acquired the property either without valuable consideration, or with actual notice of the trust. A rather complex rule was built around the twin factors of consideration and notice, and the first articulation came from Pollard J. in 1552:

> If the feoffees enfeoff one without consideration, this is to the first use, even if it is without notice: but on consideration without notice the use is changed. But on notice with consideration the first use remains, and this is the difference.[163]

Both of the tools taken up to surmount the problem strongly suggest the presence of the unarticulated contractual viewpoint.[164] Coke's argument in *Chudleigh's Case* explained the doctrine of notice as being due to an enlarged notion of confidence. Because the original confidence in the feoffee arose from the notice which he had of it, confidence should, therefore, be regarded as having been reposed in all feoffees taking with notice.[165] If one could put the idea of notice into modern contractual language without unduly stretching it, it would be possible to say that notice to the second feoffee became the nearest substitute for his binding consent, as in the ratification of another's act or the assumption of someone else's obligation.

---

[162] A revealing instance of this rationale is cited in FITZHERBERT, *supra* n. 136, "Subpoena," pl. 22. Lands were directed in trust by the father to raise the daughter's marital portion, but the feoffor's heir (the elder brother) entered and took the profits. It was agreed in argument that if he had been a disseisor he would not have been bound to her. But being the heir, he was not a stranger but was privy to his father's acts. The court held that he was therefore not to be treated as a stranger, but subject to the use, and the subpoena was good. This case is discussed in SIMPSON, HISTORY OF CONTRACT, *supra* n. 21, at 362-363.

[163] Y.B. (1524) 14 Hen. VIII, 4 pl. 5.

[164] There is some evidence that a transfer with notice was sometimes regarded as a tort. The transferee upon notice became privy to the wrong to the *cestui* and would still be seised to his use. SIMPSON, at p. 361, quotes from an undated note in Spilman's MS Reports an argument along these lines.

[165] (1589-1595) 1 Co. Rep. 120a at 121b, Note(s). *See also* BILLSON, *supra* n. 7, at 188.

Interestingly, the absence of consideration produced the conclusion that the transferee had notice, though now via a presumption involving a fiction. The gratuity of the transaction was treated as an imputation of bad faith. That is, as Coke said, "the law implies notice and therefore the use remains."[166] It was said "this introduces no inconvenience in charging him with [an implied] use; because he loses nothing having given no consideration."[167] There was no room for the argument that the use resulted back to the transferor, because he never held it from the start. Instead, the legal estate actually passed to the feoffee, while the use remained in the *cestui.*[168] On any of these approaches, liability followed a theory of notice as a surrogate for the transferee's consent.

No further did the subpoena extend. The beneficiary could not reach the purchaser for value without notice, nor could he reach any of the myriad feudal figures who might take in the "post."[169] These last could be the tenant by the curtesy, the tenant in dower, the lord taking by escheat, and others, all of whom were considered strangers to the use, and who had property rights deemed superior to the equitable claim. For example, if the feoffee to uses died without heir or was attainted for treason, then the lord asserting rights by forfeiture or escheat came not in the *"per"* (*through* or *under* the feoffee) but in the *"post"* (*after* or *behind* the feoffee).[170] It was said that this had nothing to do with consideration, notice, or consent but with paramount title.[171] Furthermore, the bad man with no pretension of right--disseisor, abator, intruder--also came in the *post*, even though he may have had notice. The beneficiary's only remedy in this case was by a bill in equity to force the feoffee to recover possession, and to execute the legal estate according to the use.[172]

Holdsworth correctly stressed that the *"post"-"per"* boundary line did

---

[166] 1 Co. Rep. 120a, 122b.

[167] SIR GEOFFREY GILBERT, THE LAW OF USES AND TRUSTS 378, 3rd ed. by Sugden, (Reed, 1811).

[168] SIMPSON, HISTORY OF LAND LAW, supra n. 23, at 169-170.

[169] SPENCE, *supra* n. 71, at 465.

[170] This curious terminology is apparently taken from the forms of the old writs of entry. See Note, "Per and Post," [1888] 4 L.Q.R. 362.

[171] GILBERT, *supra* n. 167, at 369-370.

[172] HENRY MADDOCK, A TREATISE ON THE PRINCIPLES AND PRACTICE OF THE HIGH COURT OF CHANCERY vol. II 125-126, 2nd Amer. ed. (Cooke, 1822).

not correspond exactly with the dichotomy between *jus in rem* and *jus in personam*.[173] The beneficiary had less than full ownership against the world, for there was no protection against disseisors, lords by escheat, etc. Yet he had more than a purely personal right, since he could obtain redress from heirs and transferees who had neither assumed a fiduciary duty nor received actual notice of the use, nor personally dealt with the original feoffor or the *cestui*. Furthermore, the beneficiary's inability to recover from the purchaser for value without notice could not be explained in terms of the *per* or the *post*. Such a purchaser's ownership originated in the *per*, and yet he was safeguarded as if in the *post*.[174]

This boundary line did more than reflect the incomplete reach of the *cestui's* protection prior to the late 17th century. It reflected the limited utility of the contract model. Further extensions of the *cestui's* rights against those in the *post* were actually impossible without inventing more blatant fictions as to notice or, at least, without switching to the alternative theory that his rights followed the asset itself, rather than the legal owner's conscience. One searches in vain, however, for evidence that contemporaries appreciated this fact. Legal visibility was too clouded by the baffling conceptualisms at hand. The most difficult of these was Lord Coke's famous definition of the use. Coke's definition (or as Maitland carefully noted, his "description")[175] mixed *in rem* and *in personam* concepts into a dense fog of words.

Slightly before Coke had come Plowden's comparatively clear definition in 1567. The use was "a thing collateral annexed to the person touching the land."[176] That definition put most of its emphasis upon the *in personam* aspect--the person to whom the use attached. Coke, however, first in his argument as Solicitor-General in *Chudleigh's Case*,[177] and later in his *Commentary Upon Littleton*, deftly inserted the words "in privity to the estate" squarely in the middle of Plowden's definition. Coke's addition, shown below in italics, preserved all of Plowden's language but now produced a two-headed formula: "a thing collateral annexed *in privity* to the estate of the land, and to

---

[173] HOLDSWORTH, *supra* n. 11, at 433.

[174] It must be remembered that the principles here discussed are those which developed before the days of registration of title. Different principles would apply to registered land.

[175] MAITLAND, EQUITY, *supra* n. 149, at 43.

[176] *Delamere v. Barnard* (1567) Plowden 346, 352.

[177] (1589-1595) 1 Co. Rep. 120a, 121b.

the person touching the land. . . ."[178] This now had the ring of a double privity. Dodderidge picked up on it in 1626,[179] and Hale repeated it upon several occasions.[180] It became the respected rule that two things were requisite to a trust: confidence in the person *and* privity in estate. The existence of the use depended upon the feoffee's estate remaining "unaltered," for "whenever that particular estate in the land, to which the use was originally annexed, was destroyed, the use itself was destroyed."[181] There was no alteration when the transferee got title in the *per*, for then he had the same estate that the feoffee to uses had held. The *per* was only another way of saying that the trustee and transferee were linked by contract or by voluntary act. The *post* referred to transfers by operation of law. Lord Hale understood this in 1667: "a trust is created by the contract of the party, and he may direct it as he pleaseth; and he may provide for the execution of it, and therefore one that comes in the *post* shall not be liable to it . . . and therefore they only are bound by it who come in in privity of estate."[182] Even as late as 1734, when Gilbert asked in his classic work on uses, "what this privity of estate is, that is requisite to the standing seized to an use?", he saw no contradiction in answering, "and it is when a person comes into the same estate the feoffee to use had in and by the *contract* with him . . . ."[183] By process of a torturous logic, then, the answer to Gilbert's question "what is privity of estate?" turned out to be a camouflaged contractual tie between the transferee and the *cestui*.

---

[178] SIR EDWARD COKE, A COMMENTARY UPON LITTLETON, vol. II, Lib. 3, Cap. 5, sect. 377, 272b (London, 1794).

[179] *Lord Willoughby's Case* (1626) Jones, W. 96, 127.

[180] *Arguendo, King v. Holland* (1648) Style 20; *Pawlett v. Attorney General* (1668) Hardres 465.

[181] *Chudleigh's Case* (1589-1595) 1 Co. Rep. 120a, 121b, Note (S).

[182] *Pawlett v. AG* (1668) Hardres 465, 469.

[183] Emphasis added. GILBERT, *supra* note 97.

D.   The Evolution From Personal to Real Rights

So long as the *cestui* held only a personal right, he could expect only very limited protection. His remedy was confined to the person trusted, that person's heir, or sometimes his alienee if he took with notice of the use. Hence, the trust asset was still subject to the claims of the trustee's creditors, to the rights of dower and curtesy, and liable to escheat to the Crown for the felony or attainder of the trustee. It was not until the trust estate was seen as the direct property interest of the *cestui* that such intervening claims were defeated.

The actual reconceptualization of the use from a personal to a real right was completed late in the 17th century. Near the start of that century we can see that the change had not yet taken place. In *Arthur Johnson's Case* (1596),[184] J. assigned a term for years to his two brothers-in-law for the use of his wife. When J. died, his widow married Witham, who took the profit by the curtesy during her life. Upon the wife's death, her brothers, being next of kin, took administration of her estate. The Lord Keeper certified the question to all the justices and barons as to whether the brothers (trustees under the original assignment) or Witham, her husband, should have the lease. The answer given was that since her death, the brothers now held the use in addition to the legal interest. The husband was not to have the use "because it is *as* a thing in action."[185]   That statement reflected the entrenched view that all real rights rested in the trustees, and not in the wife or her second husband. The *cestui que use's* interest was still a personal right of action under a contract model.

A case that arose in King's Bench in 1648 was a genuine precursor of the forthcoming shift,[186] showing that lawyers were beginning to have difficulty classifying the trust. Land was put in trust for the use of an alien, and the question was whether this violated the rule forbidding aliens to "purchase" English lands. Mountague argued on behalf of the *cestui* that the alien owned solely a thing in action, rather than an estate, and so there was no violation. Hales replied for the King, "The trust was not a thing merely in action, but an hereditament; and partly in possession, and cited *Cooks* (sic) *Institutes*." Chief Justice Rolle argued that its nature was not fixed, but was dependent upon that of the asset placed in trust. Trusts were not by nature

---

[184] 1 Popham 106.

[185] *Ibid.*

[186] *King v. Holland* (1648) Style 20.

choses in action, "but may be an inheritance or a chattel as the case falls out."[187] The case was adjourned, however, without a reported conclusion. Yet, in 1662, in a case in which the Chancellor was assisted by the Chief Justices, the old learning was reaffirmed. It was held in *Bennet v. Box*[188] that trust lands were not assets in equity, and that the heirs of the trust estate would take free of the unpaid loans incurred by the *cestui*. Lord Keeper Bridgeman adhered to this position in 1669.[189] Then in *Sir George Sand's Case* (1670), Chief Baron Hale held that the *cestui que trust's* felony did not cause the estate to attaint to the King, because the estate itself was never in him.[190] The trust was still basically an *in personam* right.

E.   The Transformation Under Lord Nottingham (1673-1682)

During Lord Nottingham's tenure, the trust changed dramatically along two lines. He placed an *in rem* foundation under the trust and successfully overcame the once-impregnable defense of coming in the "*post.*" The result of this reconceptualization was not to supplant, but only to supplement, the traditional *in personam* characteristics which the trust also retained. Concurrently, Lord Nottingham saw fit, with the help of agency notions, to extend and enlarge the concept of notice, so that the defense of purchaser for value without notice was reduced in scope. The result of both extensions was to enlarge the beneficiary rights more nearly against the world.

The proprietary hypothesis, as Mr. Yale has shown, can be well demonstrated by testing two corollaries that follow from it.[191]

(a)   The existence of a real interest in the *cestui* is indicated where there is recognition that the trust assets are not to be counted as assets of the trustee, or subject to claims against the trustee's estate.

(b)   The same hypothesis is confirmed where the trust

---

[187] *Id.* at 21.

[188] (1662) 1 Chan. Cas. 12.

[189] *Prat v. Colt* (1669) 1 Chan. Cas. 128.

[190] *Attorney General v. Sir George Sands* (1670) Nelson 130.

[191] The discussion of these two points is heavily based upon Yale's analysis of Lord Nottingham's contribution. *See* YALE, NOTTINGHAM'S CHANCERY CASES, *supra* n. 74, at 88-96.

assets are in fact treated as the assets of the *cestui*,
and are thus made liable to the claims of the
cestui's creditors.

Lord Nottingham advanced rapidly to these positions. Support for
corollary (a) is clear from his ruling that neither the dower rights of the
trustee's wife nor the execution claims of the trustee's creditors could be
satisfied out of the trust assets.[192] Formerly, the position had been that
dower and creditor rights came in the *post*, but these lines of cases were
overturned.[193] In support of the second corollary, Lord Nottingham said
that where the trust consisted of a lease that the *cestui* had mortgaged, then
the lease should be sold to pay off the *cestui's* indebtedness.[194] Likewise, in
Creed v. Coville (1683)[195] he ruled that the trust of an estate would be liable
for the satisfaction of a bond upon which the *heir* had made himself expressly
liable.[196] By virtue of such decisions, the "real" aspect of trusts became
settled and known, and a certain emphasis was placed upon the substantial
nature of the trust interest. The position became entrenched by the Statute
of Frauds, which said that lands in trust would be liable to the *cestui's*
judgment creditors, but exempted from the debts and incumbrances of the
trustee.[197]

Now that the *cestui* was recognized as an owner, there was far less
readiness to uphold "privity" objections that would interfere with his ability to

---

[192] See *e.g.*, *Bevant v. Pope* (1681) 2 Freem. 71 (dower rights); *Medley v. Martin* (1673) Rep. Temp. Finch 63 (creditors).

[193] See *e.g.*, *Noel v. Jevon* (1678) 2 Freem. 43, and the express overruling of *Nash v. Preston* (1631) Cro. Car. 190.

[194] *Tooke's Case*, referred to in Pollexfen's argument in *Baden v. Earl of Pembroke* (1688) 2 Vern. 52, 54.

[195] 1 Vern. 172.

[196] This case affords a glimpse of the revolutionary effect of Nottingham's decisions, and the attempt to overthrow them after his tenure on the woolsack. In *Creed v. Covile* (1683) 1 Vern. 172, Lord Nottingham had decreed the trust to be assets of the heir, but upon rehearing before Lord Keeper North, the previously authoritative case of *Bennet v. Box* (1662) 1 Chan. Cas. 12 was resurrected. *Bennet v. Box*, it was said, had settled the issue differently than Lord Nottingham, and "upon great advice" from the judges, Lord Keeper North seemed ready to reverse Lord Nottingham's previous decree and return to *Bennet v. Box*, but it does not appear from the reports that a new decree was issued.

[197] (1677) 29 Car. II, c. 3.

protect his own estate. For example, in *Harvey v. Baker* (1677),[198] Lord
Nottingham easily overcame this issue now that the internal development was
complete. In that case, a son demanded an account of the real and personal
estate of his father that had been set up in trust for him. The suit was
brought against the agent appointed by the trustees to be receiver, and the
defendant's counsel (in a rare example of the common law term being used
in Chancery) specifically pleaded "no privity" with the son, in that, "the trustees
of this estate made him receiver, and that he was to account to them, for
under them only he intermeddled. . . ."[199] But Lord Nottingham overruled
the objection by emphasizing the *cestui's* ownership of the estate in trust:

> [I]t is reasonable that the plaintiff should pursue his demand by
> following *his estate* into such hands to which he can trace it. For it
> is not fit to oblige the plaintiff to charge the trustees for the [agent's]
> acts when he thinks he may have a readier and juster satisfaction by
> setting the saddle on the right horse.[200]

Thus, the servant of the trustee was susceptible to a double account: once to
the trustee because of their contractual "privity," and secondly to the
beneficiary because of their real "privity."[201]

Chancellors of the late 17th century began to use agency principles
to extend the beneficiary action under the contract theorem. This had no
effect upon defendants in the *post*, for notice was irrelevant to their rights in
title. But the logic that anything within the notice of the agent also lay within
the notice of the principal became a new weapon against the purchaser for
valuable consideration. The rule could not be otherwise, it was said, or else
notice could always be avoided by employing an agent.[202] One of the first
examples appeared in 1663, in which the defendant's plea of being a *bona fide*
purchaser without notice was rejected. Sir Harbottle Grimstone, M.R.
declared, "Notice to the father, who transacted, is notice to the son, and shall
affect him; so notice of a dormant incumbrance to one who purchaseth for
another, is notice to the purchaser."[203] Lord Nottingham distinguished

---

[198] 79 Seld. Soc. 631.

[199] *Ibid.*

[200] *Ibid.* (emphasis added).

[201] *Pollard v. Downes* (1682) 2 Chan. Cas. 121.

[202] *Sheldon v. Cox* (1764) Amb. 624.

[203] *Merry v. Abney* (1663) 2 Freem. 151.

himself as the first Chancellor to express the point in agency terminology, which he possibly borrowed from the law merchant.[204] Thus, in *Green v. Gardner*[205] a trustee, who was nephew to the mortgagee, mortgaged lands that had been set aside in trust to pay the plaintiff's portion. Lord Nottingham rejected the defense that the mortgagee had no notice. As to the notice, he stated, "here was legal notice, for Francis, the nephew, having notice, his notice who was agent for [his uncle] Thomas of Salisbury must affect him who employed him. For it is not reasonable that special confidence in the agent should prejudice a third party. . . ."[206]

The principle of vicarious notice became settled and was applied frequently in the 18th century.[207] It was also applied retroactively to ratify the notice of a constructive agent. For example, a *per* was decreed bound by the notice of one who negotiated the sale, even though the purchaser had not hired him nor obtained actual notice prior to the transaction.[208]

Lord Nottingham's reconceptualization represented many things at once: a progression from contract to property, the concurrent extension of the doctrine of notice, and an assault upon the citadel of the purchaser and the *post*. The transformation, as Mr. Yale described it, was one in which

> as the influence of the use recedes, so does the dominance of the notion of confidence reposed in the feoffee by the beneficiary, and the emphasis shifts rather to the beneficiary's interest with its increasingly proprietary tinge, from the relationship to the equitable right, from power to property.[209]

Furthermore, as Billson observed, the earlier theory had been predicated upon the assumption that the successors of the feoffee were pursued "not by force of any real or proprietary right of the beneficiary, but by virtue of a train of personal rights against a succession of persons each acting

---

[204] *See* Charles Allen, "Agent & Servant Essentially Identical," [1894] 28 Amer. Law Rev. Journal 9.

[205] (1675) 73 Seld. Soc. 170.

[206] *Ibid.* See also, *Preston v. Tubbin* (1685) 1 Vern. 286.

[207] *Brotherton v. Hatt* (1706) 2 Vern. 574. *Sheldon v. Cox* (1764) Amb. 624; *Le Neve v. Le Neve* (1748) 3 Atk. 646.

[208] Ld. Chancellor Cowper, *Jennings v. Moore* (1708) 2 Vern. 609.

[209] YALE, NOTTINGHAM'S CHANCERY CASES, *supra* n. 74, at 90.

unconscientiously."[210]   Under the property theory, however,

> The binding of the husband, wife and creditors of the trustee
> irrespective of notice, though all took by operation of law and in
> consideration of marriage or general credit, denoted clearly that the
> fictitious presumption of knowledge to which recourse had been had
> two centuries before for the binding of the innocent volunteer had
> outlived its usefulness . . . .[211]

Yet, from the standpoint of third party beneficiary theory, another
effect must be considered equally fundamental. Although to a large extent the
property theory had deterred the rise of a "privity" objection, it broke with the
former tradition whereby the *cestui* was only a beneficiary with rights and no
liabilities. Lord Nottingham made the *cestui's* interest into a tangible estate,
but he exposed that estate to the burdens of ownership, particularly the claims
of the *cestui's* creditors. In this he was in fact counteracting the previous lack
of mutuality in the trust. At common law nearly two centuries later, the
beneficiary action would be called a "monstrous proposition" which, if
recognized, would give the beneficiary the right to sue but not to be sued.[212]
Nottingham protected the trust from a similar criticism.

Part of the reason for his success was that the new results were
eminently practical from the commercial standpoint. Furthermore, the timing
may have been propitious, because by the time of the Restoration, the
complex motivations behind the Statute of Uses[213]--political, fiscal and
feudal--had largely evaporated. Also, as an innovator, he was equipped with
great prestige and immense learning in the common law. His civilian view of
precedent was an asset, for it allowed him to view future legal development
as an open road and to make radical departures from the decrees of his
predecessors within a relatively short period of time.[214] The final result was
to put an *in rem* foundation under the beneficiary's position, and this made
the trust better able to absorb and to deal with the very problems which led

---

[210] BILLSON, *supra* n. 7, at 199.

[211] *Ibid.*

[212] Per Crompton J., in *Tweddle v. Atkinson* (1861) 1 B. & S. 393, 30 L.J. Q.B. 265, 4 Law
Times 468.

[213] (1535) 27 Hen. VIII, c. 10.

[214] "Precedents do not make law; they are only evidences of it . . . ." Quoted from Yale's
introduction to LORD NOTTINGHAM'S CHANCERY CASES, *supra* n. 74, at XLIX.

to rejection of the beneficiary action at common law.

F.   The Constructive Trust

The use of the constructive trust to enforce third party promises is not directly treated by Dr. Waters in his learned work, but it is noteworthy that generally he could find no substantive doctrine in it at all. It was only imposed, he argued, in miscellaneous cases without real connection to one another save in one respect--they all happened to be adjudicated by a separate tribunal. The mother tongue of the Chancellor was the language of trust, and he was simply creating a verbal unity. "Unlike the doctrine of *Moses v. Macferlan*," Dr. Waters writes, "there was never a theme behind the use of the constructive trust by Chancery. It was never more than a convenient and available language medium through which for the Chancery mind the obligations of the parties might be expressed or determined."[215] If he had applied his general view to the contract beneficiary, perhaps Dr. Waters would have said that the process which he calls the common application of analogous thinking[216] was often a matter of form, not substance. When relief for the beneficiary occurred, it was not because there was a trust in the sense of a pre-existing fiduciary relationship with the beneficiary, but because some wrong, such as fraud or unjust enrichment, had been done and needed to be rectified.

Professor Corbin maintained, however, that the Chancellor was using the constructive trust in a more purposeful or instrumental manner. It was more than a matter of semantics. When it was attached to a promise for the benefit of a third person, the constructive trust was essentially a privity-creating device. The Chancellor moulded the simple exchange of promises into a trust (though the parties never said or intended anything of the sort, and though there was no trust *res* other than the promise itself) in order to hurdle the obstacles of consideration and privity. This view is at first plausible because nearly all cases involving constructive trusts have three features in common: (i) a three party relationship (ii) the lack of a contractual link or direct dealings between the litigants, and (iii) a remedial hiatus at common

---

[215] P.W.M. WATERS, THE CONSTRUCTIVE TRUST 39 (Athalone Press, 1964).

[216] *Ibid.*

law.[217]   However, this point must not be pressed further than the extent to which privity and the doctrine of consideration were actually substantive barriers in Chancery. The weakness in Corbin's analysis is a tendency to exaggerate these barriers, as if they were originally comparable to those faced in assumpsit by common law courts, and thereby to insist that the constructive trust must have been, not a natural language medium or perhaps a reassuring method of stating jurisdictional competence, but a *deus ex machina* device.[218]

(a) Analysis of Tomlinson v. Gill

A misunderstanding of the historical context led Corbin to overestimate the importance of his centerpiece, the case of *Tomlinson v. Gill* (1756).[219]   In his eyes, it was a novel case, marking the first occasion on which the Chancellor regarded the promisee as a trustee for the third party, and on which the promise made and received was construed to be the *res* of a constructive trust. The same view echoed in the 1937 Report of the Law Revision Committee, which declared that *Tomlinson* is "the case in which the origins of the rule is (sic) to be found."[220]

On its face, however, the case was a creditor beneficiary action for an accounting. Tomlinson was the creditor of a man who died intestate. The

----

[217] These features are often evident in situations involving the following trustees: the vendor before completion, the mortgagee prior to foreclosure, the acquirer of property by fraud, the misuser of a fiduciary relationship, the intermeddling stranger, and the agent. A notable exception is the variety found in *Keech v. Sandford* (1726) Eq. Ca. Abr. 741. *See* GEORGE W. KEETON AND L.A. SHERIDAN, THE LAW OF TRUSTS, 191 and ff., 10th ed. (Professional Books, 1974).

[218] Corbin's viewpoint must be gathered from throughout his article, but the following quotation seems to express it well:

> If in this process he [the Chancellor] was disregarding and in a measure nullifying the *sacred* requirement of 'privity' of contract, if he was putting into the hands of a stranger one end of the 'vinculum iuris' that had previously been beyond his reach, if he was overlooking the requirement in the action of assumpsit that a promise was enforceable only by one who had given something for it or suffered a 'detriment' in reliance on it, what of it? . . . [He] had at his command something that the common law judges did not yet have at theirs--the magic word 'trustee.' By its use and with this single word, he rendered innocuous the threatening magicians ensconced within the phrases 'lack of privity' and 'stranger to the consideration.' Corbin, [1930] 46 L.Q.R. 12, 19 & 20.

[219] Amb. 330.

[220] Sixth Interim Report of the Law Revision Committee, Sec. 42, 1937 (Cmd. 5449).

debtor's widow was made administratrix of his estate, and the debtor's father came to the widow promising that if she would permit him to be joined with her in the letters of administration, he would make good any deficiency in order to discharge his son's debts. The widow agreed to this, and the father was made an administrator. Later, there proved to be insufficient assets to pay all the son's debts, and Tomlinson brought a bill for an accounting against both administrators, citing the father's promise to the widow.

One defense raised by the father was that his promise was not in writing and, therefore, was void under the Statute of Frauds. The Chancellor evaluated that contention (we shall return to it shortly), and found it had no merit. He then decreed that the creditor was entitled to an accounting, and in the event of a deficiency, to have the benefit of the contract between the defendant father and the defendant widow. The Chancellor's reasoning was that,

> The plaintiff is proper for relief here for two reasons: 1st, He could not maintain an action at law, for the promise was made to the widow; but he is proper here, for the promise was for the benefit of the creditors, and the widow is a trustee for them. 2dly, The bill is brought for an account, and that draws to it relief, like the common case of a bill to be paid out of assets.[221]

In Professor Corbin's analysis, the parole promise from the father to the widow created a trust, and when Lord Hardwicke called the widow a trustee he did so "merely as a device for making the defendant pay as he promised." Thus, the distinguished author argued:

> there was no trust fund to be administered either by the defendant or by the promisee. There was merely a contract between two persons by which one of them promised to pay a debt due to the plaintiff, a third party; and the promisee is called a trustee merely as a means of sustaining a bill in equity by the beneficiary against the promisor.[222]

The reason the widow was called a trustee, however, was not a result of receiving a promise from the father, but was related to three other factors.

---

[221] *Tomlinson v. Gill* (1756) Amb. 330, 331.

[222] Corbin, [1930] 46 L.Q.R. 12, 18.

(i)   **The decedent's estate was a trust for creditors**

The estate, at the time she received the promise, was deemed by Lord Hardwicke to be a trust for creditors. The creditors could have sued for an accounting against her irrespective of whether the father had promised to be surety. Contrary to Corbin's statement that "there was no trust fund to be administered," the *personal* estate itself was the fund to be administered, and the father's promise became a valuable asset of the estate, since the consideration given for it by the wife was sufficient to make the promise binding rather than voluntary. Two years later, Lord Keeper Northington made reference to *Tomlinson v. Gill* solely as good authority for the proposition that the permission to join letters of administration was sufficient consideration to make a promise binding between the promisor and promisee.[223] These creditor trusts were often implied in Chancery when a testator directed by his will that his assets be sold to pay his debts.[224] Although the decedent died intestate in this case, the Chancellor was imposing a constructive trust upon his personalty for the benefit of creditors. The promise did not create this trust, nor was the promise the sole asset of the trust thus created. The promise was simply received as an asset in trust for creditors. This is why Lord Hardwicke minimized Tomlinson's request for an accounting by comparing it to the "common case" of a bill to be paid out of estate assets.

(ii)   **An executrix was customarily called a trustee**

A second reason to call the widow a trustee was that the office of executor or executrix had long been treated as a "trust" in the sense of the general trust of any executor to pay debts and legacies.[225] Maddock emphasized that this usage had been well-settled in the previous century--

> Certain it is, however, that in *Lord Nottingham's* time an Executor was considered as a *Trustee*; and the opinion then prevailed, that a Legatee is entitled to bring his Bill in Equity against an Executor for his Legacy, upon the foundation, that the *office of Executor is a Trust*.[226]

---

[223] *Griffith v. Sheffield* (1758) 1 Eden. 73.

[224] *Cook v. Fountain* (1672) 3 Swans. App. 585; *Pitt v. Pelham* (1670) 2 Freem. 134.

[225] *Anonymous* (1602) Cary 21.

[226] MADDOCK, *supra* n. 172, at 2 (emphasis and capitalization in the original.)

Thus, Lord Hardwicke was not innovating a "device" or devising an appellation to make the defendant pay. To refer to an executrix as a trustee in equity, was to use a generic term.[227] When the father was permitted by contract to join in the letters of administration, he, too, became a trustee in the same sense, and thus, nothing follows from Corbin's repeated speculation[228] as to why the Chancellor called the promisee (rather than the promisor) a trustee. He could, and probably did, regard them both as trustees. Furthermore, Lord Hardwicke might have reached the same result even if the promisee had not already been a trustee, since he might constructively impose some other relationship linking up the three parties. A few years earlier, in *Hook v. Kinnear* (1750),[229] he had decreed specific performance at the instance of a contract beneficiary by making the promisee into the beneficiary's agent. There was no actual agency agreement between the beneficiary and the promisee, but Lord Hardwicke said

> I must take it that [the promisee] contracted not only on behalf of himself, but also of the Plaintiff; . . . and it is certain that if one person enters into an agreement with another for the benefit of a third person, such third person may come into a court of equity and compel a specific performance; and there are many instances where stewards have made agreements, and yet the masters for whose benefit they were made, have come into this court, and obtained

---

[227] 2 Eq. Ca. Abr. 421, pl. 4.

[228] Corbin never clearly explained why he repeatedly attached importance to the distinction between cases in which the promisee was called a trustee (e.g. *Tomlinson*) and those more numerous instances in equity in which the promisor was treated as a trustee. There is no particular shortage of cases in which the promisor was treated as a trustee and so made liable. *Thynn v. Thynn* (1684) 1 Vern. 296; *Jones v. Nabbs* (1718) 1 Eq. Ca. Abr. 405; *Drakeford v. Wilks* (1747) 3 Atk. 539; *Gregory & Parker v. Williams*, (1817) 3 Mer. 582. Apparently Corbin intended to demonstrate the fictional nature of these promisee trusts; in the case of a promisee-trustee, the only trust *res* would be the promise received, thus amounting to a clear exception of the accepted notion that the trust must hold a fund or a property. His distinction is illuminating for another reason. When the promisor is the defendant and is deemed a trustee, then the purpose of the characterization could merely relate to the grounds of liability, that is to the process of declaring conscience-based duties. On the other hand, to call a promisee a trustee could seem to be linked to the problem of creating privity between the promisee and the beneficiary. In that instance the characterization is only a privity-creating device. The "trustee" is the conduit to the beneficiary. It is for that reason significant that while we find that the Chancellors treated both promisors and promisees as trustees, leaving open speculation as to their motive, the privity-minded judges of the common law invariably made promisees into trustees. (See below at pp. 136-137).

[229] 3 Swans. 482.

decrees.[230]

Lord Hardwicke could have summoned forth the trust in this context, but he had other magic words as well.

(iii) The logic of the Statute of Frauds analysis

An equally strong refutation of the Corbin theory of a promissory trust can be made by examining the court's analysis of the Statute of Frauds. Surely if the Chancellor had meant to say that the father's parole promise created a trust, then he would not have analyzed the Statute of Frauds aspect as he did. According to Ambler's report, the Chancellor focussed exclusively upon section 4 of the statute in determining whether such a promise needed to be in writing. He found that it did not fall under the section, but he noted that this interpretation put him in disagreement with Chief Justice Holt in *Burkmire v. Darnell* (1705).[231] If Corbin's hypothesis that the promise had created a trust were true, then the court probably would have avoided the difficulty of a section 4 analysis by citing the exemptions contained in sections 7 and 8. He would not have failed to note that sections 7 and 8 expressly exempted trusts of personalty and choses, as well as constructive trusts. The alleged "trust" of promises would have been doubly exempt under these provisions.

(b)   The Tomlinson issues in historical context

Corbin's analysis clashes with the contemporary evaluation of the decision. Two years later, in *Griffith v. Sheffield* (1759),[232] Lord Northington drew from the *Tomlinson* case the proposition that permitting the father to join in letters of administration had been a sufficient consideration to enforce his promise to pay the debts of his son. It is interesting to ask why the consideration question had jurisprudential significance to contemporaries rather than the alleged use of a novel "device" to overcome the creditors' lack of privity with the father. The answer lies in the fact that the doctrine of consideration had now greatly replaced Conscience as the test of promissory liability, while privity (in the sense that only the promisee could sue upon a promise) was not a contemporary doctrine in Chancery.

---

[230] *Ibid.*

[231] 6 Mod. 248, 2 Ld. Raym. 1085.

[232] 1 Eden. 73.

Similar cases decided in Chancery in the previous century will bear out this contention. In *King v. Hatchett & Bindon* (1675)[233] and in *Hatchett v. Bindon*, (1677)[234] Lord Nottingham adjudicated two cases arising out of the same transaction. In the first case a creditor sued upon a parole promise given by the defendant Bindon to his deceased brother's administrator (Hatchett), in which he promised to pay off the creditors. Lord Nottingham refused to enforce Bindon's promise of indemnity. He said quite clearly that it was "against conscience" to make Bindon pay for his brother's debts. Relief was denied upon the purely ethical ground that such a promise was not fit to be enforced in a forum of Conscience. He stated, "let Hatchett [the administrator] sue John Bindon [the promisor] at law, but 'tis not fit the plaintiff should sue him here or force a losing bargain upon John Bindon in equity . . . ."[235]

Subsequently, Hatchett the administrator (who was also the promisee) brought a second bill against the brother upon the same promise. On this occasion, Lord Nottingham not only reiterated that to make Bindon liable went against Conscience, but he also explained that the brother's promise had been voluntary. Lord Nottingham enumerated the ways in which the promise lacked consideration.[236] Thus, the ethical principle espoused in the first case became a technical ground in the second. It was not at all impossible to restate a matter of conscience as a matter of consideration. The promise had not created a change in position in reliance upon it, and the promisor had not received a benefit. The absence of consideration was an alternative way of restating the Chancellor's ethical objection.[237] Had Lord Nottingham found that the brother's promise was given in return for something valuable, he would have permitted the creditor or the administrator to sue upon it.

When *Tomlinson* was decided 81 years later, however, the consideration doctrine had then gained the upper hand.[238] Lord Hardwicke believed it was imperative to ascertain whether the promise was supported by

---

[233] 73 Seld. Soc. 263, 344.

[234] 79 Seld. Soc. 565.

[235] *See King v. Hatchet* (1675) 73 Seld. Soc. 263, 344. See also, *Barber v. Fox*, (1671) 2 Wm. Saund. 136.

[236] See quotation p. 103.

[237] This view of the case seems to be in accord with Mr. Atiyah's view concerning the substantive role of consideration in equity. Atiyah, op. cit. 158-162.

[238] This was made clear in *Honywood v. Bennett* (1675) 73 Seld. Soc. 214.

valuable consideration not because it might otherwise offend Conscience to enforce it, but because the doctrine of consideration was now the principal test of enforceable promises.[239] The theme 'lack of consideration' had squarely replaced the factors that use to constitute the Chancellor's Conscience, and it is significant that Lord Hardwicke never once mentions Conscience in his decision.

Neither Lord Nottingham nor Lord Hardwicke were troubled by the fact that the plaintiff-creditor was not the promisee; that element was not then, if it had ever been, a requirement in equity. In 1675 the defendant's promise, even when the promisee (the administrator) sued upon it, was not enforceable. Furthermore neither Chancellor went further in their analysis of consideration than to determine whether valuable consideration had passed between the promisor and promisee. There was no attempt to determine if the creditor beneficiary was a stranger to the consideration: the rule of *Bourne v. Mason* had no precedential effect in Chancery until about 1836, when it was finally recognized as the prevailing rule in Equity.[240]

Beneficial rights in the 18th century had been established on a more general plane than previously realized. Having entertained an unhistorical picture of the Chancellor's attitude to privity and consideration, Corbin attached an unwarranted significance to the role of the constructive trust in enforcing promises for the benefit of third parties.

Corbin noted the existence of two lines of constructive trust cases, those in Chancery and those at common law, but a fundamental difference between the two was perhaps not fully appreciated. The common-law line of cases began about 1840 and primarily developed under the equity jurisdiction of the Court of Exchequeur. In these cases there was relief for the beneficiary, but only because the court always turned a *promisee* into a trustee.[241] In these instances there was good reason to believe that the trust was a device designed solely to overcome the common-law notion of privity. For example in *Lamb v. Vice* (1840)[242] a creditor was damaged when the defendant, a court official, released his debtor without taking sufficient bail.

---

[239] See above, pp. 104-106.

[240] *Colyear v. Mulgrave* (1836) 2 Keen. 81.

[241] See *e.g. Lamb v. Vice* (1840), 6 M. & W. 467; *Stansfield v. Hellawell,* (1852) 7 Ex. 373; *Robertson v. Wait* (1853) 8 Exch. 299; *Touche v. Metropolitan Ry. W. Co.,* (1871) L.R. 6 Ch. 671; *Lloyd's v. Harper,* (1880) 16 Ch. D. 290.

[242] 6 M & W 467.

The plaintiff, the Knight Marshall of the court, sued upon the bond previously given by the defendant to ensure that he would take sufficient bail from all persons arrested. The Knight Marshall was party to the bond and was permitted to collect not simply such nominal damages as he himself may have sustained, but the full loss sustained by the creditor. The Knight Marshall was thus promisee on the bond and was called a trustee for the creditor, though the word trust or trustee was not contained in the bond. Lord Abinger said, "The plaintiff clearly was a trustee for Moses; he might sue on the bond in the plaintiff's name, or the plaintiff might sue for the benefit of Moses. Nothing is more common than for a *cestui que trust* to sue on a bond in the name of his trustee."[243]

In contrast, the constructive trust in the Chancery cases was conceived in a wider variety of circumstances. An executor directed by the testator's will to sell assets to pay debts was a trustee.[244] A creditor who received a conveyance of the debtor's entire estate, promising to pay out of the assets a debt to another creditor, was called a trustee.[245] The assignee of a note (the proceeds of which were promised to repay the plaintiff) was deemed to be a trustee for the plaintiff.[246] Overcoming privity could not have been the principal aim of these characterizations because in many cases the Chancellor called the *promisor* a trustee.[247] There were also instances of relief in which no reference to a trustee can be found.[248] It seems that the trust had become, as Dr. Waters has suggested, the "language medium" of obligations,

---

[243] *Accord, Stansfield v. Hellawell,* (1852) 7 Ex. 373.

[244] *Cook v. Fountain,* (1672) 3 Swans. App. 585.

[245] *Gregory & Parker v. Williams* (1817), 3 Mer. 582.

[246] *Ex parte Byas,* (1743) 1 Atk. 124. In that case the plaintiff was originally owed £91 by A who was the creditor of B and held B's note for £71. Although A did not assign or endorse B's note to plaintiff, he promised plaintiff in writing that when B paid the note plaintiff would receive the £71. When A went bankrupt and B died, payment on the note was made to A's assignees by B's solicitor, who had notice of A's written promise. The plaintiff brought a bill against A's assignees, saying that the money received ought to be paid over to him. In a typical illustration of a constructive trust, Chancellor Hardwicke treated the assignees of A's estate as trustees and granted the *cestui que trust* (plaintiff) a recovery against them. There was no inferable trace of an intention to create a trust, or confidence in the trustee. The Chancellor used the trust mechanism here as a restitutionary remedy, linking two parties who at common law were not in privity of contract.

[247] *Paterson v. Murphy,* (1853) 11 Hare 88; *Moore v. Darton* (1851) 4 De G. & Sm. 517. See *supra* note 243.

[248] *E.g. Cassy v. Fitton* (1679) 79 Seld. Soc. 729; *Oldham v. Litchford* (1705) 2 Freem. 284, 2 Eq. Ca. Abr. 44. Discussed above at p. 95.

and it was not really used by the Chancellor as a privity-creating device in Corbin's sense. There is no basis to assume that Chancery adhered to the common-law privity doctrine at this time. We must wait until 1836, some 80 years after *Tomlinson v. Gill*, to find the first suggestion that the "stranger to the consideration" objection of *Bourne v. Mason* and *Crow v. Rogers* had become the prevailing rule in Equity.[249]

III.   FREEDOM OF ASSIGNMENT IN EQUITY

A new freedom to assign choses in action was ushered in during the Chancery phase, 1680-1800.[250] The Chancellors overcame staunch objections that contract rights were "too personal" to be transferred, and that assignments posed the threat of maintenance and champerty. The Chancellor cast aside the legalism that the assignee was at best an agent who had acquired only a revocable power to use the assignor's name. He preferred to construe the assignment as an alienation of the chose itself, and he permitted the assignee to bring an independent right of action against the obligor.

Our immediate interest in assignment lies in the fact that it serves as the functional equivalent of the beneficiary action. The Law Revision Committee has pointed out that the history of assignment has been analogous to the history of third party beneficiary contracts.[251] Both types of transaction deal broadly with an effort by C to enforce an obligation originally entered into by A and B, but an assignment to C involves the complexity of two agreements and the problem of notice. An equitable assignment will be complete between the assignor and assignee (B and C) without notice and may even bind unnotified third parties such as the debtor's trustee in bankruptcy and his judgment creditors.[252] In certain cases, however, the assignment will not be binding on the debtor himself unless he has been

---

[249] *Colyear v. Mulgrave*, (1836) 2 Keen 81.

[250] This discussion will deal only with creditor assignments of the benefit of an obligation, and does not consider the assignment of the burden of an obligation. It also does not deal with all types of assignments and particularly excludes consideration of real actions, delictual actions and personal contracts, since all of these go beyond the scope and space of this work. As to all of these aspects, see generally HOLDSWORTH, *supra* n. 11, at 532.

[251] Sixth Interim Report of the Law Revision Committee, Sec. 42, 1937 (Cmd. 5449), pl. 46.

[252] SNELL, PRINCIPLES OF EQUITY 78-79 (27th ed. 1973).

notified.[253]   The beneficiary contract, on the other hand, links up these three
parties by promises exchanged at one time, and by this single exchange creates
two obligees of the obligor's performance.   Notice is not an important factor,
because by the terms of the promise, the obligor has agreed in advance upon
the recipient of his performance.   Furthermore, the beneficiary contract
reflects a common intention between A and B to benefit C, whereas in
assignment, neither A nor B would necessarily intend to benefit C at the time
that B agreed to become A's debtor.   Moreover an assignment was
enforceable upon valuable consideration that moved from the promisee
(assignee) but only to the assignor.   The debtor was a stranger to this
consideration and received no benefit from it.

The tendency of American legal thought has been to regard these
distinctions as nonessential differences of form.   An American court, in
stressing the case to be made for functional equivalence, has stated,

> C [by A's assignment to him] thereby succeeds to A's right of action,
> and, in consequence, comes into the relationship with A and B which
> we call privity of contract.   Instead of waiting to do it by assignment,
> A may, at the outset, exact from B the same promise in favor of C.
> It is enforcable by C, who thereby has come into legal relationship
> with B.[254]

Another view, which goes beyond the case for functional equivalence, holds
that C's privity to A or B is in each case "the same," by either method of
transfer.[255]   If this proposition were true, it would indeed become anomalous
to enforce assignments and yet refuse the beneficiary action upon a contract,
particularly since the latter could be treated "equally plausibly as a bilateral
contract between A and B combined with a contemporaneous assignment to
C."[256]   According to an eminent writer, the reason for such an apparent

---

[253] SNELL, *op. cit. supra*; KEETON AND SHERIDAN, EQUITY, *supra* n. 217, at 300-301;
P.S. ATIYAH, AN INTRODUCTION TO THE LAW OF CONTRACT 231-232, 239 (2nd ed.
1971).   Thus a debtor who has been given no notice of the assignment obtains a good discharge
if he pays the assignor rather than the assignee; and in the case of successive assignments, the
debtor is also discharged if he pays the assignee who gave first notice, as opposed to the first
assignee.   See *Dearle v. Hall* (1823) 3 Russ. 1.

[254] *La Mourea v. Rhude* (1940) 295 N.W. 304, 307, per Stone J.

[255] Note, "Third Party Beneficiary Contracts in England," [1968] 35 Univ. Chi. L. Rev. 544,
550.

[256] *Id.* at 551.   Professor Willis has argued that the third-party beneficiary contract could be
regarded as the simultaneous creation and assignment of contractual rights.   John Willis, "The
Nature of a Joint Account," [1936] 14 Can. Bar Rev. 457, 461-463.

anomaly would lie in the difference between the judicial attitudes of judges and Chancellors. The Chancellor simply did not manifest an equal reverence for privity of contract.[257]

This generalization undoubtedly has some validity, but whether it fits this context is not clear. For it is certainly not obvious that C's privity to A or B--whether by assignment or beneficiary contract--should be called "the same". Assignment presents important contrasts: the absence of original intent to benefit the assignee, the subsequent nexus created by notification, the differing number of promissory exchanges, and the consideration given by the assignee for the chose. Both functional similarities and real differences suggest the need for caution in drawing a parallel between assignments and third party beneficiary contracts. Although the case for functional equivalence seems sound, any further claim concerning exact equivalence seems highly doubtful.

Before turning to the work of the Chancellor, it will be helpful to summarize the common-law rules and policies with which he had to deal.

A.   Synopsis of Policies and Rules at Common Law

(a)   Basis of the Prohibition

Historically, the deep disfavor found in medieval law toward the assignment of a chose in action emanates from the inherent personal nature of obligations generally, and from the law's dread of maintenance and champerty. Certain modern writers, it is true, tend to discount maintenance as an historical factor. They ascribe its general acceptance to the sheer power of Coke's name to perpetuate error, and particularly to an oversimplified explanation given in *Lampet's Case* (1612):

> And first was observed the great wisdom and policy of the sages and founders of our law who have provided, that no possibility, right, title nor thing in action, shall be granted or assigned to strangers, for that would be the occasion of multiplying of contentions and suits, of great oppression to the people, and chiefly of terre-tenants.[258]

---

[257] JOSEPH STORY, COMMENTARIES ON EQUITY JURISPRUDENCE (1836; reprint ed., Arno Press, 1972), vol. II, p. 93.

[258] 10 Co. Rep. 46b, 48a.

Coke's critics have pointed out that the same prohibition has at various times existed in every other state of Europe, but the rationale offered on the continent has not been maintenance.[259] Pothier's explanation of the prohibition in the old French laws, for example, was on the basis that a credit was a personal right "inherent in his person"; accordingly, "the debtor, being obliged towards a certain person, cannot, by a transfer of the credit, which is not an act of his, become obliged towards another."[260] Ames correctly concludes that the rule is not only older than the doctrine of maintenance, but is a principle of "universal law."[261]

Yet the special tenacity, severity and chronological development of this prohibition in English soil may not be fully understood unless additional factors, including maintenance, are taken into account. One intensifying factor may have been the numerous personal relationships embodied in the feudal system. Bracton said the landlord-tenant relationship was too fiduciary to be assigned without mutual consent. The bond of homage could not be transferred to a strange lord against the tenant's wishes.[262] Another factor related to the gruesome hardships of forced execution and the imprisonment of debtors.[263]

Furthermore, a peculiar historical factor at English law was the apprehension generally felt about maintenance. Maintenance was an insistent theme of the cases, and specifically outlawed by early statutes. Fear of maintenance seems to explain why the prohibition was not confined to the so-called personal actions (in contract and tort, for instance), but was extended to the real actions as well.[264] The fear that old forgotten claims could be resurrected to oppress terre-tenants was exacerbated by the absence (at this time) of any statute of limitations on actions at common law.[265] The influence of maintenance persisted longer than the socioeconomic conditions that gave rise to it, but its rise and fall took place mainly between the 15th-

---

[259] SPENCE, *supra* n. 71, at 850.

[260] ROBERT J. POTHIER, TREATISE ON THE CONTRACT OF SALE 333-334, trans. by Cushing, (Little, Brown, 1839) no. 551.

[261] AMES, *supra* n. 145, at 211; *see also*, Winfield, "Assignment of Choses in Action in Relation to Maintenance and Champerty," [1919] 35 L.Q.R. 143.

[262] Bailey, *supra* n. 124, at 547.

[263] *Id.* at 549-550.

[264] HOLDSWORTH, *supra* n. 11, at 526.

[265] Charles Sweet, "Choses in Action," [1984] 10 L.Q.R. 303; [1895] 11 L.Q.R. 238.

17th centuries.[266] From the 17th century onward, both the rule and the economic order in which it flourished began to lose ground to the commercial spirit and necessities of the times. Indeed, the growing necessities of trade were as a dynamic force pushing the law toward freer assignability and increased receptivity to the Law Merchant, while the "too personal" and maintenance objections were brakes that held the development in creative check.

Our understanding of this subject would be incomplete, then, if commercial considerations, maintenance, or the "too personal" objection were completely ignored. More than one policy was usually at work in the evolution of assignment, and each shaped the peculiar configuration of its rules. For example, covenants under seal remained nonassignable in all stages of English history.[267] The highly personal nature of covenant (plus the sacrosanctness of the seal) provides a better explanation for this rule than simple fear of maintenance. On the other hand, the nonassignability of real actions is only intelligble in light of a strict policy against maintenance. The rule that permitted an assignee to sue in his assignor's name only if he owed his assignor a precedent debt was also a means to control maintenance. It could not have stemmed from the "too personal" objection: the distinction related solely to the assignor/assignee relationship, not to the absence of privity between the assignee and the original debtor.[268]

These introductory points do not cast doubt upon Ames' statement that the "too personal" objection is the older and more fundamental cause of the nonassignability of choses in action. They point out, however, that the law's fear of maintenance was a significant historical episode, and an important chronological factor affecting its development.

(b)   The Weakening of the Prohibition

By the 17th century, the state of the original prohibition was weakened by numerous circumventions and exceptions. A chose could be transferred to a party by a devise, assigned to the king, and reassigned to another.[269] A novation could produce the same result as an assignment, although there, the debtor's consent (not mere notification), fresh

---

[266] KEETON & SHERIDAN, EQUITY, *supra* n. 79, at 199.

[267] "It is against the law to assign a covenant." 1 Rolle Abr. 376.

[268] Bailey, *supra* n. 124, at 522 & 553.

[269] *George v. Chansey* (1639) 1 Chan. Rep. 125.

consideration, and complete extinguishment of the prior obligation were all required. Another circumvention was to obtain consent contemporaneous with the creation of the duty, that is, to draft the original obligation in such a form that the debtor stipulated that he would render performance in favor of anyone to whom the obligee assigned.[270]

Yet the most prevalent and effective circumvention permitted by the courts was the letter of attorney. The assignor would expressly appoint the assignee as his "attorney" to sue upon the obligation.[271] The instrument appointing the attorney typically permitted him to keep the proceeds "*sans accompt render.*"[272] Acquiescence in the attorney stratagem may be taken as a sign relaxation of the prohibition that the terror of maintenance had begun to subside, but theoretically, there was still no relaxation of the prohibition. The fundamental restriction remained, preventing the sale of this power to any stranger. A "common interest" (*e.g.*, between joint tenants) was needed as a good defense to maintenance, and such an interest also existed between assignor and assignee where there was a prior indebtedness between them.[273] The power of attorney could therefore be given to a party when the assignment was in satisfaction of the precedent debt. It was maintenance to sell the power for no other reason than fresh consideration then given.[274] The "precedent debt" idea was simply an expedient compromise between freedom of contract and fear of maintenance. It was not a consideration requirement; on the contrary, past consideration was treated as bad consideration in assumpsit. It did not stem from the "too personal" objection, since whether the debt was new or old between assignor and assignee could hardly alter the privity, or lack thereof, between the debtor and the assignee-attorney. Contemporaries freely admitted that choses were transferred by letter of attorney "everyday," but it did not negate the general principle prohibiting assignments.[275]

There were, however, many unsatisfactory aspects to the agency device. From the assignee's point of view, he would have obtained greater

---

[270] *Fenner v. Meares* (1770) 2 Wm. Black. 1269.

[271] A clear illustration was *Potter v. Turner* (1622) Winch 7.

[272] Bailey, *supra* n. 124, at 553.

[273] BROOKE, *supra* n.26, at 114 ("Maintenance"); HOLDSWORTH, *supra* n. 11, at 535.

[274] *South v. Marsh* (1590) 3 Leon. 234; *Harvey v. Bateman* (1595) Noy. 52.

[275] For this admission, see the 1647 decision of the court of King's Bench cited in JOHN LILLY, THE PRACTICAL REGISTER, vol. I, p. 103 (Nutt & Gosling, 1719).

security had courts been able to recognize his ownership of the debt, or at least admit that he had a sufficient "interest" to ground a suit in his own name. The assignor might grant the power, but later break his word by releasing his own debtor, or by revoking the power of attorney.[276] The assignor's subsequent death, incapacity, bankruptcy,[277] or marriage (in the case of a woman) automatically revoked the power of attorney.[278] To bring suit in another's name without possessing a valid procuration was a tortious act against the debtor.[279]

(c)   **The Legal Problem Posed by the "Agency" Circumvention**

The most unsatisfactory aspect of assignment through agency was the manner in which it inverted the real question facing the courts. Agency implied that even though the assignor had been paid full value for the assigned right, the agent was fiduciary to the assignor. It pictured duties owed by the assignee rather than the other way round. In truth, the fully-compensated assignor needed to be seen as fiduciary to the assignee, so that he would be prevented from interfering with the assignee's ability to collect on the debt. The entire tendency of common law development reveals an urge to protect the assignee's position, but any protection sought through manipulation of his status as agent was always inversely conceived. The question was how the law could retain this device and yet protect the assignee under it.

We would be mistaken to think that this inversion could have been readily resolved simply by discarding the agency notion and recognizing the assignee's full ownership. The agency device served as a defense mechanism, preventing deeply-held principles of privity of contract from reaching the surface. The distinctive feature was that the common law never went beyond consideration of the assignor's and the assignee's duties to one another. So long as the assignee had a common interest and possessed a power of attorney, the proceeding against the debtor was lawful. The only litigable issue was the validity of the relationship as tested by certain rules to prevent maintenance--nothing more. This explains why so many of the cases concern

---

[276] It consequently became customary for such procurations to include a covenant by the assignor not to revoke it. WILLIAM WEST, THE FIRST PART OF SYMBOLEOGRAPHY (1647; reprint ed., Garland Publishing, 1979), sec. 521.

[277] *E.g., Peters v. Soame* (1701) 2 Vern. 428, 1 Eq. Ca. Abr. 44.

[278] *E.g., Earl of Suffolk v. Greenvill* (1641) 3 Rep. Chan. 89, Nelson 15.

[279] *Thurston v. Ummons* (1640) March N.R. 47.

the revocability of the power of attorney after countermand, death or marriage. These cases conspicuously omit consideration of the assignee's or assignor's relationship with the debtor: for example, debtors do not object that the assignee was not privy to the original debt; that no consideration moved from the assignee to him; that the debtor received no discharge from the assignor and might be liable twice for the same debt; or that the debtor wished to plead an original defense against the assignor in bar of the assignee's action.[280] Such issues had no chance to surface. That the assignor remained the nominal plaintiff in the case cut off such objections at their roots. Any objection as to consideration, discharge, defenses etc. could possess merit only with respect to the party bringing the action, not his attorney. This highly formalistic device, therefore, spared lawyers a painful reexamination of their basic attitudes about privity of contract. They never conceded that the assignee was actually the real plaintiff and true owner of the right of action. The common law was never pressed for answers about this contractual triangle. Indeed, the debtor was a stranger to the assignment, and was not entitled to raise such issues.[281] We shall see that the Chancellor's problem started from the opposite direction: he freely recognized that the assignee was the owner of the action, but he was thus forced to take the matter one step further and allow the debtor to raise original defenses and equities against the assignee.

By the 18th century, after the spectre of maintenance had greatly receded, the common law stumbled upon two paths to greater security to the assignee. One road was to stress that where consideration had been given, the assignor and assignee had an enforceable contract between themselves. The attorney was to be protected by his contract rights, even though the subject matter of the contract was not by nature assignable.[282] The second road was the path previously taken in *Dutton v. Poole*: equitable trust ideas were once again brought to bear to solve problems generated by the law's privity constraints. This animated the remarkable holdings of liberal judges like Buller and Mansfield, who took "notice" that assignments were regarded in equity as trusts for the assignee.[283] These paths were indeed "two roads to the same city," but by the second one, the agent was the acknowledged beneficiary of the assignment. An assignor, conceived as a trustee, could not revoke the rights of a trust beneficiary. The theoretical dress was borrowed

---

[280] These issues are considered below in Chapter V, at 242-243.

[281] *Walker v. Bradford Old Banks, Ltd.* (1884) 12 Q.B.D. 511.

[282] See *e.g.*, *King v. Inhabitants of the Parish Aickles* (1702) 12 Mod. 553.

[283] See below, p. 148.

from equity, but the substance was not in fact true. The Chancellor was not using the trust to protect the assignee. His concern was to protect the debtor from the assignee. The difference followed from the Chancellor's premise that the assignee had actually purchased and, therefore, owned the right to bring action, although his right was subject to the debtor's equities and defenses. It can be said with some truth that the chief goal of equity was to protect the debtor, while at law it was to protect the assignee.

(d)   The Evolution from Agency to Trust

Between 1670 and 1710, nascent signs of the coming change appeared. The values of commercial and contractual freedom started to outweigh the possible taint of maintenance; and as assignments shed the presumption of maintenance, the assignor's ownership of the chose was increasingly regarded as a formal or nominal right.[284]

A revealing indication that the battle between substance and form was turning in favor of the assignee was the Kings Bench decision in *Carrington v. Harway* (1665).[285] The court ruled that the plaintiff's prior assignment in satisfaction of a debt was not revocable, and would bar his subsequent attempt to reassign the chose to a second person. This result was not clothed in analytical dress, but the clear effect was to deprive the assignor of a power associated with his ownership.[286] Another valuable signpost was *Deering v. Carringdon* (1701).[287] The assignor died while suit was being prosecuted in his name. The Court of King's Bench refused to stay the proceedings, though the assignor's executor objected and withheld consent to the use of the executor's name. The court declared that though such assignments "do not vest an interest, yet they have so far prevailed in all courts, that the Grantee hath such an interest, that he may sue in the name of the Party, his Executors

---

[284] The way the presumption gradually dissolved is shown by *Deering v. Farrington* (1674) 1 Mod. 113, where it was argued that "it was an assignment for maintenance." But C. J. Hale replied, "That ought to have been averred." It thus appears that maintenance could still be a bar to plaintiff's suit, but only upon well-pleaded and proven facts.

[285] I Keb. 803.

[286] This decision has been called a "remarkable" holding in light of developments up to 1676. MARSHALL, ASSIGNMENT OF CHOSES IN ACTION, (1950), p. 74. The irrevocability of an assignment is recognized in *Stuart v. Tucker* (1767) 2 Wm. Black. 1137.

[287] Cited in LILLY, *supra* n. 283, at 103; CHARLES VINER, ABRIDGEMENT OF LAW AND EQUITY "Assignment" (3) (1743).

or administrators."[288]   Chief Justice Hale had previously made a similar point in 1674. Counsel argued to him that "an assignment transferring when it cannot transfer signifies nothing," but Hale simply replied: "But it is a covenant."[289]   Hale's point became the basis of the rule that "assigning a *chose in action* is interpreted as a covenant against the assignor."[290] Seemingly, the assignee was vested with some limited interest to maintain the suit. In terms conspicuously innocent of the trust, the courts recognized a fine distinction between the legal property of the owner and the contractual right enabling the assignee to sue. This raises a parallel to the fleeting theory of "interest," which courts articulated in the Formative Period to support the beneficiary actions brought in assumpsit.[291]   Once again the expression went to the verge of stating that the plaintiff had the personal right to enforce the contract of another. Yet, once again, the theory failed to develop. It completely disappeared from the cases by the late 18th century. By then, the courts had turned to trust ideas inspired by equity.

If we take our stand at the end of the 18th century, we can see that recognition of the assignee's beneficial interest had progressed far with the aid of the trust concept. The case of *Delaney v. Stoddart* (1785)[292] said that every assignor who allowed his name to be used by the assignee was to be envisaged as a trustee. The court stated in *Winch v. Keeley* (1787),[293] that common law courts had taken "notice" of the trust in order to consider which party to an assignment was beneficially interested. Ashhurst J. justified use of the trust notion in terms of expense, inconvenience and injustice:

> It is true that formerly the Courts of Law did not take notice of an equity or trust; for trusts are within the original jurisdiction of a Court of Equity: but of late years, it has been found productive of great expense to send the parties to the other side of the Hall; wherever this Court have seen that the justice of the case has been clearly with the plaintiff, they have not turned him round upon this

---

[288] *Ibid.*

[289] *Deering v. Farrington* (1674) 1 Mod. 113.

[290] Argument in *Turner v. Goodwin* (1715) 10 Mod. 222, 223.

[291] See *supra*, Chap. II, p. 31 & following.

[292] 1 T.R. 22.

[293] 1 T.R. 619.

objection.[294]

Consequently, the law placed upon the assignor a fiduciary duty to act in good faith toward the assignee and not to exercise any of the legal rights resulting from the prohibition upon assignments. The old insistence upon the use of the assignor's name in litigation still remained, but that formalism was termed but a "shadow" which should never be permitted to work an injustice.[295] The court in *Legh v. Legh* (1799),[296] for example, said it was "against good faith" for a debtor, after assignment, to obtain a release from the assignor and attempt to plead the release as a defense.[297] Thus, by the end of the century the law courts had in reality negated the medieval prohibition, but they ritualistically clung to its forms. The trust notion proved useful because it stated the fiduciary relationship straightforwardly, rather than in the inverted fashion of the agency concept.

B.   Assignment in the Courts of Equity

(a)   Two Varieties of Jurisdiction

The Chancellor's jurisdiction markedly differed according to the nature of the chose assigned. Over so-called *legal* choses (*e.g.*, an obligation to repay borrowed money), his jurisdiction was oblique and limited, because courts of equity generally abstained from enforcing debts and claims arising *ex contractu*.[298] Assignees of legal choses sought the Chancellor's protection to prevent their procuration from being unfairly revoked.[299] Relief in these instances went no farther than to compel the assignor to lend his name to a suit brought at law.[300] Such procuratory relief was available provided the attempted revocation had been arbitrary or motivated by bad faith, but not

---

[294] *Id.* at 622-623.

[295] *Master v. Miller* (1791) 4 T.R. 320, 341, per Buller J.

[296] 1 B. & P. 447.

[297] "In order to defeat the real Plaintiff, this Defendant has colluded with the nominal Plaintiff to obtain a release; and I think therefore the plea of release may be set aside consistently with the general rules of the Court." *Id.* at 448.

[298] *Hammond v. Messenger* (1838) 9 Sim. 327; *Keys v. Williams* (1839) 3 Y. & C. Ex. 462.

[299] *Meechett v. Bradshaw* (1634) Nels. 22.

[300] KEETON AND SHERIDAN, EQUITY, *supra* n. 79, at 201.

when it resulted from mere operation of law, such as by death or marriage.[301]   However, the Chancellor did not limit himself to mere procuratory relief for attorneys. When an "equitable reason or consideration" for the assignment was alleged and proven, the assignee of a legal chose had a remedy in Equity in his own name. The report of *Midloton v. Edwards* (Lincoln's Inn manuscript, 1650-1658)[302] relates that B's debt to A was assigned to plaintiff, who exhibited his bill in Equity to have the debt of B. The defendant (B) demurred on the ground that a chose in action is not assignable in law.

> "The court sayd that a chose in action is assignable in Equity if there be an Equitable reason for the assigning of it, but here is no Equitable reason sett forth in the bill for the assignment, therefore the Court did direct the plaintiff to amend his bill to sett downe upon what Equitable reason and Consideration the chose in action was assigned unto him, for Nota generally no more in Equity than in law is a chose in action assignable unlesse it be upon an equitable Reason, as for payment of debts, etc.

The Chancellor regarded the discharge of a debt as an acceptable reason to enforce an assignment, but he refused relief in other circumstances. In 1675 Lord Keeper Bridgman declared that he would not

> protect the assignment of any chose in action unless in satisfaction of some debt due to the assignee; but not when the debt or *chose in action* is assigned to one to whom the assignee owes nothing precedent, so that the assignment is voluntary or for money then given.[303]

In contrast, the enforcement of *equitable choses* in action (*e.g.*, a life interest under a trust of personalty) fell within the direct and primary jurisdiction of the Chancellor. The doctrines of Chancery gave rise to a

---

[301] *Mitchell v. Eades* (1700) Prec. Ch. 125, 2 Vern. 391; *Earl of Suffolk v. Greenvill* (1641) 3 Rep. Chan. 89, Nelson 15.

[302] Reports in Chancery by a Commissioner (John Lisle?) (1650-1658) p. 27, (Eng. Leg. Ms. Project, Ed. J.H. Baker, mf. 962). See also *Earle of Lincolne v. Serjt. Shield & Lady Delaware, Ibid.*

[303] *Anonymous* (1675) 2 Freem. 145.

distinct class of equitable interests cognizable only in that forum.[304] Furthermore, "*possibilities*" became assignable subject-matter that only the Chancellor would enforce.[305] Although such interests were first recognized in a noncommercial setting, they later proved of great utility to trade. For example, *a future cargo* of a whaling ship, including the oil, head matter, and all that might be caught, could be assigned for the money advanced to finance the expedition.[306] Such forward contracts were of first-rate importance to credit and capital formation during the commercial expansion of the 18th century.

(b)   Contractual Nature of Equitable Assignments

In contrast to the theory at law, the Chancellor treated assignment as a contract that transferred title in the chose to the assignee. "An assignment," said Ld. Hardwicke, "always operates by way of agreement or contract, amounting in the consideration of this court to this, that one agrees with another to transfer, and make good that right or interest; which is made good here by way of agreement."[307]   Given this contractual premise, the Chancellor made consideration the test of the transfer's validity, and allowed the assignee to sue as owner in his own name.[308]   Giving notice to the debtor was important, not to the validity of the assignment, but to bind the debtor to the assignee.[309]

The contractual nature of equitable assignment is not universally accepted. Eminent writers have maintained that all assignments in equity

---

[304] SPENCE, *supra* n. 71, at 855. A legal chose in action would include a debt, bill of exchange, policy of insurance, share in a Company, and a sweepstake ticket, while an equitable chose would refer to such things as a legacy share in a trust fund, a legatee's rights in an unadministered estate etc. SNELL, *supra* n. 252, at 69.

[305] At common-law, by contrast, such assignments were invalid, because a man may sell wool to be shorn from sheep he has, but not from those he is about to buy. *Robinson v. Macdonnell* (1816) 5 M. & S. 228, 236; SPENCE, *supra* n. 71, at 866.

[306] *Langton v. Horton* (1841) 3 Beav. 464.

[307] *Wright v. Wright* (1749) 1 Ves. Sen. 409, 412.

[308] Though the assignor was joined as a party to allow him to dispute the assignment. KEETON & SHERIDAN, EQUITY, *supra* n. 79, at 84; STORY, COMMENTARIES ON EQUITY JURISPRUDENCE, *supra* n. 257, at 305.

[309] Where the agreement to assign a debt was made between the debtor and the debtor's own debtor, or took the form of a direction by a debtor to his agent to pay the plaintiff-creditor, it was necessary for the creditor himself to receive notice. This notice marked an appropriation of a fund to him. *Ex parte South* (1818) 3 Swans. 392; *Kirwan v. Daniel* (1847) 5 Hare 493.

were conceived as being in the nature of a trust.[310]   However, there is really no direct evidence for this generalization. Bailey has denounced the trust theory as a "prevarication of the truth" which, if correct, would mean that no agreement or consideration would be required.[311]   In fact, the trust theory, besides lacking direct support, is rebutted by two facts: (1) the repeated insistence upon consideration by courts of equity, and (2) instances of enforcement without mention of the trust.[312]   Nevertheless, by a variety of means the trust notion has infiltrated into orthodox thought. First, the form that written assignments took was frequently couched in language that described the assignor as a trustee, and this description was simply recognized and echoed by courts of equity.[313]   Second, the trust itself was assignable subject-matter in equity, and the resulting interaction between the contractual vehicle and its equitable contents entailed an inevitable blending of terminology and concepts.[314]   Third, the Chancellor sometimes created and invoked constructive trusts in an unpredictable manner. It may have appeared that he did so in order to enforce the assignment, when oftentimes his purpose in treating the assignee as a trustee was to recognize the equitable property interest of a third person in the assigned chose.[315]   Fourth, the common law judges codified the error by continually saying it was so.

However blended and analogous they may appear, the rules of

---

[310] MARSHALL, *supra* n. 286, at 84; STORY, COMMENTARIES ON EQUITY JURISPRUDENCE, *supra* n. 257 at 305.

[311] Bailey, *supra* n. 124, at 573-574.

[312] *E.g., Peters v. Soame* (1701) 2 Vern. 428, 1 Eq. Ca. Abr. 44.; *Crouch v. Martin* (1707) 2 Vern. 595.

[313] BLACKSTONE, *supra* n. 137, at 442 ("the form of assigning a chose in action is in the nature of a declaration of trust."); Butler's note to Coke's A COMMENTARY UPON LITTLETON, *supra* n. 178, at 232 b ("the form of assigning a chose in action is in the nature of a declaration of trust, and an agreement to permit the assignee to make use of the name of the assignor, in order to recover possession."); Ld. Hardwicke in *Wright v. Wright* (1749) 1 Ves. Sen. 409, 411: "why may not it be put into such shape as to be disposed to a stranger to make him (*i.e.*, the assignor) trustee for a stranger?"

[314] Nevertheless, wherever the trust preexisted the attempted assignment, *e.g., Tyrell v. Hope* (1743) 2 Atk. 558, it was clear that the assignment was not itself regarded as a trust, but simply the mode of transferring it. On the other hand, the separate concepts could be merged in one transaction where the thing assigned was thereby placed in trust. Here, it was said that if the assignment lacked valuable consideration, it was neither valid as an assignment nor as a trust. *Meek v. Keetlewell* (1843) 1 Ph. 342.

[315] *E.g., Ex parte Byas* (1743) 1 Atk. 124; *Bennet v. Davis* (1725) 2 P.Wms 316; *Tyrell v. Hope* (1743) 2 Atk. 558.

assignment have grown up independently of the trust.[316]   Chancery's main achievement was to establish the modern law of assignment upon a contract model.   Three significant facets of this model may now be considered.

(i)   The assignee may sue in his own name

By the late 17th century, it could be observed that certain assignees had brought their own action in equity. There are no decisive holdings on this point, and yet the cases show that soloist actions were permitted. This fact strongly suggests that the Chancellor was not wedded to the "too personal" objection, nor to the formal devices thought necessary to circumvent it. In *Hurst v. Goddard* (1670),[317] a husband who served as adminstrator of his second wife's estate assigned his wife's claim to her unpaid marital portion over to his son by an earlier marriage. The husband then died. On his son's suit to enforce this obligation (originally owed to his stepmother), the chancellor decreed in his favor. This suit was brought in the assignee's own name. The assignor and the original obligee were both dead, the suit was styled under the son's name, and no mention was made of a power of attorney, which in theory would have been revoked in any event by the death of the assignor.[318]   In *Fashion v. Atwood* (1679),[319] certain debts owed to the merchant Atwood were assigned by parol to his factor Pearson in order to even out their account. Pearson thereupon reassigned these same debts to one of his own creditors, "to the use" of all his other creditors. The creditors of Pearson then sued the executrix of Atwood (Atwood having died) to have the benefit of the debts which were due. The Lord Chancellor said,

> By the agreement *Pearson* had a good Title in Equity to the Debts, which in Equity are become his, and are no longer *Atwood's*; and therefore decreed for the Creditors of *Pearson*.[320]

The plaintiff creditors brought suit in their own names without power of attorney and obtained relief. In another case brought in 1701, the report explains that the assignee of a bond brought suit in equity in his own name,

---

[316] WATERS, *supra* n. 215, at 118.

[317] 1 Chan. Cas. 169.

[318] Another case of this type is *Crouch v. Martin* (1701) 2 Vern. 595. The facts show that assignor was dead, and there was no mention of a power of attorney.

[319] 2 Chan. Cas. 6, 36.

[320] *Ibid.*

since the assignor had become a bankrupt, and accordingly the assignee could not sue at law in his assignor's name.[321] Such cases show an uncontested acceptance of the assignee's right to sue, and there is apparently no case in equity in the 18th century in which the assignee was actually denied relief because of this issue.[322] The Chancellor was now enforcing contracts, not actions by "attorneys."

(ii) **The precedent debt fetter is replaced by the consideration test**

The question asked in former times--is there some common interest between assignor and assignee?--also ceased to be relevant in equity by the mid-18th century. Chancery was no longer preoccupied with finding "precedent" debt relationships as a means of rebutting the presumption of maintenance.[323] Maintenance may still have been a significant objection when specifically averred and proven, but it had ceased to be an objection *per se* to assignments.[324] The maintenance fetter gave way to an orthodox consideration requirement and caused assignments to look more contractual than before. It now proved possible to enforce assignments made upon fresh consideration, regardless of the lack of pre-existing ties or prior dealings between the parties.[325] The "stranger" who paid valuable consideration purchased an enforceable assignment.

For example, in *Bates v. Dandy* (1741),[326] a husband borrowed funds from the plaintiff, and as security for the loan he promised to make an assignment of certain mortgages which had been previously assigned to his wife. The question was whether this bare promise to assign, without more, amounted to a disposition to the plaintiff for purposes of satisfying the loan. It was held by Lord Hardwicke that the husband had the power to assign his wife's chose for his own use, and had done so validly. The Chancellor did not

---

[321] *Peters v. Soame* (1701) 2 Vern. 428, 1 Eq. Ca. Abr. 44.

[322] Some authors have stated that Blackstone held the view that the formalism was as fully requisite in equity as it was at law. But Blackstone, in fact, while he clearly said that the action at law must be in the creditor's name, made no such assertion about equity. BLACKSTONE, supra n. 137, at 442. *See* MARSHALL, *supra* n. 286 at 73.

[323] HOLDSWORTH, *supra* n. 11, at 536.

[324] We have already noted that by 1677, there was no longer a presumption at common law. *Deering v. Farrington* (1674) 1 Mod. 113.

[325] *Row v. Dawson* (1749) 1 Ves. Sen. 331; *Whitfield v. Fausset* (1740) 1 Ves. Sen. 387.

[326] 2 Atk. 207.

inquire about a precedent debt between the borrower and the lender, and there apparently was none. The consideration of the assignment was the money then advanced by the plaintiff. The Chancellor stated: "The husband may assign the wife's chose in action, or a possibility that the wife is entitled to . . . so that it be not voluntary, but for a valuable consideration."[327]

The mention of "valuable consideration" points to the reason for the disappearance of the precedent debt rule. The influence of consideration in equity had become as nearly important as the waning fear of maintenance. The Chancellor saw little to differentiate assignments from agreements generally. If assignments were to be conceptually fit within a contractual framework, the requirement of valuable consideration ought to apply.[328] One of the earliest traces of such a development is found in a declaration by Lord Nottingham in 1675: "although such a note is not assignable in Law, yet is it in Equity, when there is a valuable consideration.[329]

The insistence upon consideration led to the rule that voluntary assignments should not be aided.[330] The Chancellor was not willing to enforce the functional equivalent of a third party beneficiary contract without this element. Of course, in shifting from precedent debt to concurrent consideration, the Chancellor was also making more than doctrinal adjustments. He could not have been unaware that, commercially speaking, he was reaching a highly supportable result that permitted freer transferability of choses in action.

---

[327] *Id.* at 208.

[328] "Consideration is necessary to the assignment of a *chose in action* unless a trust is declared or created..." W.R. Anson, "Assignment of Choses in Action," [1901] 17 L.Q.R. 90, 94. Jenks' claim that valuable consideration was never established as a general requirement for equitable assignments, except for the assignment of possibilities, is not persuasively demonstrated by his evidence. EDWARD JENKS, A SHORT HISTORY OF ENGLISH LAW, 5th ed. (Methuen, 1938), pp. 302-303. The considerable controversy on this point is surveyed in R.E. Megarry, "Consideration and Equitable Assignments of Legal Choses In Action," [1943] 59 L.Q.R. 58.

[329] *Corderoy's Case* (1675) 1 Freem. 312.

[330] *Squib. v. Wyn* (1717) 1 P.Wms. 378.

(iii)   **The assignee takes subject to equities against the assignor**

The lineage of this rule may well be very old, but no trace of it could be found before the 17th century.[331] We know almost nothing about its source or inspiration. The rule linked the creditor, debtor and assignee together, as if all three had been the original contracting parties. Undoubtedly, this would have served to reduce a multiplicity of suits, and it also tended to make irrelevant the old legal argument that assignments exposed the debtor to the danger of double payment. There would be natural concern in allowing A's debt to be transferred to C, where B had not in fact discharged A.[332] The Chancellors' procedures, however, reduced the risk of double exposure by permitting the joinder of B, as a party to the suit. Furthermore, the rule reflected the mutual dependency of contractual promise. The debtor's assertion of equities against B, let alone against B's assignee, could hardly have been recognized if equity were a system that adhered strictly to the independent covenant rule.[333] Some evidence suggests that, at least in the beginning, the rule may have been conceived by analogy to the procuration at common law. The Chancellor may have thought that an attorney should not escape from the equities available against his principal.[334] It had been decreed that the fraud of an agent bound his principal.[335] Therefore, why should the fraud of the principal not bind the agent? But whether or not the Chancellor originally conceived the rule from this model is not only uncertain, but historically moot. For such an explanation would have become extremely anachronistic after assignment became freely contractual in the 18th century. When assignments made on fresh consideration to any stranger could be brought in the assignee's name, then the source of the rule could no longer lie in a fictitious agency notion.

---

[331] Two of the earliest examples are *Porter v. Hubbart* (1672) 3 Ch. R. 78, and *Ashcomb's Case* (1674) 1 Chan. Cas. 232.

[332] Brooke, Dette, pl. 177; citing Y.B. (1496) 11 Hen. VI 7, 16.

[333] Chancery freed itself at any early date from the independent covenant rule. William McGovern, *supra* n. 16, at 674. Mutuality was inherent in the rule that a party demanding the execution of an agreement had to show that there had been no default in performing all that was to be done on his part. GILBERT, A TREATISE OF EQUITY, *supra* n. 97, at 42-43.

[334] "And the principle arises on this ground, that they are considered not as purchasers for a valuable consideration, in the proper sense of those words, but as voluntary assignees and *personal representatives* and are therefore distinguished from particular assignees." *Peters v. Soame* (1701) 2 Vern. 428, 429, 1 Eq. Ca. Abr. 44. note (1).

[335] *Jennings v. Moore* (1708) 2 Vern. 609.

Whatever the origin of the rule, it clearly possessed one important advantage. It guaranteed that the original property rights and defenses of debtors and third persons would not be lost through an assignment. In one case, the marital portion due to a wife was protected against the claims of her husband's assignees. The Chancellor conceived her marriage settlement to be in the nature of a trust, and then reasoned that since her husband (the assignor) was a trustee for her, so his assignees became her trustees also.[336] In another case, it was held that a moneylender's security interest in his debtor's assets were vested prior to the assignment and should prevail over subsequent claims by assignees of those assets.[337] Also, where a bond was originally obtained from the debtor by an "underhand agreement," the debtor would not be liable to assignees of that bond. Due to this defense, it was reasoned that the property to the bond had not entered into the assignor's estate *ab initio*.[338]

These examples show that in protecting vested interests, the Chancellor often invoked constructive trusts and made the debtor the *cestui que trust* thereunder.[339] He could also protect the debtor by stressing that no assignor could transfer greater rights or title than he actually had.[340] These familiar rationales also meant that even the purchaser for a valuable consideration was not freed from this defense.[341] Assignees of bills and notes, however, took them free of defenses. This was a special negotiability, however, created in favor of trade, which prevailed in equity from at least the early part of the 18th century.[342]

Throughout the 18th century, the Chancellor was conscious of strong commercial pressure to repudiate the proprietary rule of offsetting equities, and he sought to assist the assignee through use of the consideration doctrine. For ranged against the obligor's vested interest was the contractual interest of the assignee who had given full and valuable consideration. An assignee who had paid *valuable* consideration had a strong case for relief, but his interest

---

[336] *Tyrell v. Hope* (1743) 2 Atk. 558.

[337] *Ex parte Byas* (1743) 1 Atk. 124.

[338] *Turton v. Benson* (1718) 1 P.Wms. 496.

[339] *E.g., Tyrell v. Hope* (1743) 2 Atk. 558; *Ex parte Byas* (1743) 1 Atk. 124; *Bennet v. Davis* (1725) 2 P.Wms. 316.

[340] *Purdew v. Jackson* (1824) 1 Russ. 1, 69.

[341] *Trott v. Dawson* (1721) 1 P.Wms. 780.

[342] *Peters v. Soame* (1701) 2 Vern. 428 1 Eq. Ca. Abr. 44.; *Coles v. Jones* (1715) 2 Vern. 692.

was not automatically deemed superior.[343] The effort to protect the wife's marital portion from her husband's power to assign it was an illustration of the struggle between two interests. Considerable headway in favor of the assignee was made in *Sir Edward Turner's Case* (1681).[344] Parliament reversed a decision of the Chancellor in favor of the wife's rights, and held that Chief Baron Turner had the right to alienate a term that had been placed in trust for his wife by her former husband. Following this came a series of decisions favoring the purchaser assignee over the wife.[345] In 1742, Lord Hardwicke observed in retrospect: "In these cases you observe the particular contract of the husband for a valuable consideration, has got the better of the wife's equity to have a provision."[346] But Lord Hardwicke now countered with his own contribution: the wife's right to a provision "attached to the thing itself," and followed the assignment wherever it went.[347] The assignee of the husband took subject to the same equity. Thus, the Chancellor would not allow the creditor to receive the whole fortune of the wife without making provision for her.[348] By the end of the century, the question was settled in favor of protecting her vested rights.[349] With or without consideration, a husband not in possession of his wife's chose in action could not transfer to another a right superior to hers.[350] It was said in retrospect that,

> An opinion has certainly prevailed that a distinction subsists between an assignment by operation of law and an assignment for a valuable consideration to an individual by contract; that the former is no bar to the right of the surviving wife, but that the latter is. Yet the earlier prevailing opinion was erroneous, because all assignments pass only the interest which the husband had: How can he for valuable

---

[343] 2 Eq. Ca. Abr. 85.

[344] 1 Vern. 7.

[345] *Hill v. Caillovel* (1748) 1 Ves. Sen. 122.

[346] *Jewson v. Moulson* (1742) 2 Atk. 417, 421.

[347] *Id.* at 419.

[348] *Tudor v. Samyne* (1692) 2 Vern. 270; *Pit v. Hunt* (1681) 1 Vern. 18; *Packer v. Wyndham* (1715) Prec. Ch. 412; *Walter v. Saunders* (1703) 1 Eq. Ca. Abr. 58; *Bosvil v. Brander* (1718) 1 P.Wms. 458.

[349] *Jewson v. Moulson* (1742) 2 Atk. 417.

[350] *See* the lengthy note by Peere Williams appended to *Bosvil v. Brander* (1718) 1 P.Wms. 458. *See also*, the exhaustive argument and opinion in *Purdew v. Jackson* (1824) 1 Russ. 1.

consideration or otherwise convey more than he has?[351]

The Chancellor had opted for a proprietary rule, and he declined to carve out protection for the *bona fide* purchaser.

V.   THE CLOSE OF THE CHANCERY PHASE AND THE DECLINE OF EQUITY

In the period 1680-1800, Chancery stood in marked contrast to the common law. While the latter entertained almost no actions and gave no recoveries, equity continued to expand the beneficiary action through a variety of means. In doctrinal terms, three factors explained the Chancellor's nonobservance of the privity of contract limitation: the delayed reception (and early unimportance) of consideration; the recognition of proprietary and promissory rights of the beneficiary under the trust; and the enforceability of assignments of choses in action.

By the year 1800, however, equity itself had begun to decline in influence, and the vigor of its doctrines was accordingly diminished. The doctrine of consideration became technical, and the privity conception in *Bourne v. Mason* would be in time accepted. The once-flexible trust, particularly one in favor of creditors, would be reclassified as a contract of agency. The Chancellor began to practice abstention in the use of the constructive trust. In short, advantageous doctrines were changed or were no longer serviceable. Furthermore, the next century marked the rise of a new privity principle in contract, and the Chancellor himself was instrumental in imposing the new privity limitation upon his remedial freedom. The close of the Chancery Phase evidenced a growing convergence of the two systems.

---

[351] *Burnett v. Kinnaston* (1700) 2 Vern. 401; *Purdew v. Jackson* (1824) 1 Russ. 1, 63 & 69.

CHAPTER IV

THE RISE OF THE PARTIES-ONLY PRINCIPLE (1800-1890)

I. INTRODUCTION AND SUMMARY

The fate of the beneficiary action in the 19th century was one of decline and eventual demise. The explanation was the emergence of peremptory objection to the third party claim. A new principle stipulated that only the parties to a contract could enforce it, and it now operated concurrently with the older rule requiring the plaintiff to be "privy to the consideration." This chapter is primarily concerned with three general questions about this development: When did the parties-only principle arise, from where did it originate, and what legal institutions and doctrines were instrumental in its development? These questions require us to follow many winding paths of law and equity. Therefore, before proceeding with detailed discussion the reader will benefit from a brief summary.

The arguments of this chapter must be in part negative. The first aim is to counter the orthodox assumption that the "parties-only" principle originated as an interior development of assumpsit.[1] Contrary to what modern contract texts maintain, the principle was not introduced by the cases of *Price v. Easton* (1833)[2] and *Tweddle v. Atkinson* (1861).[3] These cases were decided on the basis of the traditional consideration rule, and they were concerned with adapting that rule to the mutuality requirements of the modern law of contract.

The second aim is constructive, the search for authentic sources lying outside of assumpsit. These nineteenth century sources were will theory received from the Continent, native principle in the action of covenant, and

---

[1] As to the interior function of privity, see above Chap. I, pp. 15-19.

[2] (1833) 4 B. & Ad. 433.

[3] (1861) 1 B. & S. 393, 30 L.J.Q.B. 265, 4 Law Times 468.

the rise of this principle in the fields of trust, tort and quasi-contract.

These sources, are cumulative, may not be exhaustive, and are referred to in the narrow sense appropriate to a doctrinal account of legal development. Only limited attention can be given to the larger background, but mention will be made of the rise of contract as a systematic subject, the decline of equity as a legal force and with this decline, the debilitation of its key beneficiary doctrines.

II. THE CONTINUITY OF THE CONSIDERATION TEST IN ASSUMPSIT

At the close of the Formative Period consideration-based privity had prevailed over several competing notions in *assumpsit*,[4] and the period between 1680 and 1800 was conspicuously inactive for the beneficiary action at common law. When we pick up this story again in the 19th century the consideration test remained the sole operative test of privity in assumpsit. At the beginning of the century, prestigious judges like Mansfield and Buller and learned authors like Livermore and Story declared themselves in favor of the beneficiary action, stating that when a contract is made with A for the benefit of B, B may sue upon it.[5] The consideration-based test had changed remarkably little over the years. From the beginning of the century down to 1861, the most-cited formulation was that "consideration must move from the *plaintiff.*" This phraseology is found in the first edition of Selwyn's *Nisi Prius* (1808).[6] It is thereafter continued in the Exchequer Chamber decision of *Bowen v. Morris* (1810),[7] in *Price v. Easton* (1833),[8] in Joseph Chitty's treatise

---

[4] *Supra*, Chap II, pp. 74-83.

[5] Ld. Mansfield said in *Martyn v. Hynde*, (1776) 2 Cowper 437 that "as to the case of *Dutton v. Poole*, it is a matter of surprise, how a doubt could have arisen in that case." In *Marchington v. Vernon* (1787), 1 Bos. & Pul. 98, 101 n.(c), an action of assumpsit upon a bill of exchange, Buller J. said that independent of the rules which prevail in mercantile transactions if one person makes a promise to another for the benefit of a third, that third person may maintain an action upon it." *See also Company of Feltmakers v. David* (1797) 1 Bos. & Pul. 98, 101, arg. of Serjt. Le Blanc and remarks of Ch. J. Eyre; SAMUEL LIVERMORE, LAW OF PRINCIPAL AND AGENT 12-13 (Baltimore, 1818) who describes the above rule as "the better opinion"; and JOSEPH STORY, COMMENTARIES ON THE LAW OF AGENCY p. 408, n.2 (Boston, 1839).

[6] WILLIAM SELWYN, AN ABRIDGEMENT OF THE LAW OF NISI PRIUS (Farrand, 1807-08), vol I. p. 45. The formula is thereafter repeated through 13 editions stretching to 1869.

[7] 2 Taunt. 374 (in argument).

[8] 4 B. & Ad. 433, 434 (per Denman J.).

(1848)[9] and in *Thomas v. Thomas* (1842).[10] There were also other versions of the rule in the books. In Petersdorff 's *Abridgement* (1843) we find it said, "Plaintiff must not be a stranger to the consideration."[11] Incidentally, this particular phraseology was taken verbatim from *Bourne v. Mason* (1669) and *Crow v. Rogers* (1720). We also find in *Comyns Digest* (1822) that "the legal interest in the simple contract resides with the party from whom its consideration moves."[12]

A slightly different version placed the accent upon the promisee's relationship to the consideration. In an 1813 case, arising when a shipping agent sued a carrier for his principal's missing or misdelivered goods, Lord Ellenborough stated--

> This action well lies. There is a privity of contract established between these parties by means of the bill of lading. That states that the goods were shipped by the plaintiffs and that the freight for them was paid by the plaintiffs in London. To the plaintiffs, therefore, from whom the consideration moves, and to whom the promise is made, the defendant is liable for the non-delivery of the goods.[13]

In 1842, Henry Stephen substituted the word "promisee" for that of plaintiff in the consideration formula,[14] and in *Tweddle v. Atkinson* (1861), Crompton J. could say "the promisee cannot bring an action unless the consideration moved from him.[15]

Clearly all of these renditions were species of the consideration

---

[9] JOSEPH CHITTY, A PRACTICAL TREATISE ON THE LAW OF CONTRACTS NOT UNDER SEAL, (7th Amer. Ed. by Perkins; Merriam, 1848) p. 53.

[10] 2 Q.B. 851, 859 (per Patteson J.).

[11] CHARLES PETERSDORFF, A PRACTICAL AND ELEMENTARY ABRIDGEMENT OF THE CASES (Baldwin, Cradock, & Joy 1825), vol. III, p. 40.

[12] SIR JOHN COMYNS, A DIGEST OF THE LAWS OF ENGLAND, (5th ed. by Hammond; Strahan, 1822) vol. I, p. 304, note (p).

[13] *Joseph v. Knox* (1813) 3 Camp. 320. *See also*, the argument in *Dawes v. Peck* (1800) 8 T.R. 330. For a modern discussion, see "The Albazero" [1976] 3 All E.R. 129.

[14] HENRY J. STEPHEN, NEW COMMENTARIES ON THE LAWS OF ENGLAND (1842 reprint ed., Garland Publishing, 1979), vol. II, p. 115.

[15] 1 B. & S. 393, at 398.

doctrine, and did not lead of themselves to markedly different substantive results upon application. They do not yet assert that only a party to a contract may sue upon it. The dominant privity test at law, both before and at the time of *Tweddle v. Atkinson,* was still the test of consideration.

A.   The "Promisee in Law" Corollary

As we noted in Chapter II[16] a corollary to the consideration test was a rule of pleadings requiring the beneficiary to allege that he was the promisee even though he was not. This fictional allegation was based upon the so-called "promisee in law" theory. The distinction between a promise in law intended for the beneficiary and a promise in fact made to the actual promisee came to light in 1651.[17] This rule was still accepted in the 19th century. It required that where B had made a promise to A for C's benefit, but the consideration for B's promise actually moved from C rather than A, then C (the plaintiff) had to declare *as if* he had received the promise directly from B. Saunders, in his treatise on pleading, understood this fiction to mean that it will be "intended" that the contract was made with the party from whom the consideration proceeded.[18]   Addison used the metaphor "the consideration may be said to draw after it the promise, so that the promise to whomsoever in fact made, shall follow the consideration."[19]   The notion of consideration "drawing" or pulling the promise to it was an accepted figure of speech. C. J. Gibson of Pennsylvania said in *Edmundson v. Penny* that "The plaintiff must unite in his person both the promise and the consideration of it; and if the action, in such a case, cannot be sustained on the foundation of the consideration by drawing the promise to it, it cannot be sustained at all."[20]   "In other words," wrote Thomas Street, "the consideration may draw the legal promise to it, but the promise alone cannot draw the right of action to the promisee in fact, where the consideration moves from another

---

[16] *See* pp. 50 ff.

[17] *Starkey v. Mill* (1651) Style 296.

[18] JOHN S. SAUNDERS, THE LAW OF PLEADING AND EVIDENCE IN CIVIL ACTIONS, 2nd ed. by Lush, (Small, 1851), p. 193.

[19] CHARLES G. ADDISON, A TREATISE ON THE LAW OF CONTRACTS, 3rd Amer. ed. by Morgan, (Crockcroft, 1875-76), p. 246. *Accord,* SIR ROBERT LUSH, LUSH'S PRACTICE OF THE SUPERIOR COURTS OF COMMON LAW AT WESTMINSTER, 2nd ed. by Stephen (Butterworths, 1856), p. 7

[20] (1845) 1 Pa. St. 335.

source."[21]

These authorities not only show that the beneficiary had to allege as if he were the promisee,[22] but that far into the 19th century, a dualist objection had not been recognized. The parties-only or promisee-only rule was still subordinated and suppressed at the level of the pleadings. The orthodox lawyer in the first half of the 19th century took a monist view of privity, but his unitary view was substantively the reverse of that put forward today. The modern reversal took place during the second half of the century. Somehow the old rule of pleadings became a substantive principle; the old corollary became a major premise of the law of contract. It has been often asserted that this remolding of the law came about as a result of two judicial precedents. This view is a serious misunderstanding that mandates reexamination of these alleged sources of the parties-only privity rule.

B.   A Review of Two "Precedents"

Price v. Easton (1833)[23]

In *Price v. Easton*, William, who was an employee of the defendant, owed plaintiff £13. The defendant-employer promised William that if his future earnings were left in defendant's hands, then he (the defendant) would pay off the debt to the plaintiff. The plaintiff was not a party to this promise. It was averred that William thereafter earned a large sum of money and left it in defendant's hands, but the debt was not paid. Plaintiff sued for breach of promise, but the court rejected the claim.

Both Anson and Pollock maintained that this rejection stemmed from

---

[21] THOMAS A. STREET, FOUNDATIONS OF LEGAL LIABILITY, vol. II p. 154 (Thompson, 1906).

[22] JOSEPH CHITTY, A TREATISE ON PLEADING AND PARTIES TO ACTIONS, 6th ed. (1836), pp. 4-5; ADDISON, *supra* n. 19; SAUNDERS, *supra* n. 19. *See generally, supra* n.21 at 154. For similar pronouncements in cases, see *Co. of Feltmakers v. Davis* (1797) 1 Bos. & Pul. 98, 102 (per Eyre J.); *Edmundson v. Penny* (1845) 1 Pa. St. 335 (per Gibson C. J.). STEPHEN M. LEAKE, THE ELEMENTS OF THE LAW OF CONTRACTS (Stevens, 1867), p. 221 (marginal note stating "a contract affects parties only.").

[23] 4 B. & Ad. 433.

the parties-only principle.[24] This interpretation is clearly mistaken. Let us start with the arguments made to the court. The authorities pressed by the defendant were not modern. All, save one, were cases from the Formative Period, and the consideration test of *Bourne* and *Crow* was stressed. The plaintiff, on the other hand, argued the "interest" and "benefit" theories put forward in the cases from the Formative Period. In sum, neither the authorities nor the arguments of counsel suggest that a parties-only principle was advocated to the court.

There was also no reference to the parties-only principle in the opinions of the judges in the Court of King's Bench:

Denman, C. J. I think the declaration cannot be supported as it does not shew any consideration for the promise moving from the plaintiff to the defendant.

Littledale J. No privity is shown between the plaintiff and defendant. This case is precisely like *Crow v. Rogers* (1 Str. 582) and must be governed by it.

Taunton J. It is consistent with all the matter alleged in the declaration that the plaintiff may have been entirely ignorant of the arrangement between William Price and the defendant.

Patteson J. After verdict, the Court can only intend that all matters were proved which were requisite to support the allegations in the declaration, or what is necessary to be implied from them. Now it is quite clear that the allegations in this declaration are not sufficient to shew a right of action in the plaintiff. There is no promise to the plaintiff alleged. The rule for arresting the judgment must be made absolute.[25]

It is difficult to misunderstand Denman and Littledale J. J. They quoted the consideration rule and a chief authority for it. Anson ignored their opinions, however, and descended upon Patteson J.'s opinion. Here, he italicized Patteson's statement "no promise to the plaintiff [is] alleged" as support for the proposition that plaintiff had to be a party to the contract. The operative word in that sentence, however, is the word "alleged." Patteson

---

[24] SIR WILLIAM ANSON, PRINCIPLES OF THE ENGLISH LAW OF CONTRACT, 274, 2nd Amer. ed. (Callaghan, 1887). SIR FREDERICK POLLOCK, PRINCIPLES OF CONTRACT, 195, 1st Amer. ed. (Clarke, 1881).

[25] *Price v. Easton* (1833) 4 B. & Ad. 433, 434, 435.

J. was raising a deficiency in the allegations of the declaration. He was alluding to the technical promisee in law concept, which required this fictitious allegation in order to satisfy the formal writ of assumpsit. Plaintiff did not have to be a party to the contract, but he needed to allege that he was. As we have seen, this fiction had no application unless the plaintiff had furnished consideration. Therefore, whereas Denman and Littledale J. J. stressed the substantive privity defect in terms of consideration, Patteson J. stressed a formal, and perhaps curable, defect of the pleadings. There was no justification to conclude that the court was divided over the proper test, or applied anything but the consideration test.

The Rule in Tweddle v. Atkinson[26]

The holding in *Tweddle v. Atkinson* (1861) has been almost universally acknowledged to be the origin of the parties-only rule, but this, too, is a basic misconception. The declaration was in assumpsit upon a written postnuptial agreement between plaintiff's father and plaintiff's father-in-law, who was named William Guy. The two fathers respectively undertook to pay plaintiff a particular sum by a specified date and further agreed that plaintiff could enforce their undertakings in any court of law or equity.[27] Plaintiff's father-in-law died without having paid £200, as he had promised to do, and the report also suggests that plaintiff's father, for his own part, had not yet paid £100 as he had promised. Plaintiff brought suit against the decedent's executor. The Court of Queen's Bench, composed of Wightman, Crompton and Blackburn J. J., held on demurrer that the action was not maintainable.

Each judge found plaintiff's action to be barred by a consideration rule which they enunciated with consistency. Wightman J. said, "it is now established that no stranger to the consideration can take advantage of a

---

[26] (1861) 1 B. & S. 393, 30 L.J. Q.B. 265, 4 Law Times 468.

[27] The agreement provided:

> "Memorandum of an agreement made this day between William Guy . . . and John Tweddle . . . . Whereas it is mutually agreed that the said William Guy shall and will pay the sum of £200 to William Tweddle, his son-in-law; and the said John Tweddle, father to the aforesaid William Tweddle, shall and will pay £100 to the said William Tweddle, each and severally the said sums on or before the 21st day of August, 1855. And it is hereby further agreed . . . that the said William Tweddle has full power to sue the said parties in any Court of law or equity for the aforesaid sums hereby promised and specified." *Tweddle v. Atkinson* (1861) 1 B. & S. 393, 394.

contract, although made for his benefit."[28] Crompton's rendering was, "the promisee cannot bring an action unless the consideration moved from him."[29] Similarly, Blackburn stated that "no action can be maintained upon a promise unless the consideration moves from the party to whom it is made."[30] With only slight emendation, Crompton's and Blackburn's phraseology may be regarded as being the source of the rule that consideration must move from the promisee. Yet, this exposes the enigma of the supposed provenance of the parties-only principle. If it truly derives from *Tweddle*, where is it found in the decision? No actual declaration of the principle was made,[31] and there was no attempt to overturn or discredit the competing "promisee in law" theory. Moreover, if we assume for purposes of argument that the principle is to be traced to this case, then the holding should have been much simpler. The plaintiff's suit would have been dismissed, simply because he was not the promisee, regardless of whether he had given consideration or not. In truth, the case was not decided upon that principle, but was reasoned solely in terms of the consideration doctrine and the principle of mutuality of consideration.

A Reappraisal of Tweddle's Case

A reexamination of *Tweddle's Case* might begin with this query: Why did both Crompton J. and Blackburn J. modify the existing consideration rule by insisting that consideration must move from the promisee rather than from the plaintiff? Was this an attempt to establish a parties-only rule, or was it rather a response to some other issue in the case? An overlooked issue was responsible for this modification.

---

[28] *Id.* at 397. Wightman's phrase "no stranger to the consideration," (appearing in Best and Smith's report), was reported in precisely the same terms in 4 Law Times 468 at 469. In a third report, however (30 L.J. Q.B. 266), Wightman J. is made to state a parties-only rule: "no stranger can take advantage of a contract made with another person." The discrepancy seems to result simply from the omission of the word consideration by this last report.

[29] 1 B. & S. 393, 398. The rule stated by Crompton J. was reported in 4 L.T. 468, 469 in a different manner: "a stranger to the consideration cannot sue upon it." Another report has Crompton J. saying during argument, "an action cannot be brought by the person with whom the contract is not made." While this looks to be a parties-only rule it may be an inaccuracy or may be in context referring to the consideration rule.

[30] *Id.* at 398, 399. In 30 L.J. Q.B. this is reported as "a man cannot sue in assumpsit unless the consideration runs from him."

[31] Crompton however, said: "The modern cases have, in effect, overruled the old decisions; they show that the consideration must move from the party entitled to sue upon the contract. *Tweddle v. Atkinson*, 1 B & S 393, at 398 (1861).

It will be recalled that the father-in-law's promise of marriage money or dowry was postnuptial. At the time of the agreement, plaintiff had married defendant's daughter. No valuable consideration of marriage could move from the plaintiff after the fact, because past consideration was no consideration. Wightman J. brought out this point in argument:

> "In that case *[Dutton v. Poole]* the promise was made before marriage. In this case the promise is post nuptial, and the whole consideration on both sides is between the two fathers.[32]

Accordingly, since plaintiff could not show that he had furnished consideration personally, he attempted to argue that he had furnished it in the vicarious sense approved in Dutton v. Poole, (*i.e.*, by showing his near relationship to a promisee who had made a reciprocal promise). The central problem for this argument, however, would be the authority attributed to the holding in *Dutton v. Poole*.

The three judges of the Court of Queen's Bench were all agreed that *Dutton v. Poole* (1680) was no longer law. They stated that the "near relationship" exception had not been applied by any court since 1680, and the modern decisions, particularly the case of *Price v. Easton* (1833)[33] had in the meantime established the previously-quoted rule that no stranger to the consideration can take advantage of a contract, although made for his benefit.[34] Crompton and Wightman J.J. stated that the modern cases had "in effect" (though not explicitly) overruled the old decisions. Blackburn J. believed that *Dutton v. Poole* was no longer binding for the distinct reason that the statute 27 Eliz. C.4 had struck at "the very root" of the decision and had made a consideration of natural love and affection insufficient to ground an assumpsit.[35] In short, the court reasoned that since *Dutton v. Poole* was no longer law, then the exception embodied in it was nonexistent in 1861 and the plaintiff must lose since he had furnished no consideration. The Court's judgment for defendant thus rested solely upon the consideration doctrine,

---

[32] (1861) 1 B. & S. 393, 396.

[33] 4 B. & Ad. 433.

[34] 1 B. & S. 393, 398 (per Wightman J.).

[35] 30. L.J. Q.B. 265, 267-268. Crompton and Wightman J.J. additionally indicated that a consideration of natural love and affection was an anomalous basis for a son to sue his father upon: "Your argument will lead to this, that the son might bring an action against the father on the ground of natural love and affection." 1 B. & S. 393, 396 (per Crompton J.).

and there was no reference to a parties-only principle.[36]

One aspect of the case, however, suggests the court's deep receptivity to this result. The judges found an action based upon near relationship difficult to reconcile with general contract principle,[37] and their chief concern in this regard was the lack of mutuality between the plaintiff and defendant. This issue provoked a strong objection by Crompton and Wightman, J.J. during the course of George Mellish's argument.[38]

> Mellish--But it is submitted that an exception exists in the case where a father is making a provision for his children, the nearness of the relationship giving them the benefit of the consideration; and, in truth, justice is in favour of the exception.
>
> Crompton, J.--There must be mutuality; do you say that the plaintiff is liable to be sued, as well as competent to sue?
>
> Wightman, J.--That is the great difficulty; there is no mutuality or reciprocity."

Then Crompton J. reemphasized this objection in his opinion:

> "It would be a monstrous proposition to say that a person was a party to the contract for the purpose of suing upon it for his own

---

[36] The structure and form of the argument bears out its exclusive focus upon the consideration rule and its exception. The structure was:

(i) Edward James argues that plaintiff cannot sue because he is a stranger to the agreement and the consideration, citing *Price v. Easton*. He is then stopped, the court apparently agreeing with him.

(ii) George Mellish Q.C. agrees with James as to the general rule, but argues that there is a near-relation exception embodied in *Dutton v. Poole* which he contends has never been overruled. James is not called upon to reply to this.

(iii) The court holds that *Dutton v. Poole* has no present validity and the exception does not exist. Therefore Edward James wins.

[37] Crompton J. said, "We should upset all the principles of the law of contracts if we held that the plaintiff could recover in this action." 30 L.J.Q.B. 265, 267.

[38] 30 L.J.Q.B. 265, 266. For a similar account of the argument, *see* 1 B. & S. 393, 395-397.

advantage, and not a party to it for the purpose of being sued."[39]

In the annals of the beneficiary action here was the first appearance of an objection based upon mutuality. Much could be read into this objection, perhaps the implied existence of a parties-only principle,[40] but in context the objection was directed at the lack of mutuality in the considerations and the performances under the contract. The basis of the objection was the court's fear that plaintiff's action, if allowed, would require defendant to render a present performance even though the plaintiff's father had not performed. As Professor Atiyah has correctly noted, "the *[Tweddle]* Court declined to assist him, chiefly because they seem to have thought it would be unfair if the groom could sue his father-in-law, and yet be free from liability if his own father failed to make his contribution."[41]   Accordingly if plaintiff were deemed competent to sue on his father-in-law's promise but not competent to be sued on his father's promise, then defendant would have no opportunity to assert the defense of failure of consideration.[42]   Furthermore, it was unclear what alternative remedy defendant might have. Mellish argued to the court that according to the old cases only the beneficiary was entitled to bring suit to enforce such promises.[43]   If this was true the defendant was left without any means to enforce his original inducement, and this remedial void was hardly improved by the improbable hope that plaintiff himself would sue his own father. Even if defendant was entitled to sue plaintiff's father, he would face considerable expense and uncertainty of ever recovering. In any case, a present performance in return for a future law suit was not thought to be mutuality of contract. Even modern systems that grant the beneficiary action in principle would not allow the action in similar circumstances, for in these systems the promisor would be entitled to assert all defenses and unfulfilled conditions against the beneficiary that he might have asserted

---

[39] 1 B. & S. 393, 398.

[40] If mutuality means that a beneficiary cannot sue unless he is liable on the burden of the obligation, then it follows that no beneficiary action is possible. A third person cannot be held liable on the burden of a contract between others, and even if he could be there might be a logical contradiction in calling him a beneficiary.

[41] P.S. ATIYAH, THE RISE AND FALL OF FREEDOM OF CONTRACT (Oxford University Press, 1979), p. 143.

[42] Nor indeed to assert any other defense between the original parties.

[43] *Id.* at 396.

against the promisee.[44]

It should be conceded that the thrust of the mutuality objection would lose its force had the evidence been that, at the time of suit, plaintiff's father had already paid in full. However, there was no evidence to this effect. The case was decided upon declaration and demurrer without evidence being taken. The plaintiff's declaration only stated that the defendant was in default, no mention being made of his own father's payment or nonpayment. The factual vacuum left by the plea of demurrer gave the court leeway to screen for potential unfairness to defendant and thereby to adopt the view that the contract was, or at least might be, lacking in mutuality in the event of a mutual default. Indeed the judges seemed to have gone beyond making assumptions favorable to defendant. Their remarks and arguments[45] indicate direct knowledge of plaintiff's father's default.[46]

This analysis of the case shows why plaintiff's reliance upon *Dutton's Case* was unsuccessful. In *Dutton*, the promisee (Grizil's father) had fully performed his own promise (no trees were cut), and her brother who inherited the land had received the full benefit of the promisee's performance. Grizil successfully sought counterperformance from one who had received a performance. What result, however, would have obtained had Grizil's father not performed his promise? In the 17th century promises were still independent covenants.[47] The father's nonperformance would not have affected his own right to sue, nor the derivative rights of his daughter. The 19th century courts, however, were no longer able to accept the conclusion that so long as consideration (in the sense of a promise for a promise) had originally moved from the promisee, the promisor was unconditionally bound. The 19th century judges had come to believe that in most bilateral contracts each promisor bargains for performance, as well as for a promise. They believed, as Corbin phrased it, that "something in exchange for nothing is not

---

[44] For French law, *see* WEILL ET TERRE, LES OBLIGATIONS §§ 540-545 (Précis Dalloz 1975); for American law, *see generally* RESTATEMENT (2nd) CONTRACTS §§ 302-315 (A.L.I. 1981). See the discussion below in Chapter V, pp. 246-247.

[45] For example Wightman J.'s question: "If the father of the plaintiff had paid the £100 which he promised, might not he have sued the father of the plaintiff's wife on his express promise?" 1 B. & S. 393, 397.

[46] It may have been acquired from an unrecorded remark of counsel.

[47] A.W.B. SIMPSON, A HISTORY OF THE COMMON LAW OF CONTRACT 463 (Oxford University Press, 1975).

justice even though the one getting nothing has a good law suit."[48]   Under
the independent promises doctrine prevailing at the time of *Dutton*, the
father's promise, not his performance, was the consideration; whereas in the
19th century, the father's performance as well as his promise were the
consideration.[49]

New Doctrines of Dependent Promises and Failure of Consideration

These new doctrines were brought in by linking the doctrine of
consideration with the law of conditions. The link was first forged centuries
earlier by Chancellors who had known and applied the Canon-law maxim
cessante causa cessat effectus.[50] Additionally, from civil-law sources such as
Pufendorf and Domat, the Chancellor took over the doctrine that there were
implied conditions in the notions of failure of cause and dependent promises.
In this way, failure of consideration became the equivalent of failure of cause.
The doctrine passed bodily into the common law, Lord Mansfield playing a
major role,[51] and it was then perpetuated in Serjeant Williams' famous
rules.[52]

Writing in 1737, well prior to Mansfield's time, Henry Ballow
described the role of conditions in equity's view of dependency:

> When a man takes upon him any duty, not absolutely gratis,
> but upon the prospect of the other's doing something on his side, the
> obligation to make good his undertaking is only conditional; and,
> therefore in the law of nature, it is a general rule, that the particular
> heads of a contract are in the place of so many conditions
> [Pufendorf] and in conditions all things remain, before they are
> accomplished, in the same state as if there never had been any

---

[48] ARTHUR L. CORBIN, CORBIN ON CONTRACTS 656 (West Publishing, 1951).

[49] *Id.*, sec. 1257. The view which takes performance to be the consideration is distinctly
modern. As late as 1790 John J. Powell had written, "It is promise for promise; and that is the
consideration and not the performance." I ESSAY UPON THE LAW OF CONTRACTS AND
AGREEMENTS (Chamberlaine & Rice, 1790).

[50] SIMPSON, HISTORY OF COMMON LAW CONTRACT, *supra* n. 47, at 403.

[51] *Kingston v. Preston* (1773) Lofft 194, 2 Doug. 684.

[52] *See* his notes to *Pordage v. Cole* (1669) 1 Wms. Saund. 319.

covenant.[53]

As to the necessity of a continuing consideration, he noted that equity differed from the law:

> And as a covenant without a consideration is null, it is the same thing if the cause or consideration happen to cease; so that in all reciprocal contracts, there is a warranty on both sides in equity, though not in law.[54]

Fonblanque's annotation in 1793 added, "If the cause or consideration of an agreement fail before it be mutually performed, equity will not, in general, decree the performance of such an agreement."[55]

These ideas had taken root with Mansfield and he freely cited to them. The final result was that the old law of independent covenants was overthrown by a new law of implied conditions. In Powell's treatise of 1790, for example, the common law rule was stated thus:

> In executory contracts, if the agreement be that the one shall do an act, and, for the doing thereof, the other shall pay etc. so that the considerations are mutual; the doing of the act is a condition precedent to the payment, and the party who is to pay will not be compelled to part with his money, till the thing be performed . . . .[56]

Changed Perspective on the Old Authorities

Thus, long before *Tweddle's Case*, the so-called "struggle for concurrency" had been waged and won.[57] The perspective of the 19th century judge toward the old authorities was profoundly altered. This interior shift prompted skepticism from Lord Cottenham in 1839. "If in *Dutton v. Pool*

---

[53] HENRY BALLOW, A TREATISE OF EQUITY (reprint ed., Garland Publishing, 1979).

[54] *Id.*, vol. I, pp. 361-362.

[55] *Id.*, Fonblanque's note (g).

[56] POWELL, *supra* n. 49 at 357-358. For comparable treatment in the 19th century treatises, see ADDISON, *supra* n. 19 at 1031-1033; ANSON, ANSON'S LAW OF CONTRACT, *supra* n. 24, at 92.

[57] S.J. STOLJAR, A HISTORY OF CONTRACT AT COMMON LAW (Austr. Nat. Univ. Press, 1975).

(sic) the father after the undertaking of his own, had cut down the wood, and had not applied the proceeds for the benefit of the daughter, it cannot be supposed that the son would have been liable to her for the £1000."[58] Under this view there could not be any absolute investiture of a beneficial right from the inception of the contract. If the beneficiary's "right" was to be recognized at all, it would have to be treated as merely derivative and dependent upon the continuing consideration. Under this assumption, the right of the common law beneficiary would have been no greater than that of the equitable assignee, since he could only take rights subject to the equities and defenses available against the assignor-promisee.[59] By such a rule, the beneficiary's right could not be completely detached from the underlying transaction.

The "Right to Sue" Stipulation

There is a final feature of *Tweddle's Case* requiring comment. Pollock was greatly impressed by the express stipulation in the contract attempting to confer the right to sue upon the beneficiary.[60] The rejection of the action, despite this stipulation, suggested to him a principle so strong that it could not be overcome by the fathers' freedom to contract. This was speculation at best, for the court did not once advert to or take a stand upon this point. Indeed, the reason why the stipulation had no effect upon the result seems clear. If, as submitted, the contract *in toto* was unenforceable, due to the absence or failure of consideration, then how could the court possibly single out and enforce any part of it? The stipulation fell because the contract itself fell, and not because of an implicit syllogism flowing from a parties-only principle.

Conclusion on Tweddle's Case

Tweddle's Case is a masterpiece of disguise. It was the child, not of a parties-only principle, but of a basic upheaval in the law of contract. The doctrine of dependent promises not only precluded suit by the promisee, but

---

[58] *Hill v. Gomme* (1839) 5 My. & Cr. 250, 256, 1 Beav. 540.

[59] The conceptual linkage between the doctrine of failure of consideration, the rule of dependent promises, and the operation of equitable assignment was noted by CORBIN, *supra* n. 48, sec. 895.

[60] SIR FREDERICK POLLOCK, PRINCIPLES OF CONTRACT 233, 3rd Amer. ed. by Williston (Baker, Voorhies, 1906).

since failed conditions were now failed consideration, it also blocked the consideration that could be derived by near relationship to the promisee. This may suggest why Crompton J., for one, chose to say that consideration must move from the *promisee*, instead of repeating the then-contemporary rule that it must move from the plaintiff. In other words, the self-evident objection that no beneficiary should be able to take advantage of a contract in which the consideration had failed, called for a small variation in the formula. Blackburn, J. was led to the same formulaic change when he adopted the "distinct ground" that the contract was voluntary under the statutes against Fraudulent Conveyances. Because Blackburn's objection impeached the consideration at its source, it explains his phrasing of the rule in terms of the promisee rather than the plaintiff. As Stoljar has noted,[61] the promises of the original parties were only gift-promises and it is doubtful that the promisee could have enforced defendant's promise.

Contemporaries may not have understood this rationale, for it was hidden within the impenetrable consideration test. Scholars have long maintained that the common law often uses the doctrine of consideration as a catchall means to solve various problems, such as mistake, duress, and failure of condition.[62] We have had glimpses of this in the 17th century cases in which the fear of double recoveries[63] or the desire to protect the stipulator's power to countermand[64] became lost in abstract talk about consideration. The *Tweddle* court continued that tradition. Though the judges may have reached the right result, their discussion of the consideration doctrine concealed their true concerns and led to confusion.

Within a short period, the misinterpretation of *Tweddle* made little difference anyway. For in the meantime, an authentic parties-only principle had in fact arisen from a different set of legal sources. It is ironic that *Tweddle's Case* received the credit. "As has often happened in the law," writes Professor Atiyah,

> the case became important, not for what the judges said, but
> for what the legal profession came to believe the case stood
> for. And what they believed that *Tweddle v. Atkinson* stood
> for was the proposition that it is somehow contrary to the

---

[61] STOLJAR, *supra* n. 57, at 139 n. 24.

[62] Malcolm P. Sharp, "Pacta Sunt Servanda," [1941] 41 Colum. L. Rev. 783, 796.

[63] *Bafield Administratix v. Collard* (1647) Aleyn 1.

[64] *Potter v. Turner* (1622) Winch 7.

inherent nature of a contract that it should be capable of
conferring enforceable rights upon third parties.[65]

III. THE SOURCES BEYOND ASSUMPSIT

We have seen that the new parties-only principle was not based upon
the 19th century precedents just discussed. For authentic sources of that
principle, we must turn to legal developments beyond the action of assumpsit.

A. The Recourse to Continental Principles and Sources

The Reception of Will Theory

The reception of will theory in the 19th century changed the face of
English contract, and it prepared the basis for a second theory of privity that
was strikingly different than the theory based upon consideration. The
English reception of will theory, however, was a delayed and difficult process,
at least by comparison to its seductive career on the Continent. The theory
had spread much earlier to most parts of Europe, reaching Scotland in the
18th century. But England's geographical isolation, native legal system, and
separate philosophical tradition offered greater resistance. Ultimately there
was a very basic difference in the application of will theory in England. On
the Continent the school of natural law had used will theory to justify
recognition of the beneficiary action. Yet when will theory was finally
received in England, the common lawyers used it instead to justify a parties-
only principle of privity that defeated the beneficiary action. What accounts
for these opposite uses of the same theory? To explain we must start with the
earlier background on the Continent and then consider the unusual features
of the English reception.

On the Continent, some three or four centuries earlier, will theory
began to take root with the first appearance of the principle of consensualism
and contractual" "informality."[66] Before then the will of the parties and their

---

[65] ATIYAH, RISE AND FALL, *supra* n. 41, at 414.

[66] The pre-Glossators and Glossators had been wedded to the old notion that there could
be no civil obligation "solo consensus." But the Canon Law and later Italian commercial
practice, from an early date, accorded sanctity to the promise and the given word. JEAN
BRISSAUD, A HISTORY OF FRENCH PRIVATE LAW, § 376, pp. 501-502 (AALS reprint
1968). Vinagradoff summarized the teaching of the later canonists on promises in five

underlying intent had not been of prime legal importance because real contracts and formal contracts constituted the two basic types of enforceable agreements.[67]

Civilian thought had not liberated itself from the rigid Roman system that gave such a narrow role to *causa* and denied enforcement to the simple "formless" promise.[68]   The changeover to the consensualist principle *"solus consensus obligat"* gradually took place in the course of several centuries, and it was perhaps not until the 18th century that the enforcement of executory innominate contracts was fully established on the Continent.[69]

As the consensualist doctrine gained ground, it demanded analysis of

---

propositions:

1. A promise must be intentional.
2. It is revocable in consequence of a material change of circumstance.
3. It must have a reasonable cause (material equivalent or moral consideration).
4. Liberality is a sufficient cause in the case of gifts.
5. Promises to political and religious bodies are legally valid.

"Reason and Conscience in 16th c. Jurisprudence," 24 L.Q.R. 373, 382 (1908). *See also,* AUGUSTE DUMAS, HISTOIRE DES OBLIGATIONS DANS L'ANCIEN DROIT FRANCAIS, 87-89 (1972).

[67] Jean Brissaud, a French legal historian, has noted that contractual formalism deemphasizes the role of the individual's will: "Formalism has the effect of compelling the judge and parties to adhere strictly to words and acts leaving to one side questions of intent. Or, to speak more exactly, in a law which is formalistic the will has no legal existence except to the extent to which it is expressed by exact words; it is incarnated in its material expression. . . ." *supra* n. 66 § 369, p. 486.

[68] Arthur Von Mehren, "The French Civil Code and Contract," 15 La. L. Rev. 687 (1955); BUCKLAND & MCNAIR, ROMAN LAW AND COMMON LAW 229-30 (2nd ed. 1952).

[69] Von Mehren, supra, n. 68, at 708. In the 16th century, writers such as the Frenchman Charles Dumoulin (1500-1566) and the German Matthaus Wesenbeck 91531-1586) were the most influential supporters. As this support increased it came to include the prestigious names of Hugo Grotius (1583-1645), Pufendorf (1632-1694) and Jean Domat (1625-1696). However, SEUFFERT, ZUR GESCHICHTE DER OBLIGORISCHEN VERTRAGE pp. 142-143, 168 (1881) points out that the large majority of writers in the 17th century were still of a mind that innominate contracts were unenforceable in the absence of part performance.

the relationship between consent and the will of the parties.[70] Hugo Grotius (1583-1645) and his school asserted as a principle of natural law that the will of the promisor produces a binding obligation. In the chapter "De Promissis" from his classic *De Jure Belli ac Pacis*, Grotius drew refined distinctions between three degrees of the will *(voluntas)*. The third degree of the will was the promise, which he regarded as the alienation either of some thing belonging to the promisor or some portion of his liberty.[71] It was a principle of Natural Law that a promise could not transfer a right from one person to another without an acceptance,[72] and accordingly Grotius reasoned that there could be no such thing as binding unilateral juristic acts.[73]

Mainly due to Kant's (1724-1804) influence, will theory *(willens theorie)* received even greater emphasis in the German legal tradition. In *The Science of Right*, published in 1796, Kant wrote: "The act of the united Wills of two Persons, by which what belonged to one passes to the other, constitutes contract."[74] Kant postulated that four acts of the will were comprised within a contract -- Offer (oblatio) Approval (approbation) Promise (promissum) and Acceptance (acceptation). Since the property of the promisor could not pass to the acceptor by virtue of either of their wills alone, but only by their combination, both the promisor and the acceptor were free to retract at all times before their wills finally united. [75] Will theory was also central in Hegelian philosophy. In the *Philosophy of Right*, Hegel defined a contract as "the process in which there is revealed and mediated the contradiction that I am and remain the independent owner of something from which I exclude the

---

[70] It may be noted that for civilian writers the expressions "consent" and "will" have traditionally been regarded as synonyms. *See* ALFRED RIEG, LE ROLE DE LA VOLONTÉ DANS L'ACTE JURIDIQUE, 15 (Paris 1961). Toullier, A French commentator of the 19th century, illustrates this point by saying: "The contractual obligation is the immediate effect of my will. It is my will that produces it by means of the consent which I give; but my will itself is the effect of the motive which has directed me." 3 DROIT CIVIL FRANCAIS, No. 37 (1833).

[71] For Grotius, the first degree of the will was merely an assertion of present purpose, the second was a pollicitation. 2.11.2-4 DE JURE BELLI AC PACIS (Whewell transl. C.U.P. 1853). The necessity to make promises binding came from man's natural duty to keep faith and speak the truth, and "since man's will is from its nature changeable, means had to be found to fix that will for time to come, and such means are called 'promise'." HUGO GROTIUS, THE JURISPRUDENCE OF HOLLAND 3.1.5, p. 293 (Lee Transl. 1926).

[72] GROTIUS, *supra* n. 71, at 2.11.14.

[73] *Ibid* 2.11.16.

[74] EMMANUEL KANT, SCIENCE OF RIGHT 101 (Hastie transl., 1887).

[75] *Ibid.* pp. 101-102. The primacy of the will also became important in the philosophy of Kant's disciples Fichte and Schopenhauer.

will of another only in so far as in identifying my will with the will of another I cease to be an owner."[76] These philosophical ideas became a basic premise in German legal thought, for example in Savigny's study of obligations.[77] Savigny regarded contract as a particular application of the notion of "declaration of will" (*Willenserklarunge*).[78] Elaborated into a highly abstract notion by the German pandectists (notably Windschied), the declaration of the will became the foundation for the theory of juridical acts (*Rechtsgeschaft*).[79]

By the 18th century will theory was prominent in the writings of the Scottish commentators,[80] but in England the theory encountered a rather hostile reception. It was strongly criticized by moral philosophers and utilitarians such as Hume, Smith, Paley and later Bentham, whose own explanation for the binding character of promises--the expectation theory--was more broadly compatible with the doctrine of consideration.[81] Thus David Hume wrote that promises are human inventions, and self-interest is the first law of promises. The mere exercise of the will would not be able to create a natural obligation. Promises are performed toward others not because of real kindness but only because the self-interested promisor reckons that the promisee will return the performance "in expectation" of another performance of the same kind.[82] In the utilitarian view, the true reason why the legal system enforces promises is to protect the promisee's expectations.[83] Adam

---

[76] GEORGE W. HEGEL, PHILOSOPHY OF RIGHT 58 (Knox transl. 1942).

[77] Savigny defined a contract as "l'accord de plusieurs parties qui déterminent par une manifestation de volonté commune leur relations juridiques." LE DROIT DES OBLIGATIONS, § 52, p. 147 (Gerardin & Jozon transl. 1873).

[78] 3 SAVIGNY, TRAITE DE DROIT ROMAIN, § 140 (Guenaux transl. 1845).

[79] WINDSCHIED, I LEHRBUCHES PANDECKTENRECHTS 166, (7th ed. 1891); SALEILLES, DE LA DECLARATION DE VOLONTE – CONTRIBUTION A L'ETUDE DE L'ACTE JURIDIQUE DANS LE CODE CIVIL ALLEMAND (1929); A. ALVAREZ, PROGRESS OF CONTINENTAL LAW IN THE 19TH CENTURY, Vol. II, p. 101 (C.H.L. Series 1969); BUCKLAND AND MCNAIR, *supra* n. 68, p. sv; KONRAD ZWEIGERT & HEIN KOTZ, AN INTRODUCTION TO COMPARATIVE LAW, 2 (Weir transl. 1977).

[80] P.S. ATIYAH, PROMISES, MORALS AND LAW, 33-34 (Oxford University Press, 1981).

[81] *Id.*

[82] DAVID HUME, TREATISE OF HUMAN NATURE, Bk. II, pt. II, § 5 (Edingurgh, 1800).

[83] J. BENTHAM, THE THEORY OF LEGISLATION, 81-82 (London 1931); HENRY SEDGWICK, METHODS OF ETHICS, 309 (Macmillan 1922). For a resumé of the utilitarian account of promising, see ATIYAH, PROMISES, MORALS AND LAW, *supra* n. 80, pp. 30 and ff.

Smith wrote, "It is the disappointment of the person we promise which occasions the obligation to perform it."[84] Smith especially objected to will theory because

> the obligation to perform a promise cannot proceed from the will of the person to be obliged, as some authors imagine. For if that were the case a promise which one made without an intention to perform it would never be binding.[85]

Archdeacon William Paley also rejected the "innate moral principles" of the natural law and grounded liability upon "the expectations which we knowingly and voluntarily excite" by our promises.[86]

By the beginning of the 19th century, however, both utilitarian expectation theory and will theory emerged as joint influences on English contract. Will theory fitted well with the new political economy and the ideology that legal liabilities should be based upon voluntary acts of free choice.[87] The translation of Pothier into English, first in 1802 in America and thereafter in England in 1806[88] may have been one of the most efficient means by which the theory and Pothier's fame were conveyed into the English system.[89] By the second half of the century, if not earlier,[90] will theory was

---

[84] ADAM SMITH, LECTURES ON JURISPRUDENCE, 92 (Meek, Raphael, Stein; Oxford University Press, 1978).

[85] *Ibid.* p. 93.

[86] "Men act from expectation. Expectation is in most cases determined by the assurances and engagements we receive from others . . . ." WILLIAM PALEY, THE PRINCIPLES OF MORAL AND POLITICAL PHILOSOPHY, (Boston, 1815) 91.

[87] ATIYAH, PROMISES, MORALS, AND LAW *supra* n. 80, at 33.

[88] This translation by Sir William David Evans was widely read. Three American editions of the Evans translation in 1826, 1839 and 1853 attested to its popularity in the United States. The first translation in 1802 was by F-X Martin, then a North Carolina book publisher who later became the Chief Justice of the Louisiana Supreme Court.

[89] ATIYAH, RISE AND FALL, *supra* n. 41, at 406.

[90] There is some uncertainty over matters of timing and degree. Professor Atiyah asserts that English contract was, in the first sixty to seventy years of the century, predominantly under the influence of the expectation theory and will theory took root in the second half of the century. PROMISES, MORALS, AND LAW, *supra* n. 80, at 33 RISE AND FALL OF FREEDOM OF CONTRACT, *supra* n. 41, at 407. Professor Simpson, however, inclines to the view that the expectation theory had relatively little success compared to the wholesale adoption of will theory (*consensus*) by the courts. "Innovation in Nineteenth Century Contract Law," 91 L.Q.R. 247, 267 (1975). The former theory was, however, still current in the last quarter of the

generally accepted in English law.

The theory helped to establish features in the law of contract that had not existed in the 18th century. New doctrines of offer and acceptance, intention to create legal relations, and frustration of contract all ultimately derive from this premise.[91] Emphasis upon the promise, rather than its performance, gave new importance to the formation or creation of a contract, so that the wholly executory contract replaced the partly-executed contract as the classical model of contract.[92] Furthermore the role of consideration and promise were now turned around. Whereas previously consideration had been the principal ground for the creation of the obligation, with the promise playing a subordinate role, now, the source of the obligation was seen in the promise, a voluntary act of free choice.[93]

Beneficiary Theory on the Continent

The "parties-only" principle was not an accepted corollary of will theory on the continent. Indeed by the 19th century there were, within the civilian tradition, three distinct views regarding the position of the *tertius*, two of which recognized a direct right in the beneficiary. Yet, from the English

---

century. Pollock wrote: "It is rather amusing to see your new lights trumpeting reasonable expectation as the real fundamental conception in contract: I agree of course, having put it in my 3rd edition, ad init., nearly 50 years ago, only without a trumpet obligato." HOLMES-POLLOCK LETTERS, 48 (1941).

[91] As to the development of these doctrines in the 19th century, see Simpson, "Innovation In 19th Century Contract Law" who notes (p. 261) that the fiction of the continuing will found in *Adams v. Lindsell* (1818) 1 B. & Ald. 681 ("the defendants must be considered in law as making during every instant of time their letter was travelling, the same identical offer to the plaintiffs") looks suspiciously like a borrowing from Robert J. Pothier's TREATISE ON THE CONTRACT OF SALE (Small, 1826) Pt. I, I, Sec. II, Art. III. For the link between German and English views on offer and acceptance, see Stefan Reisenfeld, "The Impact of Roman Law on the Common Law System" (unpublished paper for the Centenary of Roman-Dutch Law is Lesotho, 1984), where the learned author notes that for a long period Grotius' analysis of a contract as being brought about by a promise and its acceptance prevailed on the Continent. The use of the offer idea (rather than a promise) as a legal component of contracting was recognized only in 1861 in the German Commercial Code. The author notes that Sir Frederick Pollock, in the first edition of his PRINCIPLES OF CONTRACT, *supra* n. 24 (1876) borrowed from German sources the terminology *proposal* ("antrag") and *acceptance* ("annahme"). Later editions then employed the term *offer* as a synonym for proposal and thus clearly distinguished between an offer and a promise.

[92] ATIYAH, RISE AND FALL, *supra* n. 41, at 142.

[93] ATIYAH, PROMISES, MORALS AND LAW, *supra* n. 80, at 33; ATIYAH, RISE AND FALL, *supra* n. 41, at 140; SIMPSON, HISTORY OF CONTRACT, *supra* n. 47, at 322-323.

standpoint, the most influential and preferable of these would prove to be the minority viewpoint of Domat and Pothier, a view directly descended from Roman law.

The three views stemmed from the different tendencies in Roman law toward the *tertius*, as well as from the need of the writers to adapt Roman law to the more permissive "native principle" or custom in their own countries.[94] At Roman law third parties could not acquire liabilities or entitlements under a contract between others.[95] This rule prohibited a person (C) who was not a party from bringing an action to enforce a stipulation in his favor made between the parties (A stipulator, B promisor); if the stipulation was wholly in favor of the third person, the stipulator himself could not sue, for want of interest.[96]

Roman law was not, however, altogether rigid. In a number of instances, though denying a direct action on the contract, the Romans allowed an equitable action *(actio utilis)* for the *tertius* where justice or convenience seemed to require it, for example to enforce a donation *sub modo* in his favor.[97] Furthermore, Roman law recognized certain unilateral juristic acts that were binding without the necessity of an acceptance by the beneficiary. The best known examples were a gift promised to a divinity (*votum*) and a

---

[94] The custom in Holland and Friesland permitted the enforcement of these stipulations. *See* HUBER, HED. RECHTSG. 3.21.40; GROTIUS, THE JURISPRUDENCE OF HOLLAND, *supra* n. 71, sec. 3.3.38. Germanic customary law apparently looked with favor upon such agreements. See the authorities discussed in South Africa by De Villiers, A.J.A. in *McCullogh v. Fernwood Estate Ltd.*, 1920 A.D. 204, at 214-215. In early German law, from the Frankish period onward, contracts for the benefit of third persons were very common. After the reception of Roman law, however, the theory of the native law was somewhat displaced by the rule *alteri stipulari nemo potest*. Thereafter it was no longer held correct that the third party acquired a right directly arising from the contract. The right arose only from his joinder or acceptance and until then the promisee and promisor might revoke the agreement. At that time the German evolution closely approached the position worked out by Grotius. However, with the introduction of the modern Civil Code (§ 328), Germany returned to "native principle" and gave the third party an immediate right to compel performance without the necessity of acceptance or joinder. RUDOLF HÜBNER, HISTORY OF GERMANIC PRIVATE LAW, § 75 (1918), Vol. 4 CONTINENTAL LEGAL HISTORY SERIES (reprint 1968).

[95] *See* Inst. 3.19.19; Dig. 45.1.38.17.

[96] WILLIAM W. BUCKLAND, A TEXTBOOK OF ROMAN LAW 423 ff. (Cambridge University Press, 1921); R.W. LEE, AN INTRODUCTION TO ROMAN-DUTCH LAW, 437 (Appendix) (5th ed. 1953).

[97] *Lee, supra* n. 96 at 423. BUCKLAND & MCNAIR, *supra* n. 68, at 214.

promise to the municipality (*pollicitatio*).[98]

Grotius provided the first coherent alternative to the overall restrictiveness of Roman law.[99] He held that an acceptance by the third party rendered the promise irrevocable and bound the promisor to him. The tertius' right to accept the promise passed to him as an effect produced by the promisor's promise to the stipulator. In his theory the third party does not directly acquire a right under the contract between the other two. A declaration is required to accept the benefit. Strictly speaking the right of the third party arises from a *vinculum juris* between himself and the promisor.[100] Prior to the *tertius'* acceptance, the promise could be rescinded by the stipulator and promisor, through not by the promisor alone.[101] For Grotius, the enforcement of *pollicitation* and *votum* at Roman Law did not undermine the necessity of an acceptance by a third party beneficiary. Those institutions were regarded as special cases in which the civil law supplied the acceptance or made the offer irrevocable so that it could always be accepted.[102] Finally, Grotius rejected the Roman law requirement of an "interest" in the performance of a promise, noting simply that in Holland, "more attention is paid to equity than legal subtleties."[103]

Grotius' views, which still prevail in modern South African law, were not unanimously accepted by other commentators. Simon van Leeuwen, who clung faithfully to the Roman texts, held that stipulations *in favorem tertii* were altogether ineffective.[104] At the other extreme, Groenewegen, who was influenced by the Spanish jurist Antonio Gomezius, considered that stipulations in favor of third parties were enforceable, whether or not accepted by the *tertius*.[105] In Scotland, Lord Stair (1619-1695) conceived that, absent a specific condition in the stipulation requiring acceptance, the beneficiary

---

[98] BUCKLAND, TEXTBOOK OF ROMAN LAW, *supra* n. 96, at 454-455, note 7.

[99] M.A. Millner, "Ius Quaesitum Tertio, Comparison and Synthesis," 16 I.C.L.Q. 446, 449 (1967).

[100] REINHARD ZIMMERMAN, THE LAW OF OBLIGATIONS, 44 (Juta 1990).

[101] GROTIUS, DE JURE BELLI AC PACIS, *supra* n. 71, at 2.11.18.

[102] *Ibid.* 2.11.14.

[103] GROTIUS, THE JURISPRUDENCE OF HOLLAND, *supra* n. 71, at 3.3.38.

[104] SIMON VAN LEEUWEN, 2 COMMENTARIES OF ROMAN-DUTCH LAW, 4.2.56 (Kotze transl. 1886).

[105] T. B. Smith, "Pollicitatio — Promise and Offer, *Stair v. Grotius*," 1958 *Acta Juridica* 141, 144.

acquired an immediate irrevocable right without any acceptance on his part.[106] The *tertius'* declaration of acceptance had no constitutive effect. In Stair's view stipulations could create rights in favor of those unable to accept, such as those not yet born or who were absent. He placed the source of the right in the promisor's declaration of will, explaining that "Promises now are commonly held obligatory; the canon law hath taken off the exception of the civil law, *de nudo pacto*."[107]

The French tradition, represented by Jean Domat and Robert Pothier, followed the most conservative tenets of Roman Law. It has been widely recognized that the texts of the Code Napoleon dealing with *stipulation pour autrui* (C.C. Arts. 1121, 1165) were taken almost verbatim from Pothier's *Les Obligations*.[108] Domat (1625-1696) had briefly dealt with stipulations,[109] but it was Pothier who articulated the proposition "that agreements can have no effect except between the contracting parties . . . ."[110] Pothier's source was the text of the Institutes, *alteri stipulari nemo potest*.[111] Interestingly, many before him had understood this to be merely a rule associated with the *stipulatio*, an obsolete formal contract at Roman law. Previous French writers had not found it possible to generalize from it in the manner of Pothier.[112]

Pothier was also the first French writer to discuss this question at length. He stated rationales, and he distinguished a number of closely-related

---

[106] LORD STAIR, INSTITUTIONS OF THE LAWS OF SCOTLAND 1.10.4 (reprint Edin. 1681); Millner, *supra* note 99, at 455.

[107] STAIR, *supra* n. 106; Smith, *supra* n. 105, at 146.

[108] *See* RODOLFO BATIZA, DOMAT, POTHIER, AND THE CODE NAPOLEON, 55, 57 (1973).

[109] JEAN DOMAT, THE CIVIL LAW IN ITS NATURAL ORDER, § 162, p. 166 (Strahan transl. 1853).

[110] ROBERT J. POTHIER, A TREATISE ON THE LAW OF OBLIGATIONS, trans. by Evans (Small, 1853).

[111] Inst. 3.19.19.

[112] In his ANALYSE DES PANDECTS, Pothier made a similarly broad statement of principle about Roman Law: "Reguliérement, personne ne peut obliger un autre ni par pacte, ni par convention, ni par stipulation." Tome II, p. 7 (Nouvelle ed. 1827).

situations.[113] His first rationale for the principle centered upon the exclusive effects of the wills of the parties. Pothier argued that agreements,

> being formed by the consent and concurrence of intention of the parties, they cannot oblige or give a right to a third person, whose intention did not concur in forming the agreement.[114]

Pothier's use of will theory here differed significantly from that of Grotius. Pothier saw the wills of the contracting parties as superior to the will expressed in the third party's acceptance. He also gave superior effect to the latest act of the will, thus ensuring revocatory freedom even though they had made an earlier commitment in favor of the *tertius*. His second rationale was that the legal prohibition resulted whenever the promisee (stipulator) lacked an interest in the enforcement. Thus he explained,

> what I have stipulated in favour of the third person, not being anything in which I have an interest capable of pecuniary appreciation, no damages can result to me from a failure in the performance of your promise, and therefore you may be guilty of such failure with impunity. Now nothing is more repugnant to the nature of a civil obligation than a power to contravene it with impunity. This is the meaning of Ulpian when he says, Alteri stipulari nemo potest . . . ."[115]

The "interest" rationale, we have seen, had an antecedent in English history and it remains more comprehensible to an English lawyer than to a civilian.[116] It went far in bringing French and English ideas together. By stressing a material basis of the objection--the "interest" of the stipulator-- Pothier produced a second objection apart from the exclusivity of the parties' wills. To his English readers, the "interest" of the promisee would have appeared as a clear reference to the doctrine of consideration. When this "lack

---

[113] These were the *adjectus solutionis gratia*, a stipulation mixed with the stipulator's personal interest, a stipulation for an heir or successor in title, a stipulation *sub modo*, and a stipulation to the agent of a third person.

[114] POTHIER, LAW OF OBLIGATIONS, *supra* n. 110, at 146.

[115] *Ibid.* p. 131.

[116] *See* the surprised reaction of Justice De Villiers in *McCullough v. Fernwood Estate, Ltd.*, 1920 A.D. 204, at 214.

of interest" objection was joined to Pothier's restrictive version of will theory, it closely ressembled the dual objection that English law finally developed in the 19th century.

Will Theory and Privity

If the privity principle had been an historically fresh question in England, the reception of will theory might have logically suggested a liberal approach to the beneficiary action. The utilitarian approach suggested only a limited beneficiary action: the beneficiary should enjoy a right only when certain expectations (taking the form of reliance, trust, confidence) had been created or aroused in him by the promise or stipulation in his favor. Since these sorts of expectations broadly coincided with what the law already regarded as consideration, the expectation rationale was not significantly broader than saying that some consideration must move from the beneficiary. Will theory, however, located the source of the obligation in the promisor's promise, not the consideration. It suggested strongly that a direct obligation should be owed to the intended beneficiary. It must be faced that that result was not in accord with the common law precedents, nor perhaps with the temper of the 19th century. It would have contradicted the results of several leading cases that had been explicitly based upon the consideration theory.[117] Furthermore, recognition of the beneficiary action enlarged the freedom of the parties to bind themselves but diminished their freedom to untie the legal obligation. In practical terms it would have enlarged the normal liabilities of the immediate parties to the contract. The laissez-faire philosophical climate of the 19th century could have been unfavorable to this idea, for there was already underway a broad movement to limit the responsibility of contracting parties.[118] And English judges and lawyers, who were likely to be one of the

---

[117] For example *Bourne v. Mason* (1669) 1 Vent. 6, 2 Keb. 454, 457, 527; *Crow v. Rogers* (1724) 1 Strange 592; *Clypsam v. Morris*, (1669) 2 Keb. 401, 443, 453.

[118] For example in 1837 the scope of vicarious liability was held in check by the doctrine of common employment, *Priestley v. Fowler*, (1837) 3 M. & W. 1; in 1840 the independent contractor rule was first pronounced, *Quarman v. Burnett* (1840) 7 M. & W. 499; the rule in *Winterbottom v. Wright* (1842) 10 M. & W. 109 protected manufacturers and the rule of *Hadley v. Baxendale* (1854) 9 Ex. 341 controlling damages, also fit this pattern. Thus Roscoe Pound seems justified in saying, "Later in the 19th century men came to think more about freedom of contract than about enforcement of promises when made. To Spencer and the mechanical positivists conceiving of law negatively as a system of hands off while men do things, rather than as a system of ordering to prevent friction and waste so that they may do things, the important institution was a right of free exchange and free contract deduced from the law of equal freedom as a sort of freedom of economic motion and locomotion." SPIRIT OF THE COMMON LAW, p. 149.

most conservative segments of society, seemed philosophically averse to increasing the duties of the individual.[119]

Thus, despite a general current in favor of will theory, other factors must have suggested the desirability of importing a version with some limitation upon it. If will theory had not been received so late, perhaps Grotius or Stair might have provided the favored model. But the resistance that made the reception late were the same factors that proved hostile to the beneficiary action. The French model outlined by Pothier was a logical choice, for Pothier enjoyed an impressive reputation in England,[120] and his views on this subject were quite compatible with English doctrine.

The Civilian Intermediaries in England

Contract, the subject that "lacked a literature"[121] in the 18th century, inspired a vast literary output in the 19th century. More than a dozen contract treatises were published in England and America between 1790-1895,[122] and the great majority presented the privity issue in the orthodox

---

[119] Professor Atiyah has pointed out that while no influential body of persons in the 19th century ever believed in laissez-faire as a total system, nevertheless ideas based on laissez-faire principles were clearly linked to freedom of contract and may well have had more influence on judges and judge-made law than on any other organ of the State. RISE AND FALL OF FREEDOM OF CONTRACT, *supra* n. 41, at 235. *See also* A.J. TAYLOR, LAISSEZ-FAIRE AND STATE INTERVENTION IN 19TH CENTURY BRITAIN, p. 53 and ff (1972).

[120] *See generally*, C.K. ALLEN, LAW IN THE MAKING, pp. 270-272 (7th ed. 1964); J.H. BAKER, AN INTRODUCTION TO ENGLISH LEGAL HISTORY, 293 (2nd ed. Butterworth's, 1979); ATIYAH, RISE AND FALL OF FREEDOM OF CONTRACT, *supra* n. 41 at 399-400, 406. Professor Atiyah notes that both Jones (Essay on Bailments) and Byles (Bills of Exchange) paid particular tribute to Pothier in their books. His influence on such judges as Best C.J. and Lord Blackburn was openly acknowledged. *E.g.*, Best J.'s statement in *Cox v. Troy* (1822) 5 B. & Ald. 474, 480, and Ld. Blackburn's statement in *McLean v. Clydesdale Banking Co.* (1883) 9 App. Cas. 94, 105.

[121] Simpson, "Innovation In 19th Century Contract Law," *supra* n. 91 at 250, and see A.W.B. Simpson, "The Rise and Fall of the Legal Treatise," 48 U. Chi. L. Rev. 632 (1981).

[122] *See e.g.*, POWELL, *supra* n. 49; SAMUEL COMYN, A TREATISE OF THE LAW RELATIVE TO CONTRACTS AND AGREEMENTS NOT UNDER SEAL (Riley, 1809); CHITTY, LAW OF CONTRACTS NOT UNDER SEAL, *supra* n. 9; WILLIAM W. STORY, A TREATISE ON THE LAW OF CONTRACTS NOT UNDER SEAL, (Little, Brown, 1844); SIR WILLIAM FOX, A TREATISE ON SIMPLE CONTRACTS AND THE ACTION OF ASSUMPSIT (Stevens & Norton, 1842); ADDISON, *supra* n. 19; JOHN W. SMITH, THE LAW OF CONTRACTS (Johnson, 1847); LEAKE, *supra* n. 22; POLLOCK, PRINCIPLES OF CONTRACT, *supra* n. 24; ANSON, PRINCIPLES OF THE ENGLISH LAW OF

terms of the consideration rule. Yet an exceptional group of authors espoused a markedly different doctrine. They were key figures who favored the parties-only principle. William Story, Stephen Martin Leake, Frederick Pollock, and William Anson were the first commentators to state a new principle logically detached from the consideration doctrine. Their individual approaches differed significantly. Story and Leake conceived two independent rules. Leake stated both the parties-only rule ("A Contract affects parties only.") and the consideration test, and located each in a separate section of his book.[123] Story, on the other hand, noted both elements but amalgamated them under the single heading "privity of contract."[124] Leake's principle was not overtly based upon will theory or continental sources, and Story did not refer in this particular instance to such a basis, but throughout his work one finds copious references to civilian sources such as D'Aguessean, Erskine, Barbeyrac, Grotius, Justinian and, most frequently of all, Pothier.

The most radical approach was that of Anson and Pollock, who suppressed the consideration test altogether, offering in its place a self-evident principle deduced from the nature of contract. Here the continental link was openly avowed. Both writers belonged to a select circle of common lawyers who served as civilian intermediaries. By virtue of their broader horizons, cosmopolitan training or reading, and equally important, by their strategic position inside the profession, Anson and Pollock were able to filter the learning, interpret its significance, and implant civilian ideas in the common law.[125]

Pollock cast the matter with typical boldness: "No third person can

---

CONTRACTS, *supra* n. 24; CLAUDE C. PLUMPTRE, A SUMMARY OF THE PRINCIPLES OF THE LAW OF SIMPLE CONTRACTS (Butterworths, 1879); JOSEPH A. SHEARWOOD, AN OUTLINE OF CONTRACT (Reeves & Turner, 1879); WILLIAM E. BALL, PRINCIPLES OF TORTS AND CONTRACTS (Stevens, 1880); DEVEY RANKING, THE LAW OF CONTRACT (1895); WILLIAM TAYLOR, TREATISE ON THE DIFFERENCE BETWEEN THE LAWS OF ENGLAND AND SCOTLAND RELATING TO CONTRACTS.

[123] LEAKE, *supra* n. 22, comparing pp. 221 and 331 *et seq.*

[124] "As between the plaintiff and defendant, there must be privity of contract, and if the plaintiff be a mere stranger to the consideration, *and* no promise be made by the defendant to him, founded in privity upon it, the action is not maintainable by him, although a promise may have been made by the defendant to pay the plaintiff." (Emphasis added). STORY, A TREATISE ON THE LAW OF CONTRACTS NOT UNDER SEAL, *supra* n. 122, at 83.

[125] *See* V. V. Palmer, "Common Lawyers as Civilian Intermediaries," *Tulane Lawyer*, p. 40 (Winter 1986). Other intermediaries in this circle would certainly include Bracton, Holt, Mansfield, Kent and Story.

become entitled by the contract itself to demand the performance of any duty under the contract.[126] Anson's phrasing was equally bold, and he elaborated in greater detail.[127] He denied that the principle flowed from the effect of the consideration doctrine, but from "the very conception we form of a contract." He explained that the reason *Dutton v. Poole* was no longer good law was simply the fact that the plaintiff there had not been a party. "The point," he explained, "is connected with the effect of a contract rather than the nature of the consideration."[128] The very *concept* of contract had become for Anson the real explanation behind the saying that consideration must move from the plaintiff.[129] Thus, by the 1870's Anson and Pollock had reached a highly conceptualized monistic viewpoint, and Leake and Story had moved into a bifurcated middle ground, an area that was also new and distinct, for it contrasted with contemporary efforts of traditional writers to explain contractual privity solely in terms of the consideration doctrine.[130]

As civilian intermediaries and treatisewriters, Anson and Pollock were both fountains and mirrors of legal development. Their borrowings from continental writers like Savigny and Pothier were undisguised and extensive.[131] In one sense they reflected or relayed the light of romanist systems to the common law. Yet, the role of intermediary also brimmed with creative possibility, and in formulating a general rule in terms of "parties," Anson and Pollock literally poured assumpsit into the analytical framework of civilian obligations. This "civilianizing" of the beneficiary problem was

---

[126] POLLOCK, PRINCIPLES OF CONTRACT, *supra* n. 24, at 195. The phrase "consideration must move from the plaintiff" was conspicuously omitted from the treatise.

[127] ANSON, PRINCIPLES OF THE ENGLISH LAW OF CONTRACT, *supra* n. 122, at 274.

[128] *Id.* at 101.

[129] *Ibid.*

[130] That focus, for example, led Joseph Chitty to surmise that the true policy behind denying recovery to the stranger was that the stranger was merely a donee, and unexecuted gifts must not be irrevocable. CHITTY, A PRACTICAL TREATISE ON THE LAW OF CONTRACTS NOT UNDER SEAL, *supra* n. 122 at 57.

[131] There were many cites to these civilians in the footnotes. William Anson was, according to Fifoot, "even more fervently the disciple of Savigny and it was through the superior vision of the master that he hoped to irradiate the concepts of obligation and agreement." C.H.S. FIFOOT, JUDGE AND JURIST IN THE REIGN OF VICTORIA (Stevens, 1959), p. 28.

premised upon the will theory of contracts as the basis of the objection.[132] Reference has been made to the reception of will theory in England.[133] It was inescapable and self-evident to Pollock that the English law of contract shared common principles with the civilians. Thus, he wrote:

> The fundamental notion from which we *must* take our departure is one that our system of law has in common with the Roman system and the modern law of other civilized countries derived therefrom. . . . The legal effects of a contract are confined to the contracting parties.[134]

This outlook accounts for the liberty taken in suppressing the consideration rule and for a rather ruthless manner of interpreting the contemporary cases.[135] There were no cases establishing the parties-only principle at the time, but Pollock and Anson vigorously claimed that *Price v. Easton* and *Tweddle v. Atkinson* had completely settled the question. Leake also overstated these same cases, and this reflects the pull of the tide. The notion of privity was somehow acquiring a parties-only meaning, which retrospectively infused new meaning in old cases in which the word had been used. The appeal of external legal ideas was matched by the search for "native" principle in the Common Law, a second source of principle to which we now may turn.

B. The "Party to the Deed" Concept: Revival and Reception

The parties-only principle is more than a legal transplant from civilian sources. There was a native principle whose roots extended far back in time to the old action in covenant upon deeds under seal, and some lawyers and

---

[132] This theory suffused Savigny's analysis of the Roman law of contract. In defining a contract he said, "a convention, in its most general aspect, is the agreement of several persons who by a common act of the *will* determine their legal relations . . . ." ARCHIBALD BROWN, AN EPITOME AND ANALYSIS OF SAVIGNY'S TREATISE ON OBLIGATIONS IN ROMAN LAW (Stevens & Haynes, 1872), p. 86 (emphasis in original).

[133] *See supra* p. 182 ff.

[134] Emphasis added SIR FREDERICK POLLOCK, PRINCIPLES OF CONTRACT 221, 3RD AMER. ED. (Baker, Voorhis 1906).

[135] The cases needed to be creatively manipulated. As Fifoot described the process, "The *a priori* postulates of German scholars were not easy to apply to the tough empirical fragments of case law, and they sometimes deflected and even distorted the instinctive grasp of practical needs and limitations which, whatever the defects of its qualities, made English law eminently serviceable. This incompatibility marred the work of Anson." FIFOOT, JUDGE AND JURIST IN THE REIGN OF VICTORIA, *supra* n. 131, at 29.

authors in the 19th century found there an internal source.

The earliest references to this native principle are sourced in Year Book colloquies concerning the *"Estraunger al fait"*.[136] This was the most rigorous rule found in any action sounding in contract. Originally, the sphere of this rule was confined to covenant and debt, for assumpsit had never been extended into the field of formal contracts.[137] In the 19th century, however, there was a new receptivity to the analogy, and an increasing tendency to think in terms of principle. The tendency was evident in Blackstone's novel way of defining a promise. "A promise," he wrote, "is in the nature of a verbal covenant, and wants nothing but the solemnity and sealing to make it *absolutely* the same.[138] Blackstone meant that covenants, once stripped of their formal robes, were in substance the same as informal promises. This suggested that the "parties-only" principle should apply to the action of assumpsit. In editing this section of the Commentaries, Coleridge criticized the "looseness" of Blackstone's definition, and said, in effect, that Blackstone was confusing distinct notions. By the 19th century, however, there was greater readiness to exploit the inner similarity that Blackstone had pointed out.

An interesting and influential step was taken in 1814 in a Note written by John Bosanquet and Christopher Puller, whom Holdsworth describes as "lawyers of great learning."[139] Their Note was appended to the report in the case of *Piggott v. Thompson* (1802).[140] This was an action in assumpsit brought by a lessor's agent to enforce a lease. As treasurer of the lessors, the agent was named in the written agreement (not under seal) as the party to whom rents should be paid. The court refused to allow the agent to sue in his own name because he had not been a party to the lease agreement.

---

[136] *See* SIR ROBERT BROOKE, LA GRAUNDE ABRIDGEMENT (1573), p. 31, fol. 297-298.

[137] STREET, *supra* n. 21, at 179; *Ld. Southhampton v. Brown* (1827) 6 B. & C. 718; *Offly v. Warde* (1669) 1 Lev. 235; *Bulstrode v. Gilburn* (1736) 2 Strange 1027. *Compare, Moravia v. Levy* (1786) 2 T.R. 483a; *Foster v. Allanson* (1788) 2 T.R. 479.

[138] Emphasis added. SIR WILLIAM BLACKSTONE, COMMENTARIES ON THE LAWS OF ENGLAND (Tippincott, 1858) vol. III, p. 157.

[139] W.S. HOLDSWORTH, A HISTORY OF ENGLISH LAW (Little, Brown, 1926) vol. Xii, p. 135. Both later became judges. Another of their famous Notes was appended to the case of *Wennal v. Adney* (1802) 3 B. & P. 247, which Holdsworth says was "largely instrumental in placing the doctrine of consideration in relation to simple contracts on its modern basis."

[140] 3 B. & P. 147, 150.

Rooke J. said, "I think the contract was made with the lessors Commissioners."[141] The matter of chief interest, however, was the legal methodology that the Note authors employed. Though the case was brought in assumpsit upon a written contract not under seal, the Note canvassed ten cases from the 17th and 18th centuries, most of which dealt exclusively with the "parties-only" rule applied to the *inter partes* deed. The use of these authorities presupposed a nexus, an analogy, or an identity between covenant and assumpsit. It was nonsense to the formulary purist to commingle authorities in this way, but apparently not to those interested in advancing deeper principle beneath the forms involved.[142] These jurists were interested in deriving substantive principle from what was originally the one true contract action. Bosanquet and Puller were aware that buried in the old learning lay a parallel that could be applied to the action of assumpsit. The parallel concerned an old debate about form and substance.

(1)   The Elevation of Substance over Form

In Maitland's lectures on *The Forms of Action at Common Law*, he stated without elaboration that "sacramental importance" attached to the seal in the action of covenant.[143] Barbour later attempted to give a reason for the seal's special effect. "To be able to write was in the twelfth century a tremendous accomplishment, and any written document was bound to be impressive to the ordinary person."[144] According to Barbour, this formality attained such importance that the deed became far more than mere evidence of an obligation-- "it was *the contract itself*."

---

[141] *Ibid.*

[142] This form of argument was not completely unknown. *See Lowther v. Kelly* (1723) 8 Mod. 115, an action in covenant in which the important assumpsit cases like *Bourne v. Mason* and *Dutton v. Poole* were thrown into argument. But there they had fallen on deaf ears. A 19th-century explanation attributed the force of the doctrine to the old concept of 'party to the deed'. Anthony Hammond said the beneficiary has no *legal* knowledge of the contract, according to the maxim (now nearly obsolete) that no stranger to a contract, real or personal, shall by his pleading derive any advantage from it. COMYNS, A DIGEST OF THE LAWS OF ENGLAND, *supra* n. 12, vol. I, p. 304, note (p). This rationalization played no role in the courts, but it served as an argument for the spread of the 'party to the deed' concept from covenant into assumpsit.

[143] FREDERICK W. MAITLAND, THE FORMS OF ACTION AT COMMON LAW, ed. by Chaytor & Whitaker, (Cambridge University Press, 1962), p. 64.

[144] WILLARD T. BARBOUR, THE HISTORY OF CONTRACT IN EARLY ENGLISH EQUITY, (Oxford University Press, 1914) p. 21.

The mere attaching of the seal to a writing bound the party to whom the seal belonged. Even if one carelessly lost his seal, and another made improper use of it, there was no defence. It follows that the use of the seal bound the owner, whether he were actually a party to the contract or not.[145]

Yet Barbour's account dealt with liability, not the enforcement rights of plaintiffs, and he did not explain the nonparty's inability to enforce the deed even when his own seal *was* affixed. It was held explicitly that a party to the deed, even though he had not sealed it, could bring covenant, but a nonparty who had sealed it could not do so.[146] To enforce a deed, it was essential to be a party, not to place a seal. The substance behind the privity requirement in covenant apparently stemmed from the parties-only notion found in contract principle, not in talismanic properties or in the formalities attached to covenant.[147] If the rule was independent of the seal, then it should not be taken as an illustration of mystical folk reverence for writings and wax, but of a general principle of contract.

(2)   The Seventeenth Century View of Levinz

In the 17th century, lawyers argued these issues forcefully in terms of form and substance. Was the right of the nonparty determined by the physical form of the deed, or determined by the nature of the party relationships embodied in the deed?[148]   One respectable view maintained that beneficiaries could sue upon a deed poll, but not upon an indenture; a third party action depended upon the particular form of the deed. A contrary opinion said the right depended upon the type of relationship formalized by the deed, that is, whether the deed was a bilateral contract between particular parties (an *inter partes* deed) or a unilateral declaration.[149] This view said that a nonparty could not sue upon a deed *inter partes*, whether it was by indenture or deed poll.

---

[145] *Ibid.*

[146] *Clement v. Henley* (1643) 2 Rolle Ab. 22.

[147] Covenant at an early time could be brought on informal promises. *See* SIR FREDERICK POLLOCK & FREDERICK MAITLAND, THE HISTORY OF ENGLISH LAW, 2nd ed. (Cambridge University Press, 1968), p. 222.

[148] *See generally*, NORTON, NORTON ON DEEDS, 2nd ed. (1928), pp. 27-29.

[149] This would take the form of a statement uttered in the first person—" Be it known that I hereby declare, *etc*. . . . "

The controversy took shape in the inconclusive case of *Gilby v. Copley* (1684).[150] An action of debt was brought upon a deed which, though by its own terms was called an indenture, had not been in fact indented. The deed set forth the sale of plaintiff's sheep to the defendant, and it recited defendant's promise to pay £244 to the plaintiff (the vendor). Yet the deed had been actually entered into between defendant and plaintiff's agent, Wawen; the plaintiff-vendor had supplied the consideration, but was not a party. Plaintiff's suit for nonpayment was met by the demurrer that only Wawen, the agent, could bring the action. Three judges were inclined to think that plaintiff should be permitted to proceed. According to their thinking, the case turned upon a physical attribute of the writing--the deed was not an indenture. They reasoned that the principal might sue on the nonindentured deed, while on an indenture only his agent (the promisee) could sue.[151] Levinz J., however, disagreed entirely with this approach. Being the reporter of this case, he naturally gives us his own reasoning in greater detail. He would have denied the plaintiff's action because,

> the indenting or not indenting of the Deed is not material, but the matter is his being party or not party; for it is common erudition that one not party to a deed made *inter partes* cannot take by the deed, unless by way of remainder.[152]

The beneficiary's right to sue, Levinz was saying, turns upon a natural principle, not the manner in which a document happens to be cut. Apparently, the time was not yet propitious for such "substance over form" thinking to be accepted. But a seed had been planted for Bosanquet and Puller to cultivate.

Sir Cresswell Levinz enjoyed the "postponed power," as Holmes called it, of those who write for another day. His triumph was deferred for more than a century. In 1814,[153] Christopher Puller, playing the dual role of legal revivalist and counsel for plaintiff, argued the Levinz position to a successful

---

[150] 3 Lev. 138. Bosanquet and Puller's Note discussed this case.

[151] Plaintiff's counsel relied upon the case of *Dutton v. Poole*. This illustrates the use of authority from the sister action in assumpsit.

[152] 3 Lev. 138, 139.

[153] Coincidentally, the same year that his famous Note was published.

conclusion in King's Bench.[154] Thereafter, the "parties-only" principle, now reasoned in the substantive manner of Levinz, was established in a series of decisions.[155] In *Carnegie v. Waugh* (1823),[156] an action in debt for rent due on a salmon lease was brought by the lessor, a minor who was not a party to the lease (his tutors were), though he was bound by it. The defendant objected that the lease *resembled* a deed *inter partes*, and, therefore, a nonparty could not sue. It was admitted, however, that the deed, in keeping with Scottish usage, was not sealed, and the court allowed the action. Abbot C. J. said that the case fell within the exception mentioned in Bosanquet & Puller's Note, and added: "I am not aware of any case which has extended the rule that a third person cannot take advantage of a deed *inter partes*, to contracts not under seal."[157] The impact may not have been immediate in assumpsit,[158] but in Chancery the influence of contract principle was not compartmentalized by the writ system. The Chancellor was in a better position to think of assumpsits, covenants, and debts as contracts rather than actions.

(3)   The Influence Upon Equity

As early as 1815, Lord Chancellor Eldon was following the parties-only principle. This may be evidence of the decline of equity or of the power of contract ideas generally, or both. Lord Eldon often quoted the principle when a contract or a trust formalized by a deed was before him. In *Wallwyn v. Coutts* (1815),[159] he held that a trust for payment of debts, under which lands were conveyed to trustees to pay debts, was, nevertheless, revocable between the parties without regard to the cancellation of the rights of the creditor beneficiaries. Plaintiff was a scheduled creditor who failed to obtain a lien in his favor, and he also failed to block a subsequent disposition of the

---

[154] *Storer v. Gordon* (1814) 3 M. & S. 308.

[155] *Metcalfe v. Rycroft* (1817) 6 M. & S. 75; *Berkeley v. Hardy* (1826) 5 B. & C. 355; *Ld. Southhampton v. Brown* (1827) 6 B. & C. 718.

[156] 2 Dow. & Ry. K.B. 277.

[157] *Id.* at 281.

[158] There is one interesting sign found in the 1817 edition of Buller's *Nisi Prius*: "Assumpsit lies only for the person to whom the promise was made." SIR FRANCIS BULLER, AN INTRODUCTION TO THE LAW RELATIVE TO TRIALS AT NISI PRIUS, 7th ed. by Bridgman, (1817; reprint ed., Garland Publishing, 1979); p. 133(a).

[159] 3 Mer. 707.

trust assets. Lord Eldon reportedly said, "the trust being voluntary, the Court would not enforce it against the Duke and Marquis, who might vary it as they pleased."[160] The reasoning is at first sight puzzling, for while it should have been possible to revoke a contract, an *executed* trust was irrevocable.[161] On closer analysis, however, it becomes evident that the deed was treated as if it were a contract, and both a "parties-only" and a consideration objection were fully argued and accepted. The report reads:

> To this deed no creditor was a party, nor was it made by agreement with any creditor, nor was there any release, or other consideration, moving from any creditor.[162]

This emphasis upon the contractual defects in plaintiff's cause--a nonparty, a volunteer, no consideration moving from him, the power to revoke--was novel in equity jurisprudence. The components for a dualist objection were present, even if they were not yet compressed into a maxim or formula.

A case two years later better explains Lord Eldon's analysis. *Ex parte Williams* (1817)[163] attracted another doctrinal Note by a reporter and again the authorities on assumpsit and *inter partes* deeds were commingled. The facts were that the petitioner was one of the scheduled creditors of the bankrupt partnership of Hughes and Joseph. The partnership had been formed by articles providing that debts owed to the pre-partnership creditors of Hughes (set out in a schedule) should, thereafter, become the legal responsibility of the partnership. Certain assets owned by Hughes were to be transferred into the partnership for the purpose of meeting this obligation. The partnership became insolvent, and the plaintiff creditor sought a declaration that he was entitled to a dividend out of the joint partnership estate. Lord Eldon denied the petition, saying he could not agree to the assertion that the deed alone, without any acceptance on the part of the creditor, could create plaintiff's right to maintain an action. Then he said,

There are some old cases upon this subject and in one of

---

[160] *Id.* at 708.

[161] A subsequent court took Lord Eldon to mean the deed established merely a revocable mandate for the benefit of the debtor and not the creditor. *Garrard v. Ld. Lauderdale* (1831) 2 Russ. & My. 451.

[162] 3 Mer. 707, 708.

[163] Buck. 13.

them (reported by *Levinz*, or by some of the Reporters of
his Time) where A. by Deed covenanted with B. a Party to
it, that he, A. would pay a Sum of Money to C., a Stranger
to the Deed. C. attempted to maintain an Action on the
Covenant against A. Whatever then may have been the Law,
such an action certainly could not now be supported.[164]

The statement indicates his approval of Levinz's view and a hardening attitude
in Chancery toward the beneficiary.

In the 1830's, there was steady development of the "parties-only"
principle. In *Colyear v. The Countess of Mulgrave* (1836),[165] a trust in favor
of natural daughters was revoked between the parties. Once again, the view
was taken that the deed, although called a trust, was actually a contract to
create a trust and not in itself a trust.[166] One part of the opinion held that
plaintiffs were natural children and, therefore, not within the consideration;
but there was an additional bar to the claim which the court stated separately:

I apprehend that when two persons, for valuable
consideration between themselves, covenant to do some act
for the benefit of a mere stranger, that stranger has not a
right to enforce the covenant against the two, although each
one might as against the other.[167]

The concept of the "stranger" to the covenant was also invoked in *Hill v.
Gomme* (1839),[168] to explain why an intended beneficiary had no right of
redress once the original parties revoked and abandoned their agreement.

By the end of the century, the equitable privity principle was distinctly
freed from any confusion with consideration. A case in 1879 was
indistinguishable from *Dutton v. Poole*, except that the son's promise to his
father was embodied in a deed. The Court refused his sister any remedy
against her brother because she was not a party. "But the deed is not one
between the defendant and the plaintiff or Alice Clitheroe. It is between [the

---

[164] *Id.* at 15-16.

[165] 2 Keen. 81.

[166] *See* CORBIN ON CONTRACTS, *supra* n. 48.

[167] *Colyear v. The Countess of Mulgrave* (1836) 2 Keen. 81, 98.

[168] 5 My. & Cr. 250, 1 Beav. 540.

father] and defendant. The case . . . is simply an action on a deed to which he [she] is a stranger and grounded on the deed."[169]

Although the earliest articulation of the parties-only principle may have come from Pollock's or Anson's influential pen,[170] the strongest judicial statement was made after the Judicature Act by Lindley, L. J. in *Re Rotherham* (1883):

> . . . an agreement between A and B that B shall pay C gives C no right against B. I cannot see that there is in such a case any difference between Equity and Common Law; it is a mere question of contract.[171]

It was now an easy transition to the magisterial tone of Viscount Haldane in 1915:

> My Lords, in the law of England certain principles are fundamental. One is that only a person who is a party to a contract can sue on it. Our law knows nothing of a *jus quaesitum tertio* arising by way of contract. Such a right may be conferred by way of property, as for example, under a trust, but it cannot be conferred on a stranger to a contract as a right to enforce the contract in personam.[172]

We need not trace the matter further. Here emerged the principle that cannot be found in *Tweddle v. Atkinson*. This principle carried the beneficiary problem far beyond the various arguments in previous centuries concerning the boundaries of assumpsit, the need for consideration, whether a trust existed, and so forth. Haldane's grand manner soared above the categories of contract and across the divisions of law and equity. It was now clear that the beneficiary problem was governed neither by the peculiar necessities of assumpsit, nor by the property rights bestowed under a trust, but by something self-evident about contracts. To an important extent, the "party

---

[169] *Clitheroe v. Simpson* (1879) L.R. 4 Ir. 59.

[170] In his PRINCIPLES OF CONTRACT, *supra* n. 24, Pollock wrote: "a third person cannot sue on a contract made by others for his benefit ...."

[171] *In Re Rotherham Alum & Chemical Co.* (1883) 25 Ch. D. 103, 111.

[172] *Dunlop v. Selfridge* [1915] A.C. 847, 853. Lord Parmoor, in the same case at p. 864, said something similar: "The appellants are not in form parties to the contract which they seek to enforce."

to the deed" was the native principle that had played an important role in the internal evolution of this principle.

C.   The Privity Principle Ventures into the Field of Tort

The rise of the privity doctrine in the field of tort has been one of the most enigmatic, controversial, and misunderstood phenomena of 19th century law.   There is scarcely any agreement, except upon the episode's vital importance in the development of tort and contract.   The center of the controversy has been the case of *Winterbottom v. Wright* (1842) which, 140 years later, still flourishes in modern casebooks on torts.[173]

Often, the historical rise of privity is derisively ascribed to the spell of a contract fallacy which allegedly confused or entranced the *Winterbottom* court; others place the blame upon the ignorance of successor courts, who misinterpreted the narrow "mispleader" aspect of the original cases and mistakenly broadened an intent confined to contract into a fallacious proposition in tort.   Still others stress economic policy or economic preconceptions as the predominant factor influencing the court. Such views can be somewhat misleading and historically unsound. Generally, they ignore the actual sequence of doctrinal development and the fact that the doctrine arose in the context of three factors which are no longer true today.   These were: (i) a rigid tort law not yet in possession of the tort of negligence, (ii) the analytical inability to distinguish between tort and contract except in procedural terms, and (iii) a strong bias, if not a rule, against concurrent actions in tort and contract. Thus, we shall see that the privity rule was first brought into the field of tort as a method of controlling concurrent actions. In suits brought nominally in case, in which a contract was alleged but no independent tort existed, plaintiff would be nonsuited unless he was a party to the contract. Considerably later, when the tort of negligence came into being, the privity doctrine was subsequently utilized as an independent restraint upon the expansion of that action. Still, the original impetus must be distinguished from subsequent uses, if we are to understand the peculiar career of this doctrine.

---

[173] PROSSER, WADE, SCHWARTZ, CASES AND MATERIALS ON TORTS 458 (6th ed. 1976); GREGORY, KALVEN, EPSTEIN, CASES AND MATERIALS ON TORTS 360 (3d ed. 1977).

(1)   An Example: Tollit v. Sherstone

The case of *Tollit v. Sherstone* (1839)[174] shows the original impetus for the doctrine. The plaintiff brought an action in "case" alleging that his horse had been stabled at defendant's establishment for a certain charge, and that one Young had delivered the horse there and dealt with defendant. It was alleged that all charges demanded by defendant had been paid, and that Young had requested redelivery of plaintiff's horse, but the defendant "not regarding his said duty . . . wrongfully kept and detained the said horse from the plaintiff . . . for the space of four weeks next following; by means whereof the plaintiff, for and during all that time, lost and was deprived of the use, profit and advantage which he otherwise would have derived. . . ."[175] The jury gave plaintiff a verdict for £15, but a rule to arrest judgment was obtained in the Court of Exchequer. The entire court agreed that the plaintiff could not make out a case of trover, because by the contract between Young and defendant, Young had a certain interest in the horse, and thus, the refusal to deliver to plaintiff was not necessarily conversion. The wrong, if any, must have been done to Young and not to plaintiff.

The court turned next to a question of contract principle. "Then if," said Lord Abinger, "the count be not maintainable as a count in trover, is it so on the ground of a duty resulting to the plaintiff? In the cases cited by [counsel], the persons claiming were parties to the original contract; but here the only contract of the defendant was with Young. . . ."[176] Baron Maule formulated the same objection to a claim in contract, and we recognize it as the modern privity principle: "It is clear that an action of contract cannot be maintained by a person who is not a party to the contract; and the same principle extends to an action of tort arising out of a contract."[177] Here, it is clear that Maule B. invoked the parties-only principle precociously. He cited no authority for such a principle, but it did not prevent him from saying the *same* principle extends to a tort action arising out of a contract. Alderson B. also invoked this principle during the argument of the case.[178]

---

[174] 5 M. & W. 283.

[175] *Id.* at 284.

[176] *Id.* at 288.

[177] *Id.* at 289.

[178] "The person suing for a breach of duty arising out of a contract must be a party to the contract." *Id.* at 286.

All three Barons presupposed the nonexistence of an independent duty owed in tort, and reached the privity principle as a second step of their reasoning. This was not an isolated example; it was a general reasoning pattern in numerous cases of this type.[179] The best-known example was the case of *Winterbottom v. Wright* (1842),[180] but before turning to that decision, it will be helpful to look more closely at the context and background.

(2.)   The General Problem of Concurrent Remedies

It is generally accepted that, prior to the 19th century, negligence existed only as an element in various torts. It was a pleader's adverb, but not a tort unto itself. The birth of negligence as a tort did not occur until the last half of the 19th century.[181] Furthermore, it has been correctly noted that

---

[179] *See further, Burnett v. Lynch* (1826) 5 B. & C. 589; *Legge v. Tucker* (1856) 1 H. & N. 500; *Bretherton v. Wood* (1821) 3 Brod. & B. 54; *Boorman v. Brown* (1842) 3 Q.B. 511 (Exchequer Chamber).

[180] 10 M. & W. 109.

[181] The birth of negligence as an independent tort was undoubtedly a lengthy and gradual process, and it is hardly surprising that there are various views as to the actual date.

The traditional view, which was based on Winfield's ["The History of Negligence in the Law of Torts," 42 L.Q.R. 184 (1926); "Trespass and Negligence," 49 L.Q.R. 359 (1933); "Duty in Tortious Negligence," 34 Col. L.R. 41 (1934)] and Fifoot's [HISTORY AND SOURCES OF THE COMMON LAW 154-166 (1949)] research placed the development in the 19th century. "The prime factor," wrote Mr. Fifoot, "in the ultimate transformation of negligence from a principle of liability in case to an independent tort was the luxuriant crop of 'running-down' actions reaped from the commercial prosperity of the late eighteenth and early nineteenth centuries. Their significance lay rather in their number than in their nature." Winfield particularly stressed that early railway accidents were the chief agent of the tort's development, and he found confirmation from the nineteenth-century abridgments that the profession had recognized the new title "Negligence" in that period. But if Winfield's research put the development late by insisting upon evidence of conscious recognition in the books, other research could put the development earlier by stressing the doctrinal steps which served as prologue.

Many historians argue that the critical point was reached in the last quarter of the 17th century when the action of trespass on the case was given a wider scope. *See* BAKER, *supra* n. 120, at 342-47; Prichard, "Trespass, Case and the Rule in *Williams v. Holland*" 1964 Cambridge L. J. 234; Prichard, *Scott v. Shepherd* (1773) and the Emergence of the Tort of Negligence (Selden Soc. Lecture, (1676); STREET, *supra* n. 22, at 189. *See also*, Neward, "The Boundaries of Nuisance" 65 L.Q.R. 480, 485, n. 39 (1949); W.S. HOLDSWORTH, A HISTORY OF ENGLISH LAW 453 (Little, Brown, 1926). This expansion emerged from a "thin trickle" of running-down cases (Prichard, 1964 Cambridge L. J. 234, 235) in which the plaintiff sued in case as opposed to trespass, and recovered even though there was no previous undertaking by

"Winterbottom was decided in 1842 before clear recognition of negligence as an independent basis of liability and of the distinction between tort and contract.... The duty to use care toward this plaintiff could not be supported as an incident to the contract, nor did it arise from status, public calling or the like; no broader basis had yet been worked out, so no duty was found."[182]

Indeed, Winfield theorized that the privity doctrine in *Winterbottom*, far from blocking recognition of an action in negligence, furthered the tort's development by serving as a kind of shield against which the peculiar "duty of care" element in negligence would either ricochet off or, occasionally, penetrate through.[183] Winfield frankly acknowledged that this explanation might seem backhanded, and, with respect, it is backhanded. The duty notion was more immediately affected by the issue of concurrence, since comparing and recognizing the type of duty owed to the plaintiff was the crux of that issue. As lawyers sought the essence between tort and contract, they found that the duty element of tort originated from and was imposed by law, not the will of the parties. The search for a public duty became so critical to the concurrent remedy problem that contemporary jurists sometimes contrasted the words "duty" and "contract" in such a way as to show they were speaking

---

the defendant, no custom of the realm, nor allegation of force and arms. BAKER, *supra* n. 120, at 344. The landmark case of *Mitchil v. Alestree* (1676) 1 Vent. 295, 2 Lev. 172, 3 Keb. 650 was viewed as the start of a liability in negligence (though negligence is not a word referred to in the case) which, as Prichard put it, was "independent of trespass, yet independent also of any prior relationship between the parties other than that brought about by the injury." 1964 Cambridge L.J. 234, 235. In other words, the action on the case started to shed an old privity restriction (the restrictive prior relationship ordinarily presented by an undertaking or custom of the realm) and was thereby enabled to become a nonrelational remedy for accidents between strangers. This insight is not incompatible with the traditional account given by Winfield. It appears right to say that contemporaries did not recognize the tort until the nineteenth century, yet in terms of necessary doctrinal groundwork, 1676 was at least as significant as 1825 in the final development of negligence.

[182] FOWLER V. HARPER AND FLEMING JAMES, THE LAW OF TORTS (Little, Brown, 1956), vol. II, 1039-40.

[183] "The process of reasoning," said Winfield, "was this. There is here a contract between A and B. C is suing A because he has been injured. C has alleged a duty towards himself on A's part. That duty does not *ex hypothesi* arise from the contract. C has not shown that it arises from any other source; not from deceit because there was none, as there was in *Levy v. Langridge*; nor from negligence because in all the old cases of inadvertence (in public calling, public office and the like) the duty did not extend beyond the two persons immediately concerned. Therefore A is not liable. But *semble* he would have been liable if C could have proved a legal duty to take care like that in the public office, public calling *etc.* type of case." Winfield, "Duty in Tortious Negligence," 34 Colum. L. Rev. 41, 54, (1934).

about diametrically different categories.[184] Though no definition was ever attempted, contemporaries spoke as if they understood the nature of these two categories very well.[185]

The dominant focus of the pre-negligence era was fixed upon the difficult problem of concurrence. The early common law was traditionally hostile to double remedies,[186] and this attitude, though less intense in the 19th century, was still alive. Mansfield presupposed in *Hambly v. Trott* (1776)[187] that the remedies of the common law occupied exclusive spheres of application. A plaintiff should never have a second remedy except in the truly exceptional case when the interests of justice required it. Blackstone, too, accepted that tort and contract were disconnected spheres, not co-arising actions.[188] The most consistent policy behind the reluctance to allow co-existing remedies was thought to be the general unfairness of increasing the scope of the defendant's liability if plaintiff was accorded the unilateral right to frame his action in tort.[189] Plaintiffs would enjoy several substantive and procedural advantages. Firstly, the plaintiff in tort was thought to be entitled to higher and more extensive damages than the action in assumpsit would allow.[190] A claim in conversion, for example, could expose defendant to pay the full value of the goods, though a claim on a co-existent contract would

---

[184] Thus, "if the liability of the defendant arises not from the contract, but from a duty, it is perfectly unimportant by whom the reward is to be paid; for the duty would equally arise, though the payment was by a stranger," Per Jervis C. J., *Marshall v. The York, Newcastle & Berwick Ry. Co.* 11 C.B. 655, 663.

[185] *E.g.,* "Without altogether destroying the well-known distinction between actions of contract and actions of tort, I think we cannot hold the counts in this declaration to be well-joined. Per Jervis C. J., *Courtenay v. Earle* (1850) 10 C.B. 73, 83.

[186] The rule against double remedies was in force long before *Slade's Case* (1602) 4 Co. Rep. 92b. And its source is often attributed to the Statute of Westminster II, (1285) 13 Edw. I, c. 24 A.W.B. Simpson, "The Place of Slade's Case in the History of Contract." 74 L.Q.R. 381, ff. (1958).

[187] 1 Cowp. 371.

[188] BLACKSTONE, *supra* n. 138 vol. III, 117 *et seq. See also* the arguments in *Kinlyside v. Thornton* (1776) 2 Wm. Black. 1111:*Stuart v. Wilkins* (1778) 1 Dougl. 18.

[189] W.D.C. Poulton, "Tort or Contract," 82 L.Q.R. 346, 369 (1966).

[190] "During many years when I was a junior at the Bar, when I was drawing pleadings, I often strove to convert a breach of contract into a tort in order to recover a higher scale of damages, it having been then as it is now, I believe, the general impression of the profession that such damages cannot be recovered in an action of contract as distinguished from tort. . . . That view, which I was taught early to understand was the law in olden days, remains true to this day." Per Lord James of Hereford in *Addis v. Gramophone Co., Ltd.* (1909) A.C. 488, 492.

entail no more than loss of plaintiff's bargain.[191] Tort, it was additionally thought, took in a broader causation that was not subject to the contract principle of remoteness.[192] Secondly, sometimes tort actions were viewed as naked attempts to bypass a protective rule of contract. For example, if an infant sold a horse to the plaintiff and allegedly deceived the plaintiff by saying the horse was sound, clearly plaintiff should have no action in assumpsit since the minor lacked the capacity to give a binding promise. If plaintiff brought a suit in trespass against the infant (special action on the case), it was thought that he should be nonsuited, because the clear foundation of the action was assumpsit and the attempted conversion of a contract into a tort was simply an attempt to hold a minor liable on his contract.[193] The courts would block the conversion attempt for other incapacitated persons as well.[194] Thirdly, procedural protections were often at stake and increased liability could flow from less-protective tort rules concerning joinder and joint liability. For example, unlike tort, a contract cause of action required the joinder of all co-contractors, and no single contractor could be liable unless all co-contractors were found liable. Additionally, contract counts could not be mixed with tort counts. Winfield argued that the result of repeatedly locking horns over procedural issues such as these caused the courts to develop a scientific distinction between tort and contract.[195]

In the 19th century, however, the mutual exclusivity of remedies began to break down, even as the clarification of tort and contract differences made headway. It was settled by 1821 that tort and contract were coincident in the field of common calling.[196] By 1842, there seemed to be a serious

---

[191] PERCY H. WINFIELD, THE PROVINCE OF THE LAW OF TORT, 79 (Cambridge University Press, 1931).

[192] *Burrows v. The March Gas & Coke Co.* (1870) L.R. Ex. 67.

[193] *Green v. Greenbank* (1816) 2 March 485. *But see Burnard v. Haggis* (1863) 14 C.B. (NS) 45.

[194] *Wright v. Leonard* (1861) 11 C.B. (NS) 258 (married woman); *Liverpool Adel-phi Loan Assn. v. Fairhurst & Wife* (1854) 9 Ex. 422 (married woman).

[195] WINFIELD, THE PROVINCE OF THE LAW OF TORT, *supra* n. 191, at 40 *et seq.* This was particularly difficult for a system whose contractual and tortious actions had remedies of common origin. Tom Hadden, "Contract Tort and Crime: The Forms of Legal Thought," 87 L.Q.R. 240, 241-242 (1971). The distinction was once thought to lie in the nature of the wrongful act--the distinction between misfeasance and nonfeasance--but this line was casustry-prone and had to be abandoned. *Boorman v. Brown* (1842) 3 Q.B. 511, per Tindal C.J.

[196] *Bretherton v. Wood* (1821) 3 Brod. & B. 54; PERCY H. WINFIELD, A TEXTBOOK OF THE LAW OF TORT, 3d ed. (Sweet & Maxwell, 1946), 644.

possibility that the entire field of contract had been made concurrent with tort. Obviously, it was not conceivable that torts between strangers could be manipulated into contracts, short of using gross fictions to make it seem that there was a meeting of minds between plaintiff and defendant. But it required no fiction to say that any breach of a contract would constitute a tortious wrong. The danger of conversion was essentially one-directional, namely, from breach into wrong, and not *vice versa*.

This was at the heart of the controversy in the House of Lords decision of *Brown v. Boorman* (1844).[197] The defendant was retained as an oil broker with instructions to sell on a cash-only basis. However, in violation of his instructions, he sold and delivered the plaintiff's linseed oil on credit to a buyer who went bankrupt, causing the plaintiff to lose the oil and the price. The plaintiff declared in case against the broker, and alleged that defendant was under a duty to use all reasonable care not to deliver the oil without the price being paid. Nevertheless, he so negligently and carelessly conducted himself that plaintiff lost both the oil and the price. Plaintiff obtained a verdict at the trial, but the Court of Queen's Bench arrested the judgment on the ground that the duty of the broker was pleaded as a duty flowing from defendant's character as broker. The court said such a duty did not fall within the ambit of a broker's calling as defined by statute and common law. The Exchequer Chamber, however, reversed upon a different ground, holding that an equivalent duty arose from the express contract of the parties, and the plaintiff in privity of contract might always elect to sue in tort upon it. After a review of such cases as *Govett v. Radnidge* (1802),[198] *Marzetti v. Williams* (1830),[199] and *Pozzi v. Shipton* (1838),[200] Tindal C. J. came to the conclusion that there should be concurrent remedies.

> The principle in all these cases would seem to be that the contract creates a duty, and the neglect to perform that duty, or the nonfeasance, is a ground of action upon a tort.[201]

This sweeping statement was open to the objection that it made every breach of contract into a tort. Tindal's view was not actually repudiated by the House

---

[197] 11 Cl. & Fin. 1.

[198] 3 East 62.

[199] 1 B. & Ad. 415.

[200] 8 Ad. & E. 963.

[201] *Boorman v. Brown* (1842) Q.B. 511, 526.

of Lords,[202] for the Lords cautiously based their decision for the plaintiff upon the procedural ground that, whether or not the duty in question stemmed from a public duty or a contractual obligation was immaterial once plaintiff had obtained a verdict.

Subsequently, the wide statements in *Boorman* were scaled down, and the danger of full concurrence somewhat abated.[203]   In 1852, the Court of Exchequer held that a sheriff's breach of contract could not, in the circumstances, be sued upon in "case."[204] Yet, in the interim period when *Winterbottom* arose, the *Boorman* thesis reflected a strong movement toward concurrence. If the coachdriver in *Winterbottom* or the horse owner in *Tollit* were remediless in tort, so too was the plaintiff in *Boorman*, but the latter successfully converted a contractual breach into a tort action. The difference in result stemmed from privity of contract: the *Winterbottom* and *Tollit* plaintiffs were not owed a duty in contract which could be converted into a tort.

(3)   The Case of Winterbottom v. Wright

The most notable use of the privity principle in the tort-contract *catena* came in the famous case of *Winterbottom v. Wright* (1842). It was there held that a coachdriver, employed to drive the Post Office's mail carriage, had no action upon the case for personal injuries caused by the breakdown of a defective coach which the defendant coachmaker had supplied to the Post Office. Part of Lord Abinger's opinion stated, "There is no privity of contract between these parties; and if the plaintiff can sue, every passenger, or even any person passing along the road who was injured by the upsetting of the coach, might bring a similar action."[205]   Thus originated the famous citadel of privity in the field of tort.

(a)   Two Interpretations

Principally, there are two interpretations of the holding and its impact upon later law. By one version, the decision was a substantive blunder. The

---

[202] Indeed, Lord Campbell seemed to endorse it.

[203] In 1850, it was still held to be misjoinder to join contract and tort counts in the same action. *Courtenay v. Earle* (1850) 10 C.B. 73.

[204] *Woods v. Finnis* (1952) 7 Ex. 363.

[205] *Winterbottom v. Wright* (1842) 10 M. & W. 109, 114.

court was under the hypnotic lure of the "contract fallacy."[206] *Winterbottom* stood for the proposition that the background existence of a contract in the facts operated as a broad shield against tort duties to third parties, and thus it contained its own *petitio principii*.[207] The common law was against this proposition, having asserted from the earliest times that wrongs require no privity because they are essentially actions between strangers.[208]

A second version began with a different premise. The case, it was argued, may have been correctly decided on the basis of privity, but only because the plaintiff mispleaded his case in contract and failed to allege negligence.[209] It has been confidently argued that if plaintiff had alleged negligence or want of care, the result would have been different.[210] As the story goes, the court's narrow mispleader ruling was not perceived by contemporaries or successors, and was already long buried and forgotten when Francis Bohlen redirected attention to it in 1905.[211]

In the final analysis, these two interpretations of *Winterbottom* run together. For whether due to subsequent misinterpretation or an original fallacy, the case acquired a meaning well beyond an accepted contract principle ("if no privity, no action in contract"), and came to stand for the hegemony of contract over tort ("if no privity of contract, no action in tort"). Thus, it is immaterial whether or not the citadel of privity was intentionally or mistakenly built. The subsequent cases fortified it, and the lengthy assault was underway. The convenience of these stories is that the privity doctrine in the field of tort turns out to be a haunting tale about a judicially-created phantom. *Winterbottom*, we are told, is after all not inconsistent with *Donoghue v.*

---

[206] SIR JOHN SALMOND, SALMOND ON THE LAW OF TORTS, 16th ed. by Heuston, (Sweet & Maxwell, 1973), 11.

[207] Labatt, "Negligence in Relation to Privity of Contract." 16 L.Q.R. 168, 171 (1900): "It does not by any means follow that because a party to a contract can recover in tort only when the rights acquired by his contract are sufficient to enable him to maintain an action, a person who had nothing to do with the contract, but who subsequently finds himself damaged by what the parties to it have done or left undone, should be told that he has no remedy at all."

[208] *Tottenham v. Bedingfield* (1573) 3 Leon. 24; *Cf., Panthon v. Isham* (1964) 3 Lev. 359.

[209] Francis H. Bohlen, "The Basis of Affirmative Obligations in the Law of Torts," 53 Am. Law Reg. 209, 273, 337, particularly at 281-85 (1905); SIR FREDERICK POLLOCK, THE LAW OF TORTS , 571, 13TH ED. (Stevens, 1929), 570; Donoghue v. Stevenson (1932) A.C. 562 (Ld. Macmillan and Ld. Atkin).

[210] POLLOCK, THE LAW OF TORTS, *supra* n. 209, at 571.

[211] Bohlen, *supra* note 209.

Stevenson,[212] or the modern law of negligence. These interpretations hardly do justice to the historical facts.

(b)   Rejection of the "Fallacy" Thesis

It is a complete misconception to think that the Barons of the Court of Exchequer were deceived by the contract fallacy. They did not adopt the simple view that an action in tort was barred simply because the plaintiff coachdriver was not a party to the defendant's contract. Rather, the privity point was the third step in a lengthier analysis. The reasoning was first premised upon the nonexistence of any remedy in tort for plaintiff (irrespective of the presence of a contract), and second, upon the perception that plaintiff's action would disturb the normal rule against concurrence of tort and contract remedies. The steps of the analysis fit together in the following way. Because no independent tort duty had been shown or so far recognized in a fact situation such as this, the coachdriver had no action in tort; nor could he fill the gap by allegations creating or conceiving a tort merely from the defendant's breach of his contract, for tort and contract did not interrelate in this way. To allow such an interrelation would not only enlarge general restrictions on concurrence and permit double remedies, but in the case of a third party plaintiff, it would violate the privity principle in contract. The keys to the decision, therefore, are (1) the absence of any tort duty (irrespective of privity considerations), (2) a general rule of concurrent remedies, and (3) the privity of contract bar.

Obviously the "fallacy" argument must fall of its own weight, because it is possible to show that the court reached the conclusion that plaintiff was altogether remediless in tort quite apart from any privity considerations. This conclusion is clearly warranted by the report of the case. Lord Abinger explicitly stated that the plaintiff may be "remediless altogether" and his fellow judge, Baron Rolfe, said it was a case of *"Damnum absque injuria."*[213] As a matter of contemporary authorities, this was not an untrue statement. Abinger attempted to demonstrate the absence of an actionable tort duty by noting (a) there was no "public duty," as in the case of nuisance or public calling, and (b) the fraud recognized in *Levy v. Langridge* (1837)[214] was the distinct tort of deceit, which was not to be extended further. His duty checklist was short, but thoroughly covered. He, of course, could not discuss

---

[212] (1932) A.C. 562.

[213] *Winterbottom v. Wright* (1842) 10 M. & W. 109, 114 & 116.

[214] 4 M.& W. 337.

the tort of negligence, because it was not recognized as an independent tort at that time. There simply were no precedents authorizing recovery in tort. Then, he turned to the question of concurrence between tort and contract, and the possibility of converting the defendant's contract duty into a tort duty. Lord Abinger and his brethren feared that any relaxation of the concurrence and privity restrictions would let in "an infinity of actions," would lead to the "most absurd and outrageous consequences," and would allow contracts to be "ripped open" by actions in tort, and so forth.[215]

In one sense, Lord Abinger's contribution in *Winterbottom* was to turn away from the traditional discourse that placed emphasis upon rule-oriented objections to concurrence. His emphasis fell upon the higher ground that if a third person were entitled to convert a contract breach into a tort action, then the defendant would be burdened with a vast and limitless liability.[216] To the determinist historian, no doubt Abinger's rationale is easily ascribed to the economic philosophy of a judge sharply inclined to place limits on enterprise liability. The biographical point may well be true,[217] but it need not obscure, nor conflict with, the doctrinal point. The limitation was not being used to explain why tort liability could not theoretically exist, but rather why tort duties should not be innovated merely as byproducts of contracts. The consequentialist arguments advanced by the court flowed from the fear of a *self-generating* concurrence, which threatened to make every breach of contract into a wider liability in tort.

According to the court's conception, concurrence should be recognized only when each action was sustained by a separate root, that is, when defendant owed an independent tort duty and, in addition, had also breached a contract duty with the plaintiff. Thus, Lord Abinger admitted that concurrence might come about when the defendant's negligence simultaneously violated a duty imposed by law and a duty imposed by his contract with the plaintiff, *e.g.*, where an innkeeper failed to protect a lodger's luggage, or a building contractor constructed a public nuisance to the injury

---

[215] *Winterbottom v. Wright* (1842) 10 M. & W. 109., 113-15.

[216] The use of privity to control the extent of tort liability was clearly on judges' minds at this time. *See Gerhard v. Bates* (1853) 2 El. & Bl. 476.

[217] For example there is some direct evidence of Abinger's economic biases in an anti-Chartist speech in 1842 regarding the Plug Plots. See the extract in *Class and Conflict in 19th Century England*, 291-292 (P. Hollis ed. 1973).

of the party who had hired him.[218] Without sufficient analysis, however, he quickly assumed that Wright, the coachmaker, owed no public duty of any kind based on his calling; that is, he presumed that the duties of a coachmaker were not like the public duties of innkeepers, carriers, surgeons, etc.[219] As a result, Abinger presumed away the answer to the most important duty question in the pre-negligence system.

(c)   **Rejection of the Mispleader Theory**

Eminent writers such as Prosser, Bohlen, Pollock and Salmond have fully accepted the mispleader tale, but Atiyah says it is "almost complete nonsense."[220] Mispleader does seem, at the very least, an argument of convenience constructed upon an extremely narrow interpretation of the decision.[221] Many reasons also indicate that it is quite unhistorical.

First, the reasons stated by the court were broad policy grounds appropriate to substantive matters. It was not the contemporary practice to couch technical dismissals in this style.[222] A technical objection, had it existed in the court's mind, would certainly have been stated in the court's reasons for judgment.

Second, the mispleader interpretation was known to advocates and

---

[218] For illustrations of such cases, *see Wood v. Curling* (1846) 15 M. & W. 626 (Ct. of Exchequer); *Curling v. Wood* (1847) 16 M. & W. 628 (Exchequer Chamber); *Collett v. London & N. W. Ry.* (1815) 16 Q.B. 984.

[219] In the 19th century the list of professionals and craftsmen who were deemed to owe public duties began to shrink. Winfield suggests that a shift in economic conditions accounts for this change. This may be similarly described as the breakdown of status into contractual relationships. RONALD H. GRAVESON, STATUS IN THE COMMON LAW (Athalone Press, 1953), 41. In 1797 Wentworth's list included carriers, farriers, innkeepers, stable keepers, surgeons and mid-wives as those owing public duties. JOHN WENTWORTH, A COMPLETE SYSTEM OF PLEADING (Robinson, 1797-99). In 1793, it was held that carpenters were not to be included in this category. *Elsee v. Gatward* (1793) 5 T.R. 143. In 1830, it appeared that a banker was not to be included. *Marzetti v. Williams* 91830) 1 B. & Ad. 415. Clearly, the trade of coachmaker was not one of the old trades, such as the carrier, farrier, or smith. Coaches were not known in England until the middle of Elizabeth's reign. *Pride v. Stubbs* (1810) 2 Camp. 397. The first mail coach was not put out on the road until 1784. ENCYLOPEDIA BRITTANNICA, vol. 5, 867, "Coaching," (1960). Perhaps the relative lateness of the coaching trade pointed away from imposing a public duty upon the defendant in *Winterbottom.*

[220] ATIYAH, RISE AND FALL, *supra* n. 41, at 502-03.

[221] C. J. MILLER AND P. A. LOVELL, PRODUCTS LIABILITY (Butterworths, 1977), 7.

[222] *See e.g., Rapson v. Vubitt* (1842) 9 M. & W. 710.

courts long before Professor Bohlen's alleged 20th century "discovery." It was known well enough to be submitted to the courts on a number of occasions. It was simply never accepted.[223]

Third, it is incorrect to assert that plaintiff's pleadings failed to allege negligence, and consequently, sounded only in contract. The report in Meeson and Welby states, "The declaration then averred, that the defendant so improperly conducted himself, and so utterly disregarded his aforesaid contract, and so wholly neglected and failed to perform his duty in this behalf, that *etc.* . . ."[224] Clearly, a contractual reference is sandwiched in between others, but the allegation of negligence can be read standing on its own to refer to a duty apart from the defendant's contract. Furthermore, counsel for plaintiff used the term negligence three times in his argument, and in referring to his pleadings he said, "But there the declaration alleges the accident to have happened through the defendant's negligence and want of care."[225]

Fourth, two judges stated without qualification that the plaintiff was "remediless."[226] If they had meant to say that the plaintiff was only remediless in contract, and not in tort, they would no doubt have qualified themselves. Even then, plaintiff's counsel would have been permitted under prevailing rules of procedure to amend his pleadings. It was most likely that the court itself would have suggested to counsel the wisdom of such an amendment if it could have changed the result.[227]

Fifth, the contention that plaintiff might have obtained relief in tort, if only he had pleaded differently or correctly, is rebutted by the later case of *Longmeid v. Holliday* (1851).[228] *Winterbottom* was decided upon declaration and demurrer, so that the denial of a remedy leaves considerable room to argue that the dismissal could have been caused by the form of its pleadings. But in *Longmeid*, the court denied recovery upon an action in "case" after plaintiff had obtained a verdict from the jury. In that posture, the court was

---

[223] *Longmeid v. Holliday* (1851) 6 Ex. 761. 765; *Thomas v. Winchester* (1852) 6 N.Y. 397, at 404.

[224] *Winterbottom v. Wright* (1842) 10 M. & W. 109, 110.

[225] *Id.* at 113.

[226] *Id.* at 114 & 116.

[227] THOMAS CHITTY, ARCHBOLD'S PRACTICE OF THE COURT OF QUEEN'S BENCH, 8th ed. (1847), vol. II, 834.

[228] 6 Ex. 761.

required to rule for plaintiff if any theory of relief was possible, regardless of the original form of the pleadings.[229] This procedural posture in *Longmeid* explains why Baron Parke predicated the result upon a comprehensive review of the subjects of fraud, public duties, common callings, highway nuisance, and the delivery of dangerous chattels. He was making certain that plaintiff was indeed remediless, similar to the method employed by Lord Abinger in *Winterbottom*. Evidently, neither the tort of negligence nor any avant-garde "neighbour principle" had thus far appeared on the remedial scene. The unfavorable state of the substantive law of tort in 1851 confirms that *Winterbottom* was deemed remediless in 1842, not because of unartful pleadings, but because of a substantive gap in the law of tort.

Finally, upon the theory that the key to the discovery of the doctrine of a case is to search for the doctrine in the mind of the court,[230] then it is important to ask whether or not the *Winterbottom* decision was treated and understood to be a substantive action in tort. The Chief Baron himself called it an action "in tort."[231] A different characterization hardly accounts for the court's care in discussing and distinguishing the case of *Levy v. Langridge*. The *Langridge* case was unquestionably an action in tort that had been decided for the plaintiff upon the ground of defendant's fraud and deceit. Furthermore, Winterbottom's counsel, Mr. Peacock, told the court that he had modelled the pleadings after the pleadings in *Langridge*,[232] and that his case was "within the principle" of that decision. When Baron Abinger stated that "We ought not to attempt to extend the principle of that decision . . . ,"[233] he clearly regarded the action at bar as a substantive action in tort.

Conclusion

One difficulty with previous explanations as to why privity entered tort seems to be that they remain unproven and historically unlikely. The deeper difficulty is that they fail to provide any affirmative reason for the rule. Instead of rational doctrinal grounds, we are offered mispleaders, fallacies,

---

[229] Under the "aider of verdict" rule, defective pleadings were said to be cured by the jury's verdict. The phrase often used upon such occasions was "such defect was not a jeofail after verdict." THOMAS CHITTY,, *supra* n. 226, at 1357.

[230] EUGENE WAMBAUGH, THE STUDY OF CASES, 2d ed. (Little, Brown, 1894), 29.

[231] *Winterbottom v. Wright* (1842) 10 M. & W. 109, 115.

[232] This statement was reported in *The London Times* on June 7, 1842, p. 7 col. 6.

[233] 10 M. & W. 109, 112 & 113.

spells and economic prejudice. However, there is a more straightforward doctrinal explanation for the development. English judges in 1842 were wrestling with the difficult problem of controlling concurrence between contract and tort duties, and the privity objection was a natural bar to prevent contract-based duties from becoming actionable in tort.

D.   Privity Invades the Trust

A development of great importance was a realignment in the field of creditor trusts and, as stated earlier, this seems to be an example of the exterior function of the privity doctrine.[234] Over the period 1815-1877, the creditor trust underwent complete metamorphosis. If we go back 150 years to Lord Nottingham's day, the creditor's trust had been enforceable by the creditor beneficiary, provided it did not operate as an unlawful preference.[235] But in Lord Eldon's day, the creditor lost his status as a vested beneficiary. If the debtor properly set up an agreement in the form of a trust, the form was disregarded. The Chancellor now characterized the transaction as a mere contract of agency. The debtor thereby gained new freedoms and powers, including the power to revoke the agreement, but it created a double standard for creditor and donee beneficiaries. A voluntary trust for the family beneficiary was not categorized as a contract; it remained an irrevocable and enforceable trust at the beneficiary's insistence.[236] In the donee context it was said, "The duty which is once fixed is not to be changed by any circumstances which afterwards occur."[237] But when debtor and trustee used the same legal forms and expressions to arrange the payment of debts to creditors, the Chancellor eschewed a trust analysis and now raised manifold objections to the creditor's suit. It was said the creditor was a volunteer who furnished no consideration;[238] the agreement was intended for the sole benefit of the debtor, not the creditor;[239] and the agreement could not be

---

[234] See above, pp. 19-20.

[235] *Woodhouse v. Cotton* (1680) Rep. Temp. Finch 478; *Purefoy v. Purefoy* (1681) 1 Vern. 28; *Dunch v. Kent* (1684) 1 Vern. 260.

[236] *Fortescue v. Barnett* (1834) 3 My. & K. 36; *Fletcher v. Fletcher* (1844) 4 Hare 67; *M'Fadden v. Jenkyns* (1842) 1 Ph. 153; *Paterson v. Murphy* (1853) 11 Hare 88; *Moore v. Darton* (1851) 4 De G. & Sm. 517; *Lambe v. Orton* (1860) 1 Dr. & Sm. 125; *Wheatley v. Purr* (1837) 1 Keen 551.

[237] *Rycroft v. Christy* (1840) 3 Beav. 238, 242.

[238] *Wallwyn v. Coutts* (1815) 3 Mer. 707.

[239] *Paterson v. Murphy* (1853) 11 Hare 88.

enforced by one who was not a party to the deed.[240] In short, we find the donee beneficiary protected as one would expect a *cestui que trust* to be protected in equity; but the creditor beneficiary became as disfavoured in equity as he was at law. As the contract principle pressed against the property interest, the beneficiary's right receded. It was a central episode in the progressive articulation of the privity principle in Chancery. The outline of this development will be traced below in four prominent cases.[241] The essential facts in each case involved a conveyance in trust by A (a debtor) to B (the trustee), for the benefit of A's creditors, of whom C was one. No creditor action was allowed, however, because none was regarded as trust beneficiary.

In the *Wallwyn* case (1815), A conveyed lands to B in trust, but later A and B executed other deeds and varied the trusts of the original deed. Chancellor Eldon held that this revocation was valid, that the trust was voluntary, and, therefore, A might "vary it as he pleased." This ruling would have been unobjectionable if this had been an ordinary contract between A and B, but the parties had called it a "trust," and the trust had been completely constituted before their revocation. It would seem that Chancellor Eldon portrayed the transaction as a contract, but for a reason that he did not explain. It was later argued that the case was in conflict with Lord Eldon's other decisions, and particularly that it overruled the case of *Ellison v. Ellison* (1802),[242] which had stated two concise propositions relative to the voluntary trust:

(i)   if the legal conveyance was actually made, the equitable interest would be enforced, though the covenant was originally voluntary, and

(ii)   a trust once well-created would not be revocable by its author.

These rules would have provided the basis for an enforceable creditor's trust, and if they were applicable, it was nonsense to object that the creditor was a volunteer, or not a party to the trust deed, or that the agreement was revocable.

---

[240] *Wallwyn v. Coutts* (1815) 3 Mer. 707; *Garrard v. Ld. Lauderdale* (1831) 2 Russ. & My. 451.

[241] *Wallwyn v. Coutts* (1815) 3 Mer. 707; *Garrard v. Ld. Lauderdale* (1831) 2 Russ. & My. 451; *Acton v. Woodgate* (1833) 2 My. & K. 492; *Johns v. James* (1878) 8 Ch. D. 744.

[242] 6 Ves. Jun. 656.

But these objections made sense if the ostensible "trust" had been reconceptualized as a mere contract between A and B. Though Ld. Eldon did not say he had done that, it is clear in retrospect that he had begun the transformation.[243]

In *Garrard v. Lord Lauderdale* (1831), Chancellor Brougham decided another case in which, after the trust was constituted and already partially executed, A and B varied the trust. A paid off several of the scheduled creditors himself, and B paid back to A a portion of the trust fund. The Chancellor again held that C had no equitable interest, and upheld the revocation upon the following grounds:

> . . . no particular form of words is necessary to constitute a trust; but I take the real nature of this deed to be, like that in *Wallwyn v. Coutts*, not so much a conveyance vesting a trust in [B] for the benefit of the creditors of the grantor [A]; but rather that it may be likened to an arrangement made by a debtor for his own personal convenience and accomodation,--for the payment of his own debts in an order prescribed by himself,--over which he retains power and control, and with respect to which the creditors can have no right to complain, inasmuch as they are not injured by it, they waive no right of action, and are not executing parties to it.[244]

Note that the Chancellor did not call the agreement a contract, but only "an arrangement." Such deliberate imprecision may reflect that he did not know or care what type of contract it was. For the moment, the contract was innominate. Judging by his statement that *Williams v. Everett* (1811)[245] and *Scott v. Porcher* (1817)[246] laid down the principles applicable to this "species of arrangement," it appears that he had in mind a principal-agent relationship. Those were cases brought in *indebitatus assumpsit* against the debtor's agent, who, before a revocation, had been under instructions to pay A's asset to C.

---

[243] Even as a contract analysis, the revocability issue was open to doubt in that period. During the Formative Period at common law, an actual transfer from A to B became irrevocable immediately in favor of C, if A already had a "precedent debt" with C. *Potter v. Turner* (1622) Winch 7; Note, [1967] 35 U.Chi.L. Rev. 544, 550, note 23. If A, however, was simply making a donation to C, then A could countermand at any time prior to B's delivery to C. *Lyte v. Peny* (1542) 1 Dyer 49a; *Clark's Case* (1587) 2 Leon. 30, 89; *Gilbert v. Ruddeard* (1608) 3 Dyer 272a.

[244] 2 Russ. & My. 451, 455.

[245] 14 East 582.

[246] 3 Mer. 652.

The controlling principle of *Williams v. Everett* (1811) was that C, a creditor of A, lacked privity with A's agent (B), and could not enforce an action against him unless B consented to be C's agent. On this analogy the creditor trust was essentially an agency contract between A and B to which C was not a party.

Chancellor Brougham, like his predecessor Lord Eldon, cited no authority for this construction, and there was none to cite. Nor did he explain why the court should disregard the declared will of the parties in a formal deed. Judicial interference to protect the debtor's freedom to revoke was arguably a derogation of the debtor's freedom to contract, particularly where he could always have reserved this power in his agreement.

The case of *Acton v. Woodgate* (1833)[247] hardly deepens our understanding about the nature of A and B's revocable relationship, but the Master of the Rolls, Sir John Leach, said in dictum that A and B would lose the power to revoke their "trust" if B made a communication to C of the trust's existence. As he explained, "the creditors, being aware of such a trust, might be thereby induced to a forbearance in respect of their claims, which they would not otherwise have exercised."[248] Apparently, the Master of the Rolls meant that after a communication to the creditor, his acceptance must be presumed,[249] and detrimental reliance need not be shown.[250]

C's "acceptance," or his "reliance," provided two arguments for the creditor's right to sue. Lord Eldon had pointed in this direction in *Ex parte Williams* (1817). There, C, a scheduled creditor of A, attempted to enforce a provision in partnership articles between A and B providing that the partnership would thenceforth be liable for all of A's pre-partnership debts. Because this was an *inter partes* deed, Lord Eldon denied C any relief, but he added the proviso that if C had assented to the agreement, then he could obtain relief. He further stated that "a very little will do to make out [C's]

---

[247] 2 My. & K. 492.

[248] *Id.* at 495. See the same explanation in *Kirwan v. Daniel* (1847) 5 Hare 493.

[249] An offer-acceptance analogy seems to have been repeatedly invoked. For example, Chief Justice Campbell: "Here I think the creditor must be considered to be assenting to the deed, so far as to create privity between him and the trustee." *Harland v. Binks* (1850) 15 Q.B. 713, 719.

[250] Compare the statement in *Hill v. Gomme*: "If, indeed, the agreement had been so far acted upon as to have altered the *status* of the child . . . Dean might have been precluded from disputing . . . his liability . . ." (1839) 5 My. & Cr. 250. See, II Spence (1849) p. 251.

Assent to the Agreement."[251]

If it were about an ordinary contract rather than a trust, this reasoning would not seem odd. A and B have a revocable contract to which C is a stranger; however, before a revocation occurs, C may, in derogation of the parties-only principle, acquire rights under it by volitional act, thereby making the promise irrevocable toward him. Perhaps the Chancellor saw in A and B's "trust" a bifurcated agreement, which at first was only a contract *to create* a future trust in C so that A and B could control the point at which C's trust rights would arise, if at all. Or, ignoring the trust element, perhaps he saw that A and B simply agreed to make C a future offer, so that a second contract with C could be perfected only after A and B's offer was in fact extended, or perhaps he thought that B was A's agent, not his trustee, and B was empowered to enter into a contract that gave no rights to C until communicated to him. The clear point, however was his opposition to the notion--a normal effect of a true trust--that C's rights arise immediately upon the perfection of A and B's contract. The beneficial interest was not directly vested without further act on the beneficiary's part. His right was not immediately transmitted by the juridical act of the parties.

It may be said parenthetically that, by mid-century differing results in the donee and creditor beneficiary cases were attracting attention. The Chancellor did not note the inconsistency nor make explicit comparisons but he found a trust existed in the donee cases because of the intention to create one. In *Fletcher v. Fletcher* (1844),[252] for example, it was held that a voluntary deed of trust for a family beneficiary was constituted and complete, even though the trustee had received nothing but the settlor's promise or covenant to transfer funds to the trustee after his death. Thereafter, the settlor made contradictory dispositions by his last will, and the trustee refused to sue upon the covenant at law. The Chancellor held that the *cestui que trust* could sue in the name of the trustee, either at law or in equity. The defendant objected that: "this was an agreement by A and B for the benefit of C, a stranger to both. . .,"[253] but the court apparently believed that the intention was to create a trust, not a contract. Accordingly, the "parties to the deed" objection was rejected.

---

[251] Buck. 13.

[252] 4 Hare 67.

[253] *Id.* at 75.

Other cases like *Fletcher* seem to rest upon the same foundation.[254] In the case of *Paterson v. Murphy* (1853), the court expressly recognized two lines of cases. A mortgagee, by a voluntary declaration of trust, directed the mortgagor to pay off the debt by investing in securities for the benefit of certain children (not kin-related). The mortgagee subsequently attempted a revocation, but the court would not permit the revocation of a declaration of trust. The children petitioned as *cestuis que trust*, and were held entitled to the funds. Sir W. Page Wood's opinion carefully distinguished the authorities in favor of donees from those relative to creditors.[255] He then concluded, "In this case the lady has caused to be reduced into writing and has signed a clear and distinct statement of what she wishes to be done with the trust fund; and I cannot see what this can amount to less than a declaration of trust, and there is no power of revocation reserved by the document. I must, therefore, declare the children entitled."[256]

The fourth case in this series is *Johns v. James* (1878).[257] A had three creditors, and making two of them trustees, he conveyed and assigned certain property to them to raise sums to pay his debts to them and to a third

---

[254] *Kekewich v. Manning* (1851) 1 De G. M. & G. 176; *Moore v. Darton* (1851) 4 De G. & Sm. 517; *Clough v. Lambert* (1839) 10 Sim. 174.

[255]   "I am not aware of any authority for carrying the principle of the cases of *Walwyn v. Coutts* (3 Mer. 707) and *Garrard v. Lord Lauderdale* (2 Russ. & My. 451) farther than to arrangements for the payment of creditors. I do not know that that doctrine has ever been applied as between the settlor and persons who are purely the objects of his bounty, the former having appointed an agent to administer the bounty, and declared for whom it was intended. In the case of a voluntary declaration the obvious inference is that it is made for the benefit of the persons in whom the maker of the declaration means thereby for the first time to create an interest in the property to which it relates. A provision for payment of the debts of the party making the declaration is wholly different in its nature. The trustee of the property of the settlor, which is directed to be applied in payment of debts, may be regarded as standing in the position of a stewart or agent of the debtor, whose duty it is to satisfy the debts, according to the directions which he may receive, and hand over the balance to his principal. I am not aware that a declaration, made in favour of persons who are purely volunteers, has ever been held to constitute merely an agency for the exclusive purposes of the settlor. Nor do I know of any case in which, in order to establish a voluntary trust, it has been held necessary that the *cestui que trust* should be informed of its creation or existence—whether the effect of the transaction be to pass the trust property to the trustee or to declare an interest in property previously vested in him."

11 Hare 88, 90-91.

[256] *Id.* at 92.

[257] 8 Ch.D. 744.

creditor, C. A later became insolvent, and the trustees took charge of all his estate. Receiving no payment from the trustees, C brought suit, but the trustees objected that there was no averment in C's declaration that the trust deeds had been communicated to him, and thus, they had the power to revoke the trust as they saw fit. The Vice-Chancellor took the view that while a communication to a creditor is essential, a communication automatically took place where, as here, one or more of the creditors were trustees. Furthermore, there had not in fact been a revocation by A and the trustees.

The Court of Appeal reversed, however, holding that C could obtain no rights, except by a personal communication. It was said "in principle," that a communication to a party to the deed was not a communication to a nonparty, even if both were creditors.[258] Then James L. J. explained that this entire line of cases had originated upon "the plainest notions of common sense." When a man in pecuniary difficulty transfers assets to trustees,

> that is only making those particular persons who are called his trustees his agents or attorneys.... If it were supposed that such a deed as that created an absolute irrevocable trust in favour of every one of the persons who happened at the time to be a creditor, the result might have been very often monstrous. It would give him no opportunity of paying a creditor who was pressing; no opportunity of settling an action; no opportunity of getting any food for himself or his family the next day, or redeeming property pledged. So ... it must be assumed from the very nature of the transaction, and from the position of the assignor, that it was a thing for his own benefit, and not for the benefit of [creditors]....[259]

By 1878, the progression we have been tracing was complete. It was settled that A and B's relationship should be viewed as agency or mandate. The purpose (clothed, to be sure, in the "intent" of the parties) behind the deemphasis of the trust concept was to maximize the debtor's freedom of action, so that he might have the benefit of the trust method of discharge without being bound irrevocably. This is not surprising if we remember that philosophically, the age reflected the apogee of freedom of contract, and the power of parties to revoke or modify their agreement was held as nearly sacred as the power to form them. Professor Treitel suggests that the

---

[258] "It seems to me that on principle you cannot create a right in [C] where the deed has not given him a right, because something has occurred giving B a right, who was originally in the same position as [C.] *Id.*, p. 750, per James L. J.

[259] *Id.* at 749.

judiciary's desire to preserve the power of revocation was one of the main reasons for resistance to the beneficiary action.[260] If A and B's contract was a law unto itself, then the same individual freedom and self-interest which produced its existence argued for some maneuverability in modifying or rescinding it. The trust could be an inconvenience here, for to allow an immediate property interest to vest in C would place C's interest in conflict with such valuable contingent interests or ancillary powers normally accorded A and B in contract.[261] Furthermore, the creditor "trust" functioned as a kind of informal bankruptcy proceeding. The flexibility offered by the agency notion must be read in the context of the continuing plight of debtors in 19th century England. Until 1861, the law of England knew no general bankruptcy law for the average citizen[262] and even the imprisonment of debtors was not abandoned until 1869.[263] Until then, discharge in bankruptcy was limited to traders. If an ordinary debtor was unable to negotiate special terms with his creditors, he faced the harsh choice of flight or imprisonment. Composition was particularly difficult for the non-trader, because the voluntary cooperation of all creditors was needed. Any dissenter insisting on full payment held a practical veto over efforts to settle. Thus if a debtor did attempt to compose his debts through some mechanism like the "trust," it might well be vetoed, and as James L. J. pointed out, an irrevocable instrument like the trust would deny him the opportunity of paying a pressing creditor, of settling an action with a dissenting creditor, or of providing for his own family as his financial condition changed.

In any event, by 1878 the bold inversion of the creditor trust into a revocable agency was complete. In the process, the parties-only principle was invoked as a constant justification for the reclassification of the creditor trust.

---

[260] G.H. TREITEL, AN OUTLINE OF THE LAW OF CONTRACT 216, (Butterworths, 4th ed. 1989).

[261] The terminology "ancillary powers" and "contingent interests" is taken from Note, [1968] 35 U. Chi. L. Rev. 544, 548-549.

[262] ENCYCLOPEDIA OF THE SOCIAL SCIENCES, vol. II, p. 449, *Bankruptcy*; for a detailed history *see* HOLDSWORTH, *supra* n. 181 vol. VIII, at 229-245, and Ian P.H. Duffy, "English Bankrupts," 24 Am. J. Legal Hist. 283 (1980).

[263] SIMPSON, HISTORY OF CONTRACT, *supra* n. 47, at 593.

E.   The Resurgence of "Privity" in the Field of Quasi Contract

Introduction

Soon after the turn of the 19th century, the concept of privity suddenly surfaced in the form of a vigorous restriction upon the action of *indebitatus assumpsit*. The first sign came in *Williams v. Everett* (1811), which involved a debtor who sent funds to his banker with a letter of instructions to pay a creditor. The banker refused to pay the creditor, however, and the latter brought suit for money had and received. The claim was denied by Lord Ellenborough who said there was no "privity" between the creditor and the banker.[264]

Certain legal historians have said that when Lord Ellenborough relied upon the privity concept in 1811, he injected a foreign and novel notion into the action for money had and received.[265] However, to claim that this was the inception of the idea seems unhistorical. It was more accurately a resurgence, for the exact expression had appeared before in this sphere of assumpsit. There had been too much previous discussion by Holt and others to support the claim of novelty.[266] Furthermore, it may be misleading to maintain that plaintiffs under this action had never before been subject to a parties-only objection. Actually, this privity was at one time a substantive necessity that was later circumvented by the use of fictional pleadings. The terms of the writ necessitated that plaintiff allege he was a promisee and that the defendant was a promisor.[267] The original way of dealing with such

---

[264] 14 East 582. The Chief Justice stated in part: "It will be observed that there is no assent on the part of the defendants to hold this money for the purposes mentioned in the letter; but on the contrary an express refusal to the creditor to do so. If, in order to constitute a privity between plaintiff and defendants as to the subject of this demand, an assent express or implied be necessary, the assent can in this case be only an implied one, and that too implied against the express dissent of the parties to be charged. *Id.* at 597.

[265] R.M. JACKSON, HISTORY OF QUASI-CONTRACT IN ENGLISH LAW, 99 (Cambridge University Press, 1936); PERCY H. WINFIELD, LAW OF QUASI CONTRACTS (Sweet & Maxwell, 1952), p. 14 and following; J. D. Davies, "*Shamia v. Joory*: A Forgotten Chapter in Quasi-Contract," [1959] 75 L.Q.R. 220.

[266] *See* below, pp. 227-228.

[267] Maitland sets out this form: ". . . whereas the said X heretofore, to wit (date and place) was indebted to the said A . . . and being so indebted, the said X in consideration thereof afterwards . . . undertook and faithfully promised the said A to pay him the said sum of money . . . ." MAITLAND, THE FORMS OF ACTION AT COMMON LAW, *supra* n. 143, at 91.

actions is exemplified by a case in 1674.[268]   The action in *indebitatus assumpsit* was refused when brought against the executors of a church treasurer who had been in arrears upon his obligation to pay an annuity to the plaintiff. Apparently, the annuity was not the result of any contract between the treasurer and the plaintiff. The judges in Common Pleas reasoned, therefore, that although it was optional since *Slade's Case* (1602)[269] to bring assumpsit or debt upon a contract, "Yet where there is no contract, nor any personal privity, as in this case there is not, an assumpsit will not lie."[270] Soon thereafter, however, courts began to allow the action for the recovery of funds "belonging" to the plaintiff, or for preventing the defendant's unjust enrichment. As these cases of the late 17th and 18th centuries collided with the contract model of the writ, it came to be permitted that plaintiff could allege, contrary to fact, that he was a promisee. The collision between form and substance resulted in a fiction that in effect revised the privity required under the writ.

This change in the action's scope had begun in the mid-17th century when it was deemed to lie upon constructive obligations for the payment of money. In one of the first actions of this kind,[271] a plaintiff in 1678 brought *indebitatus assumpsit* for "money had and received" against the usurper of his office, who had collected the fees and profits and simply kept them for himself. The defendant was a literal stranger who had not promised the plaintiff anything. But the court held that since account would lie on such facts, so assumpsit would also lie. Unlike a promise or contract reasonably implied from the conduct of the parties, this "contract" rested upon no mutual dealings, no consideration and no party intention. Freed of these restraints, the action could be used to collect any sum of money owed to the plaintiff, whether by virtue of a statutory fine,[272] by a law forfeiture,[273] breach of customary duty,[274] or payment by mistake.[275] A plaintiff in 1688 used the

---

[268] *Anonymous* (1674) 1 Mod. 163.

[269] 4 Co. Rep. 92b.

[270] *Anonymous* (1674) 1 Mod. 163.

[271] *Arris v. Stukeley* (1678) 2 Mod. 260.

[272] *City of York v. Toun* (1700) 5 Mod. 444.

[273] *Barber Surgeons of London v. Pelson* (1680) 2 Lev. 252.

[274] *Mayor of London v. Gorry* (1676) 2 Lev. 174 1 Vent. 298, 3 Keb. 677; *Shuttleworth v. Garret* (1689) 1 Show. K.B. 35; *Lord North's Case* (1588) 2 Leon. 179. This last case seems to be the earliest recognition of this action, though Ames had found no case before 1666. Ames, p. 161.

action to collect knighthood fees from the defendant.[276] A woman of property in 1708 succeeded in recovering funds from a charlatan who received the rents fom her estate while she laboured under the delusion that he was her spouse.[277]

The fictional nature of this privity became increasingly blatant when extensions were justified by the device of waiver of tort. Originally, it was held that account would not lie upon a simple wrong, so that if X stole a purse, the owner had no action of account.[278] Curiously, however, *indebitatus assumpsit* outgrew the action it replaced and became concurrent with trover. Thus, assumpsit was allowed against a nurse to plaintiff's intestate, who after his death went off with the money he had had about him. It was said that the plaintiff could consent to the taking, and the law would presume a subsequent agreement.[279] Perhaps the first action involving waiver was *Howard v. Wood* (1679).[280] The high-water mark was *Lightly v. Clouston* (1808).[281]

Three devices were needed to make this "sound" in contract. The assent of the plaintiff was supplied retrospectively; the dissent of the defendant was disregarded; and the allegation of money received "to plaintiff's use" was untraversable.[282] Here, by the crudest of means, a "privity" was superimposed upon facts originating in tort.

To a purist like Chief Justice Holt, such devices were "metaphysical" notions that distorted assumpsit beyond recognition. Privity objections were raised on numerous occasions, and yet, logical as these were, they failed to arrest the development of the waiver doctrine. Defense counsel in *Howard v. Wood* vainly argued: "where a receipt depends merely upon a tort, there can

---

[275] *Lady Cavendish v. Middleton* (1629) Cro. Car. 141.

[276] *Duppa v. Gerrard* (1690) 1 Show. K.B. 78.

[277] *Hasser v. Wallis* (1708) 1 Salk. 28.

[278] *Tottenham v. Bedingfield* (1573) 3 Leon. 24. Here, the possessor of a parsonage was refused an action of account against an interloper who took the tithes and carried them off. The court said "it is merely a wrong."

[279] *Thomas v. Whip* (1714) Bull. N. P. 131.

[280] 2 Show. K. B. 21, Jones, T. 126.

[281] 1 Taunt. 112, where the defendant seduced the plaintiff's indentured apprentice from onboard ship, and employed him as a mariner. The plaintiff's action in assumpsit "for work and labour performed for the defendant at his request" was successful.

[282] *Lamine v. Dorrell* (1706) 2 Ld. Raym. 1216.

be no contract or privity, and without them no debt, and by consequence *indebitatus assumpsit* does not lie."[283] Another unsuccessful counsel in *City of York v. Toun* asked, "How can there be any privity of assent implied when a fine is imposed on a man against his will?"[284] By 1700 the law was settled, despite the efforts of a gifted opponent like Chief Justice Holt.[285] By 1772, the court of King's Bench could look back with more realism and recognize that privity had become the thinnest of strands--

> though while this action was in its infancy the Courts endeavoured to find technical arguments to support it, as by a notion of privity etc., yet that principle is too narrow to support these actions in general to the extent in which they are admitted.[286]

In view of this background, one should not be so surprised that the references to privity proliferated after 1811 into what Jackson has called "an intractable mass of conflicting opinions."[287] While Jackson saw only chaos, Davies, in a later analysis, arranged the cases into an ironical pattern. He discovered a doctrinal progression in four stages which, over a period of fifty years, cancelled itself out by turning full circle.[288] For Davies, the result of this lengthy flareup was only that the law ended up where it had begun, and privity went back into a state of remission.

But what lay behind this resurgence of privity? For Winfield it was part of the general "revival" (in quasi-contract) of the implied contract

---

[283] (1678) Jones, T. 126, 127. *See also, Lord North's Case* (1588) 2 Leon. 179, Fennor *arguendo*.

[284] 5 Mod. 444.

[285] *See, e.g., Thorp v. How* (1702) Bull. N. P. 130; *City of York v. Toun* (1700) 5 Mod. 444; *Ward v. Evans* (1702) 2 Ld. Raym. 928. *Crifford v. Berry* (1710) 11 Mod. 241; C. J. Holt was not apparently opposed to the action of a third party beneficiary so long as the assumpsit related to a consensual agreement. *See, Yard v. Eland* (1699) 1 Ld. Raym. 368.

[286] *Hitchin v. Campbell* (1772) 2 Wm. Black. 827, 830; (per C. J. de Grey). The remarks of the Chief Justice, however, were not a complete and full exposure of the privity fiction for he cautiously added in the next sentence, "Besides, (if it were necessary), there is in this case a privity between the defendant and the bankrupt, the judgment being voluntarily given." Here, he reverted to the waiver of tort method of supplying contractual privity.

[287] JACKSON, *supra* n. 265, at 99.

[288] J.D. Davies, "Shamia v. Joory: A Forgotten Chapter in Quasi-Contract," [1959] 75 L.Q.R. 220.

theory.[289] Jackson suggested several other answers. Some of these actions for money had and received were perceived by courts as forbidden assignments of choses in action; furthermore, courts had forgotten their history, notably the fact that long ago the wide extra-contractual features of account had been incorporated into *indebitatus assumpsit.*[290] His most intuitive explanation, however, linked the privity epidemic to the law's refusal to recognize the beneficiary action. The beneficiary in quasi-contract, he argued, was originally clothed as a *cestui que trust.* As the trappings of the trust were thrust aside, the beneficiary was unmasked as nothing but a stranger to the contract.[291]

Jackson's position evidently rested upon the assumption that a parties-only principle was an already well-established norm by the early 19th century. He did not generally associate the epidemic with the rise of that principle or the advent of a dual privity objection. Yet if we go behind the "intractable mass" to its beginning in *Israel v. Douglas* (1789),[292] we shall be able to distinguish this dualism in two coherent lines of authority. In one branch of those cases the courts applied the parties-only principle (*e.g.*, *Williams v. Everett*): the essential objection was to the absence of any contract or promise between the defendant, the debtor's agent, and plaintiff, the debtor's creditor. In the other branch of cases, whose facts were functionally the equivalent of the substitute-debtor cases, courts held that the plaintiff's failure to give consideration barred his recovery (*e.g.*, *Wharton v. Walker*).[293] Once properly differentiated, these cases and their rationales reflect the two basic privity objections of English contract and at the same time, all of the cases in the "intractable mass" are accounted for. Hence, these cases provide a small laboratory in which to study the beneficiary action, and their evolution is an accelerated experiment with the dualist objection. We will see, therefore, that privity's resurgence in the action for money had and received was an event related to the rise of the parties-only principle and to the inception of a dualist objection.

---

[289] WINFIELD, THE LAW OF QUASI-CONTRACTS, *supra* n. 265.

[290] A singularly unpersuasive explanation. Forgetfulness is not a serious vice of the common law lawyer. Whatever the reason for the reawakening of privity, it was not the product of legal amnesia. The law of account was fully argued and appreciated in *Israel v. Douglas* (1789) 1 H. Bl. 239.

[291] JACKSON, *supra* n. 265, at 121 *et seq.*

[292] 1 H. Bl. 239.

[293] (1825) 4 B. & C. 163.

To trace these ideas properly, we should start with the doctrinal change brought about by the famous case of *Israel v. Douglas*.

The Case of Israel v. Douglas (1789)

This case is, in an important sense, the modern precursor of all talk of privity and consideration in this part of quasi-contract. Its background significance can be easily overlooked because the decision squints in two directions. On the one hand, it sanctioned the technical extension of the count for money had and received; on the other hand, it had a disturbing effect upon contract and agency principles.

The facts were that A was indebted to B for brokerage services, and B was indebted to C for money lent. B gave an order to A to pay C the sum due between A and B as a security. C sent this order to A, which A accepted and promised to pay. On the strength of this security, C then loaned B an additional sum. Thereafter B went bankrupt and A refused to pay C. Suit was brought by C against A for "money had and received." The objection was made, however, that plaintiff had misconceived his action, in that no money had actually been "received" by A. His indebtedness for B's services had been a mere book debt or a chose in action, but neither B's money nor C's money had come into his hands. However, the court, over the dissent of Wilson J., who favoured keeping the forms of action distinct, thought this was too technical. The action should lie, Gould J. stressed, because "where is the real and substantial difference, whether I in fact pay money to you for a third person, or whether I give you an order to pay so much money, to which you expressly assent? In reason and sound law, it is money had and received to the use of such third person."[294] Thus, the element of "receipt" had been widely construed, and if Wilson J.'s dissent had articulated the problems to be faced later, perhaps this chapter of quasi-contract would have been averted.

The Effect of the Extension

The extension of the definition of "money had and received" to include constructive receipt proved instrumental in two lines of cases. In the first variety--which we shall call the Substitute Debtor case--there was a direct tie-in to the consideration rule of the beneficiary action. The pattern was usually that C was owed by B who was owed by A. An attempt was thus

---

[294] *Israel v. Douglas* (1789) 1 H. Bl. 239, 242.

made to shift B's debt onto A, and thereby substitute A in B's place toward C. This, in fact, was the pattern of *Israel v. Douglas* itself. In the second variety--which we shall hereafter call the Revocable Agency case--C is owed by B and B has an agent named A. An attempt is made by B to pay C by transferring assets to his agent with instructions to pay C, or by treating assets in his agent's hands as a fund for C. Now in either variety, B may be making a transfer, creating a fund, or substituting a debtor by means of promises that concerned bookdebts or bookassets. These are choses in action. A remedy given in such circumstances already pushes us well beyond the limits of the old action of account, simply because that action demanded a physicial receipt of something by the accountant. The extension thus made the "money had and received" count an alluring means of enforcing third party beneficiary contracts and assignments of choses in action.[295] Perhaps the consideration barrier in assumpsit and the obsolete fear of maintenance could be entirely bypassed by this new route. Hence, the technical extension created a temptation to apply the remedy to fact situations[296] indistinguishable from the famous nonsuits brought by creditor beneficiaries in *Bourne v. Mason* (1669), *Crow v. Rogers* (1720), and *Price v. Easton* (1833). As we shall see, however, when the first attempts were made, first Lord Ellenborough, and then other judges as well, immediately interposed the requirement of contractual consideration and blocked recoveries. Such talk was new to this action only because this overlap with assumpsit had just been introduced into legal discourse. Thus, talk of consideration was new, but it was not "unintelligible." It was a swift adjustment to an attempted end-run. Courts were simply unwilling to see these settled results reversed by a mere shift in remedy, particularly not when a separately evolving "parties-only" principle was coming into its own here and elsewhere and adding a certain cogency to these results. Revealingly, no mention of "privity" ever occurred in these Substitute Debtor cases.

But why was no consideration objection made from the outset in *Israel v. Douglas*? The answer lies in the fact that from a third party beneficiary standpoint, every possible objection to C's recovery was perfectly satisfied. The plaintiff was a promisee (A had promised C directly), and plaintiff had furnished consideration for A's promise (C lent money to B in return for A's promise). Thus, though the fact went unmentioned, C could

---

[295] The action had already been used successfully by an assignee of a bond against a debtor, who had actually received a loan of £1000 and had promised to pay any assignee of the lender. *Fenner v. Meares* (1779) 2 Wm. Black. 1269.

[296] *E.g., Wharton v. Walker* (1825) 4 B. & C. 163; *Cuxon v. Chadley* (1824) 3 B. & C. 591.

have chosen to declare against A in special assumpsit.[297]   Unlike the reactions later provoked by its progeny, the *Israel* case itself excited none of the old allergies of the beneficiary action.

In contrast, the Revocable Agency cases were dominated by talk of "privity." The problem was wholly different. The extension permitted the creation of an unliquidated fund in A's hands, which began as B's money, but which at some point must be irrevocably converted into C's money. The choice of some mechanism and decisive point, however, at which title and risk of loss would pass from B to C, and whereby B's power to countermand would be protected had to be made as an original proposition. The problem called forth the test of "privity."

The Consideration Objection in The "Substitute-Debtor" Cases

This variety of case is illustrated by *Liversidge v. Broadbent* (1859),[298] and *Wharton v. Walker* (1825). Structurally, it involved the relationship in which C is owed by B, who is owed by A. A is a mere debtor of B, not B's agent, and B is a mere debtor of C's, not C's agent. An attempt is then made by the parties to substitute A in B's place in relation to C. It was clear that this could be done by a novation between all three parties, whereby C would discharge B and accept A in his place. There, C plainly had a good action in assumpsit against A.[299] However, if only two of the three principals attempted this substitution, then the closely related paradigms of the third party beneficiary contract and the assignment of a chose in action exerted an influence. In *Wharton v. Walker*, B was indebted to C for £4,5s, and for payment gave C an order upon A (B's tenant) to pay this sum to C out of the next rent due. C sent this order to A, but there was no other direct communication between C and A. However, at the time B collected the rent from A, A produced the order, retained the amount due to C, and promised B to pay it to C. Payment was not made, and C sued A for money had and received.   The court held that C had no action, because there was no

---

[297] Lord Loughborough apparently recognized this, for he said, "It is admitted that the plaintiff has the law with him in *some* action. 1 H. Bl. 239, 241. In a later case, Martin B. commented that in *Israel* "there was a consideration to support the promise." *Liversidge v. Broadbent* (1859) 4 H. & N. 603, 612.

[298] 4 H. & N. 603.

[299] *Tatlock v. Harris* (1789) 3 T. R. 174.

extinguishment of the intermediate debt.[300] The objection to C's suit was the lack of consideration: B had not been discharged by C. Presumably if C had discharged B (or promised forbearance against B),[301] that would have been good consideration, and A would have been bound to him.[302]

The consideration objection also proved fatal in the case of *Liversidge v. Broadbent*. Here, B was indebted to C on two bills of exchange, and A was indebted to B for a similar amount. After one of B's bills had been dishonored, C requested security and suggested that B arrange for A to guarantee payment of B's bills. B, therefore, signed the following document:

I hereby authorize [A] to pay to [C] on his order the sum of £113.13, the amount of two acceptances together with the expenses on the bills and interest thereon, towards my account for building the cottages . . . [A] to debit my account with the above money: also [C] receipt to [A] I acknowledge shall be binding between myself and A in the contract.[303]

This was sent to A, who signed it, and wrote the word "acknowledged" at the foot of the document. C's action against A, however, was rejected by Barons Pollock, Martin, Bramwell and Watson, who held that C had not granted any forbearance nor discharged B, and thus, he had furnished no consideration.

Liversidge and *Wharton* were not only replicas of the fact pattern found in *Bourne v. Mason* (1669) and other cases of its type, but they employed the same rationale, even though consideration was supposedly irrelevant to the *indebitatus* count. It seems likely that the consideration doctrine is a mask covering underlying hostilities. Is it the court's feeling that to enforce the action in C's favor without first discharging B would give C two debtors for the price of one? Is there a fear that this could lead to double losses by B? In these facts, A's original debt to B had been discharged by B, but B had not been discharged by C, and thus potentially C, after a recovery

---

[300] *Wharton v. Walker* (1825) 4 B. & C. 163, 165. Bayley J. also stated a preliminary objection that no money was actually *received* by C. This was enough reason to deny plaintiff an action upon an account stated. Here, Bayley was flatly contradicting the holding in *Israel v. Douglas*.

[301] The creditor beneficiary's forbearance to sue was held sufficient in *Hodgson v. Anderson* (1825) 3 B. & C. 842; Bramwell J. said it also explains *Hamilton v. Spottiswoode* (1849) 4 Ex. 200.

[302] The court was also inclined to approve this as a valid equitable assignment, provided this consideration could be found. *Crowfoot v. Gurney* (1833) 9 Bing. 372.

[303] 4 H. & N. 603, 606.

against A (if permitted), could enrich himself by suing B, and thereby doubly impoverish B. Perhaps the courts saw portents of a multiplicity of actions stemming from such situations, for clearly B's next step would be to seek assistance in Chancery. One can only speculate, because the disguised reasoning is more easily discerned than the probable policy behind it.

Martin B.'s opinion in *Liversidge* was remarkable for stating "two legal principles" preventing C's suit on the facts: *One*, "that at common law, a debt cannot be assigned, so as to give the assignee a right to sue in his own name . . ." and *two*, "that a bare promise cannot be the foundation of an action."[304] This calls for two comments. His first "principle" resurrected a prohibition which was surely terminally ill in the late 18th century.[305] The common law, through Mansfield and Buller, had gone to the verge of reversing course and legalizing the assignment of debts.[306] Buller, in particular, was prepared to take "notice" of the trust obligation that he supposed[307] the assignor to be under in equity. Yet in 1800, for reasons not entirely ascribable to the sheer conservatism of Lord Kenyon and his brethren, there was a resounding reaffirmation of the strict learning. The counterattack was against the extension of the *indebitatus* action brought about in *Fenner v. Meares* (1779),[308] and *Israel v. Douglas* (1789). It is clear from *Johnson v. Collins* (1800),[309] that the simplest judicial weapon was to reassert and insist upon this hollow rule. Here, and in subsequent cases, the latent assignment present in any substitute debtor case was conveniently exploited for the purposes at hand.[310] As submitted earlier in Chapter II, the hostility to the substitute debtor cases in the Formative Period (a period encompassing the high point of the maintenance rationale) could well have been related to this policy ground. Unlike his predecessors, Martin J. explicitly made the logical connection, but by elevating a pretext into a "principle," he again clouded the

---

[304] *Id.* at 610.

[305] *See* above, at p. 148.

[306] ATIYAH, RISE AND FALL, *supra* n. 41, at 136.

[307] *See* above, at p. 152.

[308] 2 Wm. Black. 1269.

[309] 1 East 98.

[310] The connection was noted and argued in *Wharton v. Walker* (1825) 4 B. & C. 163, and in *Wilson v. Coupland* (1821) 5 B. & Ald. 228 (per Best J.) This technicality was selectively used, however. *See, Crowfoot v. Gurney* (1833) 9 Bing. 372.

underlying issue.[311] The second comment is that Martin B. stated only two principles. There is no third, namely, no sign of a privity of contract or "parties-only" principle. The omission is significant, because in *Liversidge*, the plaintiff (C) was not a promisee. We may be sure that Martin would have used this ground had the principle itself been appropriate or available to him in this category of case. Bramwell's concurrence shows that the applicable test, as late as 1859, was that "the consideration to support an assumpsit must move from the plaintiff."[312] Even where plaintiff was a promisee, courts made no note of that fact. C's action was refused because B had not been released.[313]

The "Revocable Agency" Cases

This second variety formed a distinct and numerous line of cases[314] that included *Williams v. Everett* (1811), and *Lilly v. Hays* (1836).[315] The relationship typically involved was that C is owed by B, who had an agent named A.[316] The parties did not seek to shift B's debt to any other party. A was not a third party debtor, but only B's agent. B remained the only debtor of C. In order to pay C, however, B might transfer funds into A's hands for that purpose, or might simply instruct A that certain funds or bookdebts already in A's hands should be paid to C. After such a transfer or order had been made, the question in each case was whether C, without any further connection to A and B's transaction, acquired instantaneously a right against A for money had and received. The answer of the courts, on facts such as these, was an insistent "no".

---

[311] In fairness to Martin J., however, it should be noted that in *Liversidge*, A and B's agreement (if viewed as an attempted assignment) was particularly objectionable. It was an example of the assignment of the burden of an obligation (not its benefit), and without the creditor's *formal* consent. Martin B. did not single out this fact, yet such assignments may not have been valid even in equity, and differed *toto caelo* from the one approved in *Crowfoot v. Gurney* (1833) 9 Bing. 372.

[312] *Liversidge v. Broadbent* (1859) 4 H. & N. 603, 613, quoting 2 Wms. Saund. p. 137 g.

[313] *Cuxon v. Chadley* (1824) 3 B. & C. 591.

[314] *See Gibson v. Minet* (1824) 1 Car. & P. 247; *Moore v. Bushell* (1857) 27 L.J. Ex. 3; *Scott v. Porcher* (1817) 3 Mer. 652; *Fleet v. Perrins* (1868) L. R. 3 Q.B. 536; *Walker v. Rostron* (1842) 9 M. & W. 411; *Morrell v. Wootton* (1852) 16 Beav. 197; *Malcolm v. Scott* (1850) 5 Ex. 601; *Cf.*, *Collins v. Brook* (1860) 5 H. & N. 700.

[315] 5 Ad. & E. 548.

[316] The problem where A has a subagent, who is made defendant, is separately treated below.

In the leading case of *Williams v. Everett*, B transferred assets to his agent A, a banker, with directions to pay C. But A repudiated these directions, maintained he would not hold the funds to C's use, and, in fact, made no promise to C. In denying C's action against A, Lord Ellenborough held that there was no "privity" with A; and in order for such a privity to exist, A must have given his "assent" to be C's agent and to hold the funds for C.[317] The facts showed that A assented to the receipt, but not to the instructions. Lord Ellenborough stated that until A's assent to pay C is finally given, his principal would shoulder the risk of loss and retain the power to revoke his prior instructions to A. A contrasting case in which C recovered against A was *Lilly v. Hays* (1836). Here, B sent £1100 to A with instructions to pay C. A allowed C to learn indirectly that he consented to hold the money to C's use and would pay him. The court found sufficient evidence that A's assent was communicated to C.

The Unimportance of Consideration

As we saw, the theme in the Substitute Debtor cases was the necessity of consideration. The Revocable Agency cases presented, however, a different analytical problem in which consideration is hardly mentioned. The theme here is agency, and the test of C's action is no privity without A's assent. The disappearance of the consideration question is explicable. In these cases no substitution of debtors (*i.e.*, no transfer of a chose in action) is meant to occur. Accordingly, there is no issue of discharge or forbearance. No fresh consideration is required, because the consideration which made B originally obligated to C is still sufficient to make B or B's agent liable to C. This was precisely what Lord Abinger meant in *Walker v. Rostron* (1842) in saying that C's consideration was "the existence of the debt."[318] But how does C's consideration move from C to A? In *Lilly v. Hays* (1836), the court, noting that consideration is "seldom shown" in these types of cases, answered that question by stating "there *is* a consideration moving here, through the instrumentality of [B], the original debtor, to [A] the defendant, as agent for [C] the plaintiff." Coleridge J. distilled the issue into four words: "Agency supplies the consideration."[319] This would seem to mean that when A's

---

[317] Lord Ellenborough said, "Here no agency for the plaintiff ever commenced, but was repudiated by [A] the defendants in the first instance." *Williams v. Everett* (1811) 14 East 582, 598.

[318] 9 M. & W. 411, 420.

[319] 5 Ad. & E. 548, 551.

assent made him C's agent, A was the double agent of both B and C. Three parties were thus linked by A's double agency, and the original consideration from C ran as through a conduit to A. Contemporary commentators regarded *Lilly v. Hays* as further confirmation of the contract principle that the plaintiff must not be a stranger to the consideration.[320]

Purpose of Requiring A's "Assent"

Though stress upon the single word "privity" made his thought process vague, Lord Ellenborough marshalled two policies in support of requiring A's assent to C. The first policy was to fix the limits of B's revocatory power and to define the point at which C could treat A and B's transaction as irrevocable. Thus Lord Ellenborough said,

> It is entire to [B] to give and countermand his own directions . . . as often as he pleases . . . until by some engagement entered into . . . with [C] they have precluded themselves from so doing . . . .[321]

The agent's assent, as opposed to the choice of some earlier event (such as A's *receipt* of B's assets or B's instructions), effectively postponed and prolonged the principal's revocatory power. Furthermore, as compared to a later event that might cause injustice to C, assent served as a functional compromise, marking the beginning of C's right of justifiable reliance.[322] A second policy concerned questions of ownership and risk of loss. At this stage in the history of principal and agent, title was recognized as being in the principal, though possession had been given to the agent. Lord Ellenborough saw the principal's (B's) power to countermand as a corollary of his ownership. In accordance with the rule *res perit domino*, title could not be separated from risk. Hence, he allowed the location of risk to determine the power of revocation:

> If it be money had and received . . . *when* did it become so? It could not be so before the money was received on the bill becoming due: and at that instant, suppose [A] the defendants had been robbed of the cash or notes in which the bill in question had been paid, or they

---

[320] THEOPHILUS PARSONS, THE LAW OF CONTRACTS, 5th ed. (Little, Brown, 1866) vol. I, pp. 466-467.

[321] *Williams v. Everett* (1811) 14 East 582, 597.

[322] The best example of this was *Gibson v. Minet* (1824) 1 Car. & P. 247.

had been burnt or lost by accident, who would have borne the loss thus occasioned? Surely the remitter [B] and not [C] the plaintiff and his other creditors . . . . *This appears to us to decide the question*: for in all cases of specific property lost in the hands of an agent, where the agent is not himself responsible for the cause of the loss, *the liability to bear the loss is the test and consequence of being the proprietor*, as the principal of such agent.[323]

Thus, at the point of A's assent, C acquired an insurable interest since the risk of loss shifted to him.[324] The agent's assent may seem to be a late point to pass title and risk, but the 19th-century outlook favored the revocatory power of the debtor. It will be remembered that when equity in 1831 first overtly stated reasons for the reconstruction of the creditor trust into a revocable agency,[325] the Chancellor specifically based his position upon the principle of *Williams v. Everett* (1811), and *Scott v. Porcher* (1817).[326]

A possible third policy behind A's assent may have been important though it was not openly discussed by the court. A's obligation toward the creditor of his principal was thereby made a consensual decision, not an operative effect of the agency relationship. A's option *not* to be B's agent--to terminate or to negotiate and guard his own interest--was thereby accorded an importance by the law. Agency in the 19th century was no longer a world of bailiffs and domestic servants, but a more individualistic world of middlemen, brokers and bankers. Business dealings could involve a far more impersonal agency, and oftentimes a complex web of subagency. The agent himself was often the creditor of the principal, and he might already share an interest in the asset by which B would pay C. Furthermore, A often had to protect himself not simply from C--a single creditor--but from B's other creditors as well.[327] Time and again, we see the courts using the lack-of-assent ground to protect the agent from the contending creditors of his bankrupt principal, or to protect the agent who, as creditor, had satisfied his

---

[323] *Williams v. Everett* (1811) 14 East 582, 597 & 598, emphasis added.

[324] *Hill v. Secretan* (1798) 1 B. & P. 315.

[325] *Garrard v. Ld. Lauderdale* 1831 2 Russ & My. 451.

[326] 3 Mer. 652. *Cf., Fitzgerald v. Stewart* (1831) 2 Russ & My. 457.

[327] *See, Williams v. Everett* (1811) 14 East 582.

own claims out of the funds which C claims.[328] In many of these cases, A was ultimately in the position of a stakeholder caught in the middle between the rights of various claimants.[329] If A was not in privity with these parties until his assent, then he was not held to know the validity or priority of their claims, but was insulated if he wished to be.

Certainly, too much has been made of the different terminology courts used to describe "privity." These reflected differences in degree, not kind, and it is difficult to say with Dr. Jackson that they are conflicting and unintelligible. The various terms all add up to the description of a voluntary undertaking by A toward C. None were definitional or meant to be exhaustive. Courts made indiscriminate synonyms of A's "engagement," his "promise," and his "contract" with C.[330] Contract, it will be noticed, could bear a more informal meaning here, because there was no requirement of fresh consideration between A and C. When courts spoke of A's appropriation, his communication, his being estopped or his "attorning" to C,[331] they were again referring to any range of acts broadly indicative of A's consent.

Nothing technical hinged on these words. One can hardly find a case in which the court denied C a remedy by saying, "You have shown A *appropriated* the funds, but you have not shown he *assented* to be your agent"; or "You have shown A *promised* to be your agent, but you have not shown that he contracted to do so."[332] If it is correct to stress the broad purposes of this terminology rather than its literal dissimilarities, then we must find that

---

[328] *E.g., Cobb v. Becke* (1845) 6 Q.B. 930; *Stephens v. Badcock* (1832) 3 B. & Ad. 354; *Baron v. Husband* (1833) 4 B. & Ad. 611.

[329] For example, a part owner of a ship (B) deposited certain funds (the proceeds of freight) in his own name with his banker (A). B died and his father became his executor. From these funds the father repaid himself for a loan he had made to his son (B). Then B's partner, C, who was entitled to a share of the freight proceeds, sued A for money had and received. The court denied recovery. Lack of privity of contract between C and A was argued, and was apparently the basis of the decision. *Sims v. Bond* (1833) 5 B. & Ad. 389.

[330] In *Williams v. Everett* (1811) 14 East 582, Lord Ellenborough used both *assent* and *engagement* interchangeably in his opinion. In *Moore v. Bushel* (1857) 27 L. J. Ex. 3, 4, Bramwell J. preferred to say A had "no contract" with C, but Watson J. spoke of "no communication" with C. These terms were only individual preferences, and not intended to be terms of art.

[331] *Fleet v. Perrins* (1868) L.R. 3 Q.B. 536, 542, per Blackburn J.

[332] An exception seems to be *Malcolm v. Scott* (1850) 5 Ex. 601. A apparently communicated to C that he would pay, but did not make a firm promise to C. The court held that A was not liable to the action.

previous commentators have not broken the cases down into their essential categories. Jackson has six categories grouped along conceptual lines of contract, appropriation, estoppel, etc.[333]   Davies fashioned these into a sequence of notions which marks the circular progress of the courts.[334]   The essential division, though, lay between the Substitute Debtor and the Revocable Agency cases.

The Signs of Amalgamation

Griffin v. Weatherby (1868)[335] seems to be the first case to break out of the two lines traced above. The facts were that C was owed £1000 by B, and B was the managing director of A, a company which owed him (B) £600. When C pressed B for payment, he delivered to C an order drawn on A, which C sent to A. A promised C in various letters that it would pay; it did not do so, and C's suit followed. The court found in favor of C, even though there was no finding of a discharge of B or of forbearance against B. When counsel argued the necessity of consideration, Blackburn J. betrayed a misunderstanding by stating: "*Walker v. Rostron* is a direct authority against that proposition,"[336] though that case, as we have seen, had squarely rested on the consideration issue. Then, disregarding the distinction, Blackburn stated the law in a way entirely independent of consideration:

> Ever since the case of *Walker v. Rostron*, it has been considered as settled law that where a person transfers to a creditor on account of a debt, whether due or not, a fund actually existing or accruing in the hands of a third person, and notifies the transfer to the holder of the fund, although there is no legal obligation on the holder to pay the amount of the debt to the transferee, yet the holder of the fund may, and if he does promise to pay to the transferee, then that which was merely an equitable right becomes a legal right in the transferee, founded on the promise; and the money becomes a fund received or to be received for and payable to the transferee, and when it has been received an action for money had and received to the use of the

---

[333] JACKSON, *supra* n. 265, at 99-103.

[334] Davies, *supra* n. 288.

[335] L.R. 3 Q.B. 753.

[336] *Id.* at 758.

transferee lies at his suit against the holder.[337]

The effect of this reasoning was to allow C to recover on showing a "fund" held by A and A's promise to pay it to C, despite the fact that B was not discharged or given forbearance. By taking *Walker v. Rostron* out of context, Blackburn J. disarmed the consideration issue, because, as Lord Abinger said there, "the existence of the debt" is the consideration.[338] The fundamental issue is that Blackburn's amalgamation would have enforced a beneficiary contract that would not have been enforced at common law in assumpsit without consideration "moving" from C. This the law was not prepared to do, even in quasi-contract.

---

[337] *Id.* at 758-759.

[338] Mr. Davies seems to overlook this point when he states the effect of *Griffin v. Weatherby.* "If [A] is in possession of a fund, and at B's instructions assents to hold it for [C], [C] need not furnish consideration, but if [A] is a mere debtor to B, then [C] must furnish consideration." Davies, [1959] 75 L.Q.R. 220, 228. In *Griffin v. Weatherby,* however, A *was* a "mere debtor" and yet C did *not* have to furnish consideration, at least none other than that originally furnished to B. This is the amalgamation brought about by Blackburn's mixing of the two sets of cases.

CHAPTER V

REFLECTIONS AND CONCLUSIONS

My purpose in this final chapter is to recapitulate some of the conclusions reached in this study and to reflect generally upon the the beneficiary action at English law.

I.

This study has indicated that in the field of contract privity has always had plural meanings and multiple roles. An understanding of this generic term must be related to context, function and period.[1] We have seen that four functions (the schematic, evidentiary, interior, and exterior) must be differentiated. Much confusion in the modern literature has been caused by ignoring the differences between the interior privity of assumpsit and the exterior parties-only principle. It is by this means that the case of *Tweddle v. Atkinson* (1861) has been mistaken for the source of the parties-only principle in English law. Equally important, the privity doctrine of the common law has not been carefully distinguished from the more liberal regime in Chancery where this doctrine did not originally obtain either in its consideration-based or parties-only form. We saw that confusion on this point led to mistaken and exaggerated views about the beneficiary doctrines in equity.

II.

It has been clarified that the components of what contract texts refer to as "the modern privity doctrine" entered the equation in different historical stages. The first consideration objection gained recognition in the courts in and around 1670,[2] but the final form of the objection was not finalized until about 1861.[3] The parties-only objection is an equally old, if not older idea,[4] but for a long time it played a subdued role in assumpsit thanks to the

---

[1] *See supra* Chap. I, pp. 10-20.

[2] *See supra* p. 68 ff.

[3] *See supra* p. 165 ff.

[4] *See supra* pp. 28-29, 49-52.

promisee-in-law fiction. Nevertheless, this long-dormant idea awakened in the 19th century to become a principle of English contract.[5] When that occurred it was an old phrase with a debt-related past -- "privity of contract" -- that was given new content and conscripted to this task.

III.

In light of the present account, certain theories about the underlying nature of the objection to the beneficiary action now seem less persuasive, if not unhistorical. Three of these might be briefly mentioned.

Detriment in assumpsit.

It has been suggested that the beneficiary was disqualified under the action of assumpsit because he had not suffered the detriment or damage contemplated by that action. Thomas Street wrote that, "[t]he reason for the modern rule is found in the original conception underlying assumpsit . . . giving redress for damages incurred by the nonfulfillment of a deceitful promise. Only the person who suffered the detriment or damage in question could therefore bring suit upon breach of the promise."[6] Yet this assertion glides over an elementary historical fact that emerged clearly in the Formative Period: many early cases awarded recovery to the beneficiary *because he had sustained the detriment.*[7] Indeed the reason for the brief heyday of the beneficiary action in the 17th century, short-lived though it was, seems in no small part due to the original tortious character of assumpsit which, together with its freedom from wager of law,[8] kept it relatively free of privity constraints. From the earliest times torts were said to be actions between "strangers" and thus exempt from any requirement of privity.[9] Thus it is unhistorical to argue, as Street did, that tort origins were at the root of the disqualification, for if consideration did begin as tortious detriment, then this may be the reason why courts were initially satisfied that it had moved from an injured plaintiff, whether promisee or third party beneficiary. It is clear in

---

[5] *See supra* p. 159 ff.

[6] THOMAS A. STREET, FOUNDATIONS OF LEGAL LIABILITY vol. II, pp. 155-156 (Thompson, 1906).

[7] *See supra* p. 31 and ff.

[8] *See* the cases employing the "interest" theory, above at p. 31 and ff.

[9] "Wrongs," said Manwood J., "are always done without privity." *Tottenham v. Bedingfield* (1573) 3 Leon. 24.

a formal sense that assumpsit departed from its prototype -- the action of trespass -- to become progressively contractual in appearance.[10] At the substantive level, it has been noted that by 1560 the delictual notion of consideration had been completely subsumed within the contractual.[11] Detriment had become a facet of consideration as an inducement to the promise, rather than being the result of reliance on the promise. Thus the farther assumpsit moved from its trespassory base, the more logical it became to apply the contractual notion of consideration to the beneficiary action. If this submission is correct, then the beneficiary was once enfranchised in early law for the same reason that Street thought he was disqualified.

Policy against gratuitous promises.

It has also been urged that the reason for the beneficiary's disqualification lies in the policy against enforcement of gratuitous promises and executory gifts. Professor Treitel argues, "A system of law which does not give the gratuitous promisee a right to enforce the promise is not likely to give this right to a gratuitous beneficiary who is not even a promisee."[12]
The main premise behind this view is that the beneficiary is usually a gratuitous beneficiary who, even if he is called a creditor beneficiary, is essentially a donee of a promise for which he has not paid.

Professor Treitel's analysis, however, is not completely persuasive because the analogy between the gratuitous bilateral promise and the third party beneficiary contract is not strong. In the gift beneficiary contract, the beneficiary can with justification be called a donee, but the promisor did not make a gratuitous promise. Actually, consideration moved from the promisee to the promisor. If A gives consideration to B in return for B's promise to pay a sum to C, then A is not a gratuitous promisee and B is not a donor toward C. If this were the true policy, an assignee should likewise be a

---

[10] By omitting *vi et armis* and *contra pacem*, by changing the form of the general issue from "not guilty" to "non assumpsit" and by the new rules of Hilary Term. GEORGE SPENCE, THE EQUITABLE JURISDICTION OF THE COURT OF CHANCERY (Stevens & Norton, 1846), vol. I, p. 248.

[11] Ibbetson, "Assumpsit and Debt in the Early 16th Century," [1982] Col. L.J. 142, 153, n. 69.

[12] G.H. TREITEL, AN OUTLINE OF THE LAW OF CONTRACT, 2nd. ed. (Butterworth's, 1975), p. 446; Furmston similarly maintains, "If A were to promise C to pay him £100 simpliciter, we should not say that there is a contract but that C cannot enforce it because he has not given consideration." "Return to Dunlop v. Selfridge," [1960] 23 Mod. L. Rev. 373, 383. The donative explanation given by Treitel and Furmston was originally stated by Joseph Chitty.

"donee," since he is neither the original promisee nor did he give consideration to the promisor. The analogy to donations appears more tenuous in a creditor beneficiary situation where there are two sets of consideration, no donative intent on anyone's part, and the identical economic result reached by an assignment. It may be sensible policy to refuse enforcement of promises made without consideration, but the beneficiary contract deserves enforcement if the consideration given by A to B or from C to A functions to caution and deter impulsive liberality.[13] Furthermore, on its face the test "consideration must move from the promisee" has never ruled out the enforcement rights of a donee. The test does not concern whether C furnished consideration, but solely whether it moved from A, the promisee.

Revocatory freedom.

Recognition of the beneficiary action, it is said,[14] involves potential interference with the power of the contracting parties to vary their own transaction. In return for services by A, B may promise A to deliver a certain watch to C, or B may promise A that he will pay a debt that A owes C. Thereafter, however, A and B may mutually decide that B should deliver a less valuable watch or that B need not pay off A's debt. This right of the contracting parties to vary or rescind their contract, including a third party beneficiary contract, is fundamental in English law.[15] Under this approach the beneficiary's consent to the variation or revocation need not be obtained. His "rights" under the contract are extinguishable by the parties, even though they made no provision in the contract originally reserving such a power to themselves, and perhaps even though they originally intended the contract in favor of the beneficiary to be irrevocable. This power, however, can only be exercised by mutual consent. In *Re Schebsman* (1944)[16] it was held that an attempted unilateral revocation by one of the contracting parties did not

---

[13] Following Wilmot J.'s classic statement as to the function of consideration: "But it [consideration] was made requisite in order to put people upon attention and reflection, and to prevent obscurity and uncertainty . . . . Therefore it was intended as a guard against rash inconsiderate declarations. . ." *Pillans v. Van Mierop* (1765) 3 Burr. 1663, 1670.

[14] SPENCE, *supra* n. 10, at 280; Gabriela Shalev, "Third Party Beneficiary: A Comparative Analysis," [1976] 11 ISR. L. REV. 315; Note, "Third Party Beneficiary Contracts in England," [1968] 35 Univ. Chic. L. Rev. 544.

[15] *Re Schebsman* (1944) Ch. 83; [1943] 2 AER 768 (C.A.). *See* W.P. Page "The Power of Contracting Parties to Alter A Contract Rendering Performance to a Third Person," 12 Wisc. L. Rev. 141 (1937).

[16] (1944) Ch. 83; [1943] 2 AER 768 (C.A.).

destroy or affect the beneficiary's rights, so long as the nonrevoking party desired to perform under the contract toward C or would enforce performance of the contract on C's behalf.[17] The law, as it presently stands, perhaps rests on the ground that the power is a valuable interest purchased by the consideration or simply because it is fundamental to the parties' freedom of contract. This policy is not often articulated in the cases, but it is one that underlies much of the discussion found in In *Re Schebsman* (1944)[18] and a number of 19th century decisions.[19]

Emphasis upon the conflict between the beneficiary action and revocatory freedom, however, has perhaps obscured two points that have not been answered. On the one hand, the two "rights" remain compatible until the original parties have in fact mutually revoked their agreement. Thus, a parties-only rule based upon this policy would not explain why the beneficiary has no action in cases where there has been no revocation at all or perhaps only a unilateral revocation. The beneficiary could well be accorded a defeasible right subject to the power of mutual revocation. The mere potential for interference does not persuasively explain the inflexibility of the parties-only principle.[20] On the other hand, other legal systems clearly demonstrate that it is possible to recognize the beneficiary action and at the same time retain the principle that the parties possess the power to discharge or modify the duty to the beneficiary by subsequent agreement.[21] Therefore, taken by itself the power to revoke would seem to be a weak basis upon which

---

[17] In an action for breach the party-plaintiff may recover all that the beneficiary could have recovered if the contract had been made directly with himself. *Lloyd's v. Harper*, (1880) 16 Ch. D. 190, 321; *Jackson v. Horizon Holidays Ltd.* [1975] 3 AER 92 (C.A.), 1 W.L.R. 1468.; monies recovered will be considered money had and received to the beneficiary's use.

[18] (1944) Ch. 83; [1943] 2 AER 768 (C.A.).

[19] *See* Ld. Abinger's remarks in *Winterbottom v. Wright* (1842) 10 M & W. 109 and the creditor trust cases discussed *supra* in Chap. IV. at p. 212 ff.

[20] A similar criticism has been made of the refusal of the courts to use the trust mechanism as a means to circumvent the privity doctrine. Mr. Atiyah notes that this refusal is primarily based upon the fact that the trust, once constituted, is irrevocable. Courts have hesitated to construe third party beneficiary contracts as trusts because that characterization takes away the moral right of the parties to revise their agreement, even though in the particular case no such revocation may have been attempted. Mr. Atiyah's criticism is that this treats a fiction as a fact and refuses a legitimate claim based upon what might have been, rather than upon what is in fact so. AN INTRODUCTION TO THE LAW OF CONTRACT, 237-238 (2nd ed., Oxford University Press 1971).

[21] *E.g.* § 311(2) RESTATEMENT (2nd) Contracts (A.L.I. 1981). In French doctrine the stipulator also retains the power of revocation until there has been an acceptance by the beneficiary. WEILL ET TERRE, LES OBLIGATIONS § 543 (Précis Dalloz 1975).

to explain the modern privity rule in England.

IV.

In light of the many factors that have played a part in the long evolution of this doctrine, we may be increasingly skeptical of a search for single causes. The evolution is far more complex than a single policy can take credit for. There have been waves of influences, including the advent of dependency of promises,[22] the development of the trust,[23] the reception of will theory,[24] and the drying-up of beneficiary cases after the Statute of Frauds,[25] to name only a few factors other than consideration-based explanations or the parties-only principle. Furthermore, to focus solely upon the consideration doctrine as the central cause requires us to take the deceptive simplicity of the doctrine at face value. Throughout this evolution the consideration objection was stated in a manner far broader than the precise problem. Applied like a blanket, the doctrine comforted the judges, but it also concealed the issues from themselves and others. This can be seen more clearly if we step back from English law and examine the beneficiary problem generally.

In a well-developed system affording the beneficiary action, there are three general problems that must be worked out if the beneficiary is to be accommodated.[26]

(i) The problem of double duties and double liability: does the promisor's duty to the beneficiary coexist and overlap with his duty to the promisee (both having the option to sue the promisor)? Is the potential for double liability avoided by a set-off rule?[27]

(ii) The problem of defenses and conditions: does the beneficiary

---

[22] *See supra* pp. 171-172.

[23] *See supra* p. 110 ff.

[24] *See supra* p. 175 ff.

[25] *See supra* p. 80.

[26] For French law, *see generally* WEILL ET TERRE, LES OBLIGATIONS §§ 540-545 (Précis Dalloz 1975); for American law, *see generally* RESTATEMENT (2nd) CONTRACTS §§ 302-315 (A.L.I. 1981).

[27] Under § 305, RESTATEMENT (2nd) CONTRACTS (1981), satisfaction of the duty to the beneficiary satisfies to that extent the duty to the promisee.

acquire a nondefeasible right to receive performance once there is a contract between promisor and promisee, or is his right always "subject to" defenses and conditions in the contract such as mistake, fraud, or nonperformance by the promisee?[28]

(iii) The problem of revocation and modification: do the promisor and promisee retain the power, at any time before performance, to revoke or modify the contract by subsequent agreement and thereby divest the beneficiary of his right to performance?[29] Does it matter if the beneficiary had, before receiving notice of the revocation or modification, already justifiably relied on the contract in his favor and changed position?

In the present study we have seen that English law typically declined the opportunity to devise solutions to these problems, preferring flat refusals cast in a consideration or (in the 19th century) a parties-only objection. This was evidently the case in *Bourne v. Mason* (1669)[30] where the danger of double liability (problem (i) above) was posed and perhaps perceived, but which was quickly translated by the court into a consideration objection. This was no ineluctable choice by the judges, but rather a refusal to work out some alternative rule that could have avoided the danger and satisfied consideration requirements -- *e.g.* by ruling that whole or partial satisfaction of the promisor's duty to the beneficiary satisfied to that extent the promisor's duty to the promisee.[31] Another refusal took place in *Tweddle v. Atkinson* (1861)[32] where the problem of defenses and conditions ((ii) above) was completely camouflaged by the consideration objection. Here the promisor admittedly had a good defense, one that all legal systems permitting the beneficiary action would have admitted, but the court applied the consideration objection with such disguise that the holding was taken to mean that only a promisee could enforce a promise in another's favor. As we have also seen,[33] the English courts were not able to bring about a reasonable accommodation between the beneficiary action and the revocatory power of

---

[28] The right is defeasible under American law § 303, 309, RESTATEMENT, (2nd) CONTRACTS (1981), and in French law, § 543 WEILL ET TERRE.

[29] A revocatory power is retained in American law, RESTATEMENT (2nd) CONTRACTS § 311 (1981), and in French law, WEILL ET TERRE § 543.

[30] Discussed *supra* p. 69 ff.

[31] *Cf.* § 305(2) RESTATEMENT (2nd) CONTRACTS (1981).

[32] Discussed *supra* p. 165 ff.

[33] *Supra* pp. 240-241.

the parties ((iii) above). For example, the trust's irrevocability was a leading reason for its fall from favor as a third party beneficiary device in the 19th century.

These repeated refusals point to an important characteristic of the evolution of the beneficiary action. The common lawyers used abstractions to a surprising degree and thereby committed themselves to precedents in which vital questions were passed over. The resulting inconvenience was left to Chancery and Parliament to correct. The history of the beneficiary action has largely been the dialectic of judge and Chancellor, punctuated by the statutes of Parliament.

V.

Finally, the evolution of this subject demonstrates that, despite the modern privity principle, England does have a third party beneficiary "system". A long list of statutory exceptions stretching from fire, life and motor insurance to carriage of goods by sea, grants a direct action to the beneficiary.[34] Apart from statute, enforcement of third party beneficiary contracts may be obtained by the promisee in his own name through a decree of specific performance, or it may be obtained by the beneficiary securing the promisee's agreement to use the latter's name in bringing suit. Further, the functional equivalent of a direct beneficiary action can be created and enforced by an assignment a trust, or under the wide agency principles of English law.

This is not an elegant "system" nor a particularly rational one, but its peculiar features hold the clue as to why the modern privity principle has survived. Today the principle has become, in terms of substantive coverage and effect, relatively hollow. The principle now governs a reduced and restricted sphere in which it causes only occasional inconvenience and injustice, and provokes but sporadic enthusiasm for reform.[35] The exceptions and circumventions have almost swallowed the principle itself. Furthermore, *stare decisis* --- the usual ally of the *status quo* --- is not the only source of its staying power. The long string of parliamentary statutes in derogation of the

---

[34] These are collected in 9 HALSBURY'S LAWS (4th ed.) §§ 342-343.

[35] Professor Atiyah has correctly observed: "It must be confessed that there are few circumstances of practical importance today where the principle is liable to be applicable and to work serious injustice or inconvenience. Objections to the existing law must now rest largely on its form and the lack of uniformity and consistency, rather than on its content." INTRODUCTION TO THE LAW OF CONTRACT, *supra* n. 20, at 229.

principle has in a sense limited the creative option of the judiciary. These piecemeal interventions, always justified by and limited to some precise inconvenience, may well have established the institutional precedent that derogation (or even abolition) of this principle is the domain of Parliament, not the courts who originally created it. Under these circumstances it would be a brave prophecy to say whether reform will ever come from the courts or what Parliament may someday do.

INDEX

Agency Theory (formative period)
first appearance, 55
reception in assumpsit, 58
particular command notion, 58
instrumentalist fiction, 57-58, 61
principal treated as beneficiary, 63-64
view of Finlay, 56-57

American view of privity, 9

Abinger, Lord 205-206, 208-209

Anson, Sir William, 188-190

Assignment (Chancery Phase)
Chancellor's jurisdiction, 148-149
contractual viewpoint, 150-152
consideration test, 153-155
subject to equities, 155-158
suits in assignee's name, 152-153

Assignment (Common Law)
functional equivalent to beneficiary action, 139-140
basis of prohibition against, 141-143
acceptance of trust concept, 147-148
"letter of attorney" circumvention, 143-146
precedent debt requirement, 142-144

Benefit Theory (formative period), 46 ff.
source of 46-48
judicial attitude toward gifts 46-48
Rolle C.J.'s views, 49-52

Bosanquet and Puller, 190-191

Bourne v. Mason, 68 ff.

Civilian theory of beneficiary contracts, 1-4
    relativity principle, 1
    three variants on Continent, 180-184

Civilian Intermediaries,
    English and American jurists as, 186-189

Concurrent remedies, problem of, 200-205

Coke, Lord, 11, 121-122

Conscience, as animating principle in Equity, 96-101

Conscience and Consideration, convergence of, 101-104

Consideration Theory (formative period) 68 ff.
    substitute debtor problem, 68-69
    treatment of nonpromisees, 73
    triumph of, 74 ff.

Consideration in Chancery, 88 ff
    reception, 93-110
    compared to causa, 90
    compared to equitable consideration in law of uses, 90-92
    two-tier theory developed by Chancellors, 107-109

"Consideration must move from plaintiff", 160

"Consideration must move from promisee," 21-25

Contemporary controversy over privity, 20-25
    Monist/Dualist dispute, 20

Corbin, Arthur, contribution to the subject, 85
    criticism of, 130-138

Constructive Trust (Chancery Phase), 130-138

Constructive Trust in Court of Exchequer, 137-138

Creditor Trusts, 212-220

Demise of beneficiary action (formative period), 78-83

Debtor's prison, relationship to beneficiary problem, 3

Dutton v. Poole, 75-78, 172-173

Failure of consideration, doctrine of, 171

Functions of privity, 10-20

Grotius, Hugo, 182 ff.

Hardwicke, Lord, 131-138

Hatchett v. Bindon, 135-136

Interior function of privity, the contract writs, 15-19

Interest Theory (formative period), 31-46
        distinguished from consideration, 37
        property connotation, 38
        association with use concept, 37-38, 43-44

Israel v. Douglas, 224-227

King v. Hatchett and Bindon, 135

Letter of attorney, effect in assignment, 143-146

Levinz, J., 193-194

Maintenance, historical importance of, 141-142

Maitland, Frederick, his analysis of uses, 116-118

"Marriage Money" cases, 35, 48, 50, 52-54, 80

Meanings of privity, 6-8

Nottingham, Lord
        role in reception of consideration, 102-104
        role in reconceptualization of trust, 111-112, 124-128

Parties-Only principle
    rise of, 159 ff
    civilian influence, 186-189
    reception of will theory, 175 ff, 185-186
    party to deed concept, 189 ff

"Party to the Deed" concept
    as forerunner to parties-only principle, 189-198
    influence in Equity, 194-198

Personal vs. real contracts, 1-2

Procedure and evidence (formative period), 12-14

Processual explanation of privity, 87

"Promise in law" fiction, 29, 49-52, 163

Pollock, Sir Frederick, 187-189

Pothier, Robert, 183-185

Pound, Roscoe,
    view of equitable consideration, 109-110
    view of the trust, 114-115

Price v. Easton, 163-165

Quasi-contract and privity, 219 ff

Relativity of contracts, civilian principle of, 1

"Revocable agency" cases, 230-235

Smith, Adam, 178-179

Starkey v. Mill, 49-52

"Substitute Debtor" cases
    formative period, 68-72
    nineteenth century, 227-230

Stipulaiio Alteri, 4

Tomlinson v. Gill, 130-138

Trusts
    historical origins, 110 ff
    functional equivalence, 89
    contract model, 118-122
    transformation into real right, 123 ff
    constructive trusts, 129 ff
    creditor trusts, 212-219

Tweddle v. Atkinson, 165 ff

"Use upon a use," 110-111

Utilitarian view of promises, 178-179

Will Theory
    continental development, 175 ff
    hostility in England, 178-179
    late reception, 175
    impact on common law, 179, 184-185

Winterbottom v. Wright, 205-212

Writs of action (special privities), 15-20